EVERYONE'S
MONEY BOOK

ON STOCKS, BONDS, AND MUTUAL FUNDS

JORDAN E. GOODMAN

Dearborn™
Trade Publis
A **Kaplan Professional** C

D0775762

This publication is designed to provide accurate and authoritative information in regard to the subject matter covered. It is sold with the understanding that the publisher is not engaged in rendering legal, accounting, or other professional service. If legal advice or other expert assistance is required, the services of a competent professional should be sought.

Vice President and Publisher: Cynthia A. Zigmund
Editorial Director: Donald J. Hull
Senior Project Editor: Trey Thoelcke
Interior Design: Lucy Jenkins
Cover Design: Design Alliance, Inc.
Typesetting: the dotted i

Published by Dearborn Trade Publishing
A Kaplan Professional Company

Printed in the United States of America

01 02 03 10 9 8 7 6 5 4 3 2 1

Library of Congress Cataloging-in-Publication Data

Goodman, Jordan Elliot.
    Everyone's money book on stocks, bonds, and mutual funds / Jordan Goodman.
        p.   cm.
    Includes bibliographical references and index.
    ISBN 0-7931-5379-4
    1. Stocks—United States—Handbooks, manuals, etc. 2. Bonds—United States—Handbooks, manuals, etc. 3. Mutual funds—United States—Handbooks, manuals, etc.
I. Title.
    HG4921 .G66 2002
    332.63'2—dc21

                                     2002009047

Contents

List of Figures

Introduction

Everybody wants money. That's why they call it money.
—Danny Devito, Heist

Money. Everyone wants it, everyone needs it, everyone gets it one way or the other. It's what you do with the money you make that will largely determine the kind of life you'll lead for decades to come. Invest it carefully, diversify, and continue to invest regularly through good times and bad, and you should enjoy a fulfilling life and a prosperous retirement. But blow it on fast times or speculative investments, and your golden years may lose their luster.

The vast majority of Americans reach their retirement years without an adequate nest egg. As a result, they spend their senior years pinching pennies instead of living their dreams. It doesn't take a lot of effort to set up an investment program that will lead you to a comfortable lifestyle. It does, however, take initiative, persistence, and follow-through.

You'll find much of the information you need to build a successful investment portfolio in the pages of this book, but the real lessons will begin when you open a brokerage account, mail in your check, and put your own dollars on the line. That's when you'll learn the joys of a bull market—and the agony of a bear market. You'll see some of your investments grow to a multiple of your initial stake, and others plunge to just a fraction of what you paid. You'll experience the full gamut of emotions, from disappointment and disgust to unbridled glee. But when the smoke clears and the dust settles, you will have achieved the American dream—a successful, diversified investment portfolio that affords you the freedom to lead a vibrant and fulfilling life.

In the traditional world of investing, the overwhelming favorites of individual investors have been stocks, bonds, and mutual funds. All three vehicles offer a simple and effective way to invest in the growth of America and the worldwide economy. And all three have proven to be much more profitable over the long term than the bank savings accounts and certificates of deposit (CDs) that many Americans use to invest their savings.

WHY STOCKS?

Despite the ups and downs of the stock market, stocks have outperformed every other conventional form of investment over the past century. American stocks have provided an average annual return of nearly 12 percent over the past 100 years. By contrast, CDs and bank savings accounts have provided an average annual return of around 3 percent during that same period. In dollar terms, that means that $10,000 invested in stocks 50 years ago with a 12 percent average annual return would have grown to nearly $3 million, while that same $10,000 invested in a 3 percent CD 50 years ago would have only grown to about $65,000.

That's a dramatic difference—particularly if you think of it as your retirement nest egg. Would you rather retire with $3 million or $65,000? That's why, despite the risks of the stock market, the greater risk would be to keep your money in a "safe," low-yielding investment that might not even keep up with inflation.

Stocks give you the opportunity to invest in and profit from some of the greatest and most successful companies. Bill Gates has become the richest man in the world thanks to the success of his company, Microsoft. You can profit from Microsoft, as well, simply by buying Microsoft stock. As a shareholder you become a part owner in that company. That means you can own a piece of top companies such as Coca-Cola, General Electric, Merck, and Procter & Gamble. You can also buy a stake in some young up-and-coming companies. If those companies hit it big, you'll hit it big as well because the value of your stock will soar.

Stocks give investors two ways to gain—capital appreciation and dividends. Not all companies pay dividends, but most large, well-established companies do pay dividends to investors each quarter. Those dividends—which generally range from about 1 to 5 percent of the current stock price—come from the company's profits. So as a stockholder, you share in the company's profits. Many companies raise their dividend each year, giving shareholders an increasing flow of income.

You can also profit from the stock's appreciation. As the company grows and becomes more profitable, its stock tends to increase in value. Not every

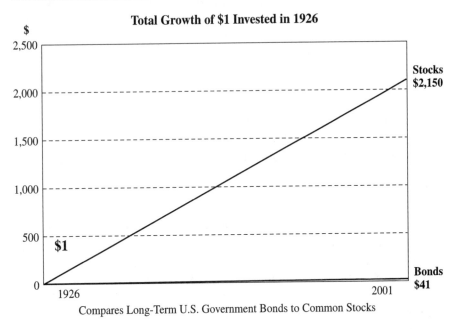

Figure I.1   Stocks versus Bonds, 1926–2001

Total Growth of $1 Invested in 1926

Compares Long-Term U.S. Government Bonds to Common Stocks

stock increases in value every year, but, on average, stocks tend to appreciate about 12 percent per year. Some do much better, but others do much worse, and can actually decline in value. That's why it is so important to diversify, building a portfolio of several stocks from several different industry groups.

In this book, you will learn how to find good stocks and how to build a solid portfolio.

As the above chart shows, stock investing can help your dollars grow at a much faster pace than bonds—and the longer the time frame, the bigger the disparity.

WHY BONDS?

Bonds are considered a much more conservative investment than stocks. The risk of losing money is lower, but so is the potential for gain. Many investors include both stocks and bonds in their portfolios to provide diversification.

Bonds are generally issued by corporations or government entities. The federal government is the largest issuer of bonds, but many municipalities also issue them, as do most major corporations. The main reason investors are attracted to bonds is because they provide a steady stream of income. Many retired people use the interest from their bonds to cover their daily expenses. Very affluent individuals often prefer bonds because they are safer than stocks. After all, if you already have millions of dollars, there is little incentive to take chances with your money to supercharge your returns. A steady stream of income from a bond portfolio is usually enough of a return to satisfy many affluent investors. In fact, certain types of bonds, called *municipal bonds,* provide income that is tax-free.

However, many investors shun bonds because the long-term return tends to be much lower than stocks would provide. But a lot of investors have holdings in both stocks and bonds. The stocks provide better potential for long-term capital growth, while the bonds offer safety and a steady income. Even when stocks are tanking, bonds can balance your portfolio by holding their value and paying interest. While bond values may fluctuate over the life of the bond, when a bond matures, you are reimbursed exactly the same amount as you paid for the bond initially, as long as the issuer does not default.

Bonds can have an important role in your investment portfolio. You will learn more about the types of bonds that are available, and how to invest in bonds later in this book.

WHY MUTUAL FUNDS?

For millions of investors who don't have the time, expertise, or inclination to invest in individual stocks and bonds, mutual funds offer the perfect solution.

Mutual funds are the simplest possible way to invest in the stock and bond markets. With a single investment, a mutual fund provides professional management and instant diversification at a very low cost. Each mutual fund is managed by a professional money manager who may invest the fund's assets in a diverse range of stocks or bonds. By buying shares of a mutual fund, you become a shareholder of that broad portfolio and, therefore, share in the gains—and losses—that the mutual fund might experience.

There are many types of mutual funds from which to choose, including funds that invest in government bonds, corporate bonds, blue chip stocks, small stocks, tech stocks, foreign stocks, high-yielding stocks, or a combination of stocks and bonds. In all, there are about 8,000 different funds on the market.

While the initial selection process may be a little difficult—narrowing your list from the 8,000 available funds to the two or three funds you finally

Figure I.2　1925–2001 Chart of Stocks, Bonds, Bills, and Inflation

From 1925 to 2001

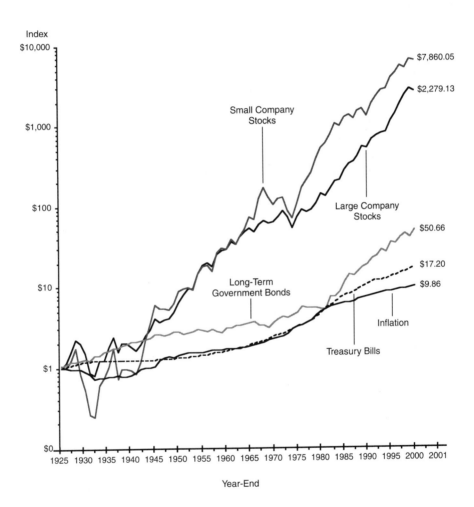

Source: (c) *Stocks, Bonds, Bills, and Inflation 2001 Yearbook™*, Ibbotson Associates, Chicago (annually updates work by Roger G. Ibbotson and Rex A. Sinquefield). Used with permission. All rights reserved.

decide to buy—the rest of the mutual fund investment process is very simple. Once you've become a fund shareholder, you can have the dividends from your fund automatically reinvested in additional shares—or automatically mailed to you. You can also set up a plan, know as an *automatic investment plan* (AIP), that automatically deducts money from your bank account each month to invest in more fund shares. That way, without ever writing a check or agonizing over your investment options, you can build a growing position in your favorite mutual funds.

This book will give you a thorough understanding of mutual funds and will guide you through the mutual fund selection process.

INVESTING FOR THE LONG TERM

Investing is a lifetime process—and the sooner you get the process started the more successful you'll be. Your goal should be to build a diversified portfolio of high-quality stocks and bonds or mutual funds—or a combination of the three. Overwhelming as that may sound, it all starts with a single investment. Buy a stock, buy a mutual fund, but buy something, and get the investment process started. Millions of working Americans never earn a dime in the stock market because they never take the first step, which is to open a brokerage account and make a purchase. The sooner you get into the investment market, the sooner you can begin to learn the game and to profit from your investments.

As the chart in Figure I.3 illustrates, the earlier you begin investing, the easier it is to reach the big money.

If you start investing at age 20, you need only invest about $1,000 a year in the stock market to reach $1 million by age 65. But the level of annual investment rises quickly. If you wait until age 30 to start, you need about $3,000 a year, at 40 you need nearly $9,000, and at 50 you need an annual contribution of nearly $30,000. After that, you might need to either win the lottery or lower your expectations. Obviously, the best plan is to start investing as early as possible.

AN INVESTMENT PLAN

There are many ways to invest in stocks, bonds, and mutual funds, but one of the very best is to enroll in an individual retirement account (IRA), 401(k) plan, or other tax-favored retirement plan.

Retirement accounts such as IRAs give you two great tax advantages. For one, the money that you contribute to an IRA may be tax-deductible. In other words, if you contribute $3,000 to an IRA, you can deduct that $3,000

Figure I.3   Reaching $1 Million

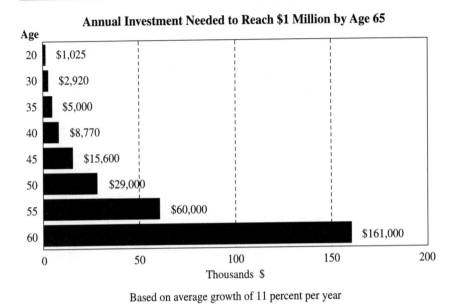

Annual Investment Needed to Reach $1 Million by Age 65

Based on average growth of 11 percent per year

from your taxable earned income for that tax year, if you meet certain conditions. (There are, however, limits on how much you can contribute each year.) The other tax benefit is that the money within your retirement account can grow and multiply tax-deferred. You can buy and sell stocks or bonds for profit within the account and collect interest and dividends without paying current taxes on those gains. You pay no taxes on your retirement money until you withdraw it from your account when you retire.

In fact, the newer Roth IRA can give you an even bigger tax break. With a Roth, you contribute after-tax dollars, but any money you earn on your Roth investments accumulates tax-free. You can build up a $1 million investment in your Roth IRA, and still pay never have to pay taxes when you withdraw the money during your retirement.

With a self-directed retirement account, you can invest in the stocks, bonds, or mutual funds of your choice. You make all the decisions on where your money is invested. It's an excellent way to participate in the growth of the economy and the stock market.

You can also invest in the market by setting up a brokerage account with a brokerage company. You have your choice between a full-service broker, such as Merrill Lynch, where you pay higher commissions but receive advice and assistance with your trades, or a discount broker, such as Ameritrade, that will charge lower commissions but offer no advice or direction with your investment decisions.

This book will help you with all phases of the investment process, from selecting a broker to building a well-balanced portfolio. Ultimately, *you* are the one who will have to make the tough decisions on what to buy and what to sell. By learning as much as possible about your investment options, and spending a little time tracking your investments and studying the market, you should be able to build an investment portfolio that will afford you a fulfilling and prosperous lifestyle.

CHAPTER 1

Stock Basics

I f you've never invested in stocks or have only limited experience with them, you might be harboring a common misperception that the stock market is a dangerous, volatile place where thousands of sophisticated professional traders and brokers lurk to steal your hard-earned money.

The reality of the stock market—if you learn a little about it—couldn't be further from that myth. Millions of small investors like you have been able to finance their dreams by successfully buying and holding for years shares of profitable companies and of mutual funds that buy such shares. Millions of other investors depend on the regular income they earn from their stock and mutual fund holdings.

Sure, stock prices go down at times, as well as up. Sometimes, like in the 508-point crash of October 19, 1987, or the 554-point drop on October 27, 1997, they can plummet so fast that your heart palpitates. But this is the exception that proves the rule. If you look over the past few decades, prices of good-quality companies' stocks have invariably moved higher, as shareholders are rewarded by the performance of the firms they own. As a device to increase your net worth so you can achieve your financial goals, stocks or stock mutual funds are your best investment over the long run (see Figure 1.1).

WHAT ARE STOCKS?

When you buy common shares in a company, you become a part owner in that firm, along with the other people and institutions that own all the

1

Figure 1.1   1925–2001 Chart of Stocks, Bonds, Bills, and Inflation

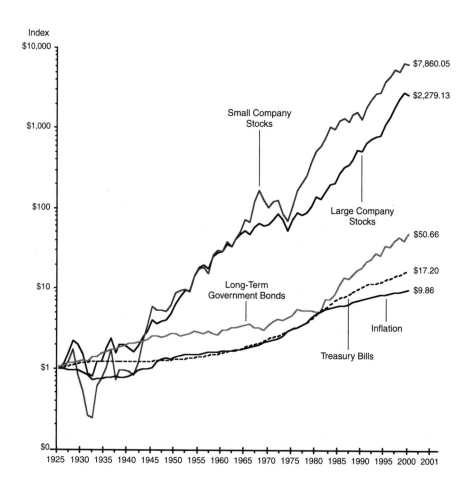

Year-End

shares that have ever been issued. Because you are a part owner, you have a piece of equity in that company. That is why stocks are often called *equities.*

The shares you own constantly rise and fall in value as investors buy and sell them based on their perception of the company. The more people want to buy because they think profits will rise, the more the share price increases. Theoretically, your opportunities for profit are boundless. However, if the firm's prospects start to sour and it looks like profits will turn down, more people will want to sell than buy, and the share price will fall.

Another way to own a piece of a company is through ownership of *preferred shares.* Owners of preferred shares, though they usually do not have voting rights on company matters, are entitled to receive their dividends before common shareholders, and if the company is liquidated, preferred claims are satisfied before common shareholders' claims. Preferred dividends are set at the time the shares are issued and therefore cannot rise over time as common dividends can if the company performs well. Preferreds yields, typically 4 percent to 8 percent, are much higher than common dividend payouts.

In general, preferred stock is not as volatile as common stock; thus, it does not offer as much appreciation or depreciation potential. They are typically issued at $25 a share and trade in the $20 to $30 range. Some preferred issues, known as *convertible preferreds,* can be converted into common shares at a preset price.

THE BASICS OF BEING A SHAREHOLDER

As a shareholder, you are also entitled to receive quarterly updates on how your company is doing. You are mailed a report that tells you whether profits were up or down and what other major corporate developments occurred in the last three months. You also get a more detailed annual report outlining how the numbers for the latest year compare with prior years, as well as the company's plan for the future. You will also be invited to vote at the firm's annual meeting, either in person at the meeting or by a mail proxy ballot. You vote on important matters, such as whether a major acquisition should be completed. At most companies, you get one vote for every share you own. So, unless you own an enormous number of shares, you shouldn't expect to have much influence over the company's strategic direction. For the most part, you are along for the ride while the professionals running the company do their best to maximize profits.

In addition to the profit potential from a rising share price, you can earn money from stocks by collecting dividends. If the corporation is profitable and the board of directors decides it is prudent, the firm will send you a dividend; that is, a quarterly check for your piece of the profits. You can often reinvest the dividend back into more shares of stock if the company offers a dividend reinvestment plan. Dividends are normally paid by large, well-established companies that believe they will achieve a certain level of profit each year. Smaller and newer firms usually do not pay dividends because they want to reinvest all of their profits back in the business to make it grow faster.

Unlike other investment vehicles, such as bonds, certificates of deposit (CDs), or futures contracts, shares in a company never mature or expire. As long as the company stays in business, the shares have some value. If the company goes out of business, however, your common stock will probably become worthless, because when a corporation is liquidated, shareholders get what's left after the Internal Revenue Service (IRS), bankruptcy lawyers, and all other creditors, including bondholders and preferred shareholders, are paid. In most cases, that means the shareholders' stake is wiped out. On the bright side, you might still appreciate your stock certificate as a wall hanging in your living room, as it might remind you of the hopes you once had for the company issuing it.

Why would a profitable company want to give you a chance to participate in its growth? Because it needs the money that the sale of stocks generate in order to run and expand the business. When a company offers shares to the public for the first time, known as an *initial public offering,* the proceeds of the sale help the company open new factories, research and develop new products, acquire other businesses, or pay down debt. Later, if the company needs more capital to grow, it can issue additional shares, in what is known as a *secondary offering.*

Most of the time when you buy shares in the secondary market, however, your money is going to the person or institution selling the shares, not to the company. The company benefits by having a constantly updated market price for its shares so it knows how much money it can raise if it wants to do a secondary offering.

The person selling you shares might be doing so for several reasons. The person might have a big profit in the shares and want to cash in. The person might have found what he or she thinks is a better investment opportunity in another stock. He or she might need the money to meet expenses. Or the person might think that the company's stock is about to fall because this year's profits will not be as high as people expect.

Whatever a person's reason may be, you will never know because you won't meet that seller. Because it would be difficult for you to find someone on your own who has shares and wants to sell, and it would be impossible for that person to find someone who wants to buy the shares, a centralized marketplace called a *stock exchange* has been set up to facilitate buying and selling. You can't just go down to the stock exchange with your certificates and sell your shares on your own, however. You must execute trades through a brokerage firm that is a member of the exchange.

PLACING YOUR ORDER

When you're ready to buy (or sell) a stock, you can choose from several different ordering options. Here are the five most common kinds of orders you can give a broker to buy or sell shares:

- *Day order.* This is an order to buy or sell a stock at a particular price on the day the order is placed. If the trade is not executed on that day, the order expires.
- *Good-this-month (GTM) order.* A GTM order tells a broker to buy or sell a stock at a particular price any time during the current month. If the trade is not executed by the end of the month, the order expires. A variation of this order is a *good-this-week order,* which expires within a week.
- *Good-till-canceled (GTC) order.* A GTC order tells a broker to buy or sell a particular stock when it hits a specific price, whenever that might be. Such an order remains in effect until it is canceled. As long as the GTC order is in effect, it is known as an *open order.*
- *Limit order.* A limit order tells a broker to buy or sell a particular stock at a certain price or better. For example, if you want to buy a stock for $27 a share that is now trading at $30, you can place a limit order at $27. If the stock falls quickly below $27, your broker would execute the order at the lower price, saving you money. On the other hand, if you want to sell a stock at $40 that is now trading at $35 and the stock suddenly shoots up beyond $40, the broker would execute the limit order and obtain an even higher price for your shares.
- *Stop order.* With a stop order, you are trying to protect a profit or limit further losses. The most frequently used stop order, known as a *stop-loss order,* tells your broker to sell your stock at whatever the market price is when the stock hits a specific price less than the price for which it is currently trading. For example, say you bought a stock at $40 a share and it has since risen to $60. If you want to protect your profit, you can place a stop-loss order at $50. However, if the company suddenly announces that its earnings were far less than expected in the latest quarter and the stock plummets to $45, your order will be executed at $45, which is the next market price after the stock hits $50. If you want to make sure you get $50 a share, you should place a limit order. If you are selling short—that is, betting that a stock will fall in

price—you can use a stop order to buy back shares at a particular price to prevent your losses from mounting. The risk in placing stop orders is that they may be executed because of a momentary setback in a stock's price. This is why you should not set stop orders too close to the current market price. Most pros leave at least a 20 percent margin to avoid losing a stock that will bounce back.

STOCK EXCHANGES

In the United States, stocks are bought and sold at three principal stock market exchanges.

New York Stock Exchange (NYSE). Founded in 1792, the NYSE is the oldest, largest, and most prestigious of the stock exchanges. Located on the corner of Wall and Broad streets in downtown Manhattan, the Big Board, as it is called, is home to about 3,000 of the largest and most well-established companies in the United States. In addition, many foreign companies offer their shares for trading on the NYSE in the form of American depositary receipts (ADRs), which for all practical purposes are the same as U.S. shares. The listing requirements to trade on the NYSE are much more stringent than those to trade on other exchanges.

The NYSE uses a specialist system for trading stocks, which means that a specialist is assigned to maintain a fair and orderly market in every stock. Under normal conditions, brokers representing buyers and sellers meet in front of the specialist's post to agree on a price. However, when there is a sudden surge of buyers or sellers because of some dramatic event, the specialist must step in to take the other side of the trade. For example, if a company announces that it is being acquired at a much higher than market price, a stampede of buyers will descend on the trading post. The specialist must sell shares to those buyers—though it would be at a higher price than the price of the shares right before the good news was announced. Similarly, if a company announces that its earnings were much lower in the latest quarter than people expected, there would be a flood of sell orders. The specialist would have to buy shares from the crowd—though it would be at a lower price than the price of the shares right before the bad news was announced, until the market for the stock stabilized.

American Stock Exchange (AMEX). Known as the Curb Exchange until 1921 because it conducted trading on the street curb, the AMEX is home to about 800 medium- and small-sized growth companies. The AMEX is now a unit of Nasdaq. However, it still operates as a stand-alone unit. The AMEX is located near the NYSE in lower Manhattan at 86 Trinity Place. Like the NYSE, the AMEX hosts many companies, particularly Canadian ones, trading in the form of ADRs. The AMEX specializes in the trading of options, index options, and Exchange Traded Funds, which index various broad and narrow industry groups. The AMEX uses a specialist system like the one employed on the floor of the NYSE.

Nasdaq National Market System. Nasdaq (National Association of Securities Dealers Automated Quotation system) stocks are, for the most part, smaller and less established than NYSE or AMEX companies. Though Nasdaq stocks may be riskier and more volatile than traditional blue chips, in many cases, they also have more growth potential. Unlike the NYSE and AMEX, the National Market System (NMS) has no centralized floor where all trading on Nasdaq occurs. Instead, Nasdaq is a network of broker-dealers connected by an elaborate telephone and computer system. Instead of a specialist system, Nasdaq uses what are known as *market makers* to compete against each other and offer the best prices to buy and sell a stock at all times. Before this system was set up in 1972, trading in such stocks was called *over-the-counter* (OTC) trading, so the Nasdaq market is still called the OTC market by some. From your perspective as a stock buyer or seller, though, it makes little difference whether your stock is traded on the NYSE, AMEX, or Nasdaq. You must know where it is traded only so that you can look up the stock's price in the newspaper, because all three exchanges are listed separately.

STOCK INDEXES AND AVERAGES

News reports about the stock market that you see or hear every day on television, on the radio, and in newspapers normally track the action of stock indexes and averages, not individual stocks. These reports can give you a sense of the general direction of stocks, though they will not tell you whether the stocks in your portfolio are up or down. Still, it is good to understand these indexes because they are commonly used as benchmarks for judging the performance of individual stocks. Each index is calculated slightly differently and measures a different sector of the market. The most commonly quoted indexes follow.

AMEX Composite Index. This index tracks the average of stocks traded on the AMEX, which tend to be medium- and small-sized growth stocks. The index is weighted by the market capitalization of its component stocks, meaning that stocks with a larger number of shares outstanding and with higher stock prices affect the index more than smaller companies with lower prices.

Dow Jones Industrial Average. This most commonly quoted average tracks the movement of 30 of the largest blue chip stocks traded on the NYSE. When people ask, "How did the market do today?" they are usually referring to the performance of this average. The Dow Jones is a price-weighted average, so it is more affected by the movement of higher priced shares than by lower priced ones, no matter how many shares are outstanding.

The 30 component stocks in the Dow Jones industrials are Aluminum Company of America (Alcoa), American Express, AT&T, Boeing, Caterpillar, Citigroup, Coca-Cola, Du Pont, Eastman Kodak, Exxon Mobil, General Electric, General Motors, Hewlett-Packard, Home Depot, Honeywell International, IBM, Intel, International Paper, J.P. Morgan Chase & Co., Johnson & Johnson, McDonald's, Merck & Company, Microsoft, Minnesota Mining and Manufacturing (3M), Philip Morris, Procter & Gamble, SBC Communications, United Technologies, Walt Disney, and Wal-Mart Stores.

Dow Jones and Co., which maintains the average, also tracks utilities (electric and gas) in the Dow Jones Utilities Average and transportation stocks (airlines, railroads, and truckers) in the Dow Jones Transportation Average. The combined industrial, utilities, and transportation averages are called the Dow Jones Composite Average.

Nasdaq Composite Index. This index tracks the movement of all companies traded on the Nasdaq NMS. These tend to be smaller, more volatile companies than the blue chips in the Dow Jones Industrial Average or the S&P 500. The Nasdaq Composite is market-value weighted, which gives more influence to larger and higher priced stocks.

NYSE Composite Index. This is the index for the trading of all NYSE stocks. It is market-value weighted and expressed in dollars and cents. When commentators say, "The average share lost 15 cents on the New York Exchange today," for example, this is the index to which they are referring.

Standard & Poor's 500 Index. The S&P 500 is the benchmark against which most portfolio managers compare themselves. It is composed of 500 blue chip stocks, separated by industry, so that almost all key industries are represented. The index always tracks 400 industrial company stocks, 60 transportation stocks, and 40 financial stocks, like banks or insurance companies. The S&P 500 is the fairest yardstick against which you can measure the performance of your stocks.

Wilshire 5,000 Equity Index. The broadest measure of all indexes, the market-value-weighted Wilshire includes all major NYSE, AMEX, and Nasdaq stocks and gives a good indication of the overall direction of all stocks, large and small.

Foreign indexes. The key indexes used to track stock prices in other countries include the CAC-40 in France, the DAX in Germany, the Financial Times 100 (known as the Footsie) in the United Kingdom, the Hang Seng Index in Hong Kong, the Nikkei 225 Index in Japan, the Toronto 300 Index in Canada, and the Zurich Index in Switzerland.

BUYING STOCKS ON MARGIN

Most of the time, you will probably pay for your shares of stock in full. However, if you're feeling so optimistic about a stock that you want to increase your risk in the hope of magnifying your return, you can look into buying on margin, or with borrowed funds. According to rules set by the Federal Reserve, brokers currently will lend you up to half the money you need to buy stocks, as long as they have some collateral of yours to seize in case your stocks lose value. That collateral must be in the form of other securities or cash, which would include money-market fund shares. A broker charges you interest on the loan at the broker's loan rate, which is typically about a percentage point over the prime rate.

By doubling your bets (borrowing to match your own funds), you can make twice as much money if your stock goes up than you would if you were paying for your stock in full. For a margin loan to pay off well, the stock should rise quickly so that you can sell the shares and pay off the margin loan.

Yet margin loans clearly have tremendous risks. The first risk is that the value of the stock you buy will either remain fixed or decrease, thereby not earning the money to repay your margin loan. For you to break even, your stock must rise by at least the amount of your interest costs. More disastrously, if your stock price falls by half, you will be hit by the second most dreaded event in investing—a margin call. (A stock market crash is the most dreaded on our list.) When you receive a margin call from your broker, you must put up additional collateral to cover your loan or your position in the stock will be sold immediately, meaning you will have lost your entire investment. Meanwhile, if your collateral has declined in value as well, you will owe your broker even more money.

Most beginning investors should stay clear of buying on margin because of the risks. Think of it as a game you can play with your excess profits when you've become a wildly successful investor.

SELLING SHORT

If you think buying on margin is risky, wait until you hear about selling short. In fact, many serious investors believe, with good reason, that selling short is more like gambling than investing. This technique is for people who think they can profit if a stock drops in price. Because, as we've said, stocks tend to rise in value over time, these people are trying to swim upstream.

In truth, stock prices do fall, and if you've sold short in the right stock at the right time, you can make a great deal of money. The flip side is that your losses are unlimited because the stock you have shorted can rise forever (theoretically). The following example illustrates how selling short works.

Assume that you want to short the stock of Smith Company because you think its new product is a flop and its earnings will be less than anyone expects, causing the stock price to plummet. You essentially borrow the shares from someone who owns them, typically your broker, with the promise that you will return them later. You then immediately go out and sell the borrowed shares at the current market price, which you think is inflated. (If the stock pays a dividend while you have possession of them, by the way, you must pay that amount to the lender.)

When the share price plunges (if your hunch is right), you buy the same number of shares in the marketplace and return them to the lender. This is known as covering your short. Your profit is the difference between the price you sold the stock for in the first place and the price at which you bought it back.

The specifics of this ideal short sale might be as follows:

- You "short" or borrow 100 shares of Smith Company stock at $70 a share, which you immediately sell for a total of $7,000.
- Smith's poor earnings report comes out, and the stock plummets to $50 a share.
- You buy 100 shares of Smith at $50 each for a total of $5,000 and return the shares to your broker. Your profit is $2,000.

However, suppose that Smith Company's earnings report is actually better, not worse, than expected, and the stock soars. You won't be happy, to put it mildly. The specifics of this short sale might be as follows:

- You borrow 100 shares of Smith Company stock at $70 a share, which you immediately sell for a total of $7,000.
- Smith's good earnings report comes out, and the stock soars to $100 a share.
- You buy 100 shares of Smith at $100 each for a total of $10,000 and return the shares to your broker. Your loss is $3,000.

From time to time, you will hear that stock prices are up one day because of short covering. That happens when stock prices start to rise and short sellers capitulate before their losses become too great; that is, they buy shares to settle their loans.

Short selling, like buying on margin, should be done only by experienced investors with nerves of steel. To make money at this game, you not only must accurately guess the direction of future stock prices but also the timing. It's a dangerous game that only a few people win.

MAKING SENSE OF STOCK TABLES

To track the value of stocks in your portfolio or look up the prices of and activity in stocks you are thinking of buying, you must be able to decipher stock tables—the way most people get this information. They may look intimidating at first, but with a little explanation, they can reveal significant data that will help you choose stocks.

Newspaper Stock Tables

Though there are slight variations between the tables displayed in your local newspaper and the ones in national publications like *Barron's, Investor's Business Daily,* or *The Wall Street Journal,* the basic elements of the stock tables remain the same. These tables describe the consolidated trading activity in individual stocks, combining data from the NYSE, regional exchanges, and the Nasdaq NMS. Most newspapers provide more detail for NYSE and AMEX listings than for Nasdaq listings. Following is a typical line in the tables:

52-Week						PE	Vol				Net
High[1]	Low[2]	Stock[3]	Sym[4]	Div[5]	Yld[6]	Ratio[7]	100s[8]	High[9]	Low[10]	Close[11]	Chng[12]
35	12	Exxon-Mobil	XOM	1.00	2.8	17	3000	34.75	33	34.75	+.50

The following explanations correspond to the number above each column:

1. *High* means the highest price that the stock has reached over the past 52 weeks, up to but not including, yesterday's trading. The difference between the high price and the low price (column 2) of the last year indicates whether the stock is stable or volatile. The wider the range, the more volatile the stock's price.
2. *Low* means the lowest price that the stock has reached over the past 52 weeks, up to but not including yesterday's trading. By comparing the numbers in columns 1 and 2 to yesterday's closing price (column 11), you can determine whether the stock is currently trading near its high or low price for the past 12 months.
3. This column displays the common stock's name. Unless the company has a short name, it is abbreviated. The stocks are listed alphabetically by their full names, so the letters you see might look out of order. Several letters occasionally follow a stock's name. Some are upper case and some, lower case. Following are the letters you will see in the tables and an explanation of what they mean.

A or *B*—There are different classes of stock, such as class A or class B, with different voting rights.

dd—The company lost money in the most recent four quarters.

f—The stock has changed exchanges within the past month.

h—The company has a temporary exception to Nasdaq qualifications.

n—The stock was a new issue during the past year.

pf—It is a preferred stock issue.

pp—The holder of the stock owes installments of the purchase price.

pr—It is preference stock, which has a higher claim on dividends than preferred stock, in case of the liquidation of the company.

rt—It is a right to buy a security at a specified price.

s—The stock has split within the past year by at least 20 percent. (For example, a 2-for-1 stock split means that for every share you used to have, you now have two shares, and the price of the shares splits in half.)

un—The stock is a unit, including more than one security.

v—Trading has been suspended in the primary market.

vj—The company is in bankruptcy or receivership or is being reorganized under bankruptcy law.

wd—Trades will be settled when the stock is distributed.

wi—Trades will be settled when the stock is issued.

wt—The issue is a warrant, giving you the right to buy more stock.

ww—The stock trades with a warrant attached.

x—The stock is trading ex-dividend, which indicates that yesterday was the first day it traded without the right to receive the latest quarterly dividend. The price change is adjusted to reflect this fact.

xw—The stock trades without a warrant attached.

4. The stock symbol is the trading symbol used to identify the stock by computerized quotations systems.

5. The dividend is the dollar amount of the dividend per share paid in cash over the past four quarters. In the example, the dividend is $1. The dividend rate may have risen or fallen since the last quarterly payment, so you should not assume you would receive this amount over the next four quarters. Several letters might follow the dividend rate.

a—extra dividend

b—the annual rate plus another dividend paid in stock, not cash

c—a liquidating dividend, which implies that a company is selling off its pieces and distributing the proceeds to shareholders as dividends

e—an irregular dividend, which means that the annual dividend rate is based on the latest dividend figure *f*—the dividend at an annual rate but increased for the latest quarter

g—a dividend paid in Canadian dollars

i—a dividend declared after a stock dividend or split

j—a dividend that was paid this year, but recently dividend payments were suspended

k—a dividend that was paid this year, which includes dividends that were owed from the past but still not paid (known as dividends in arrears)

m—the dividend on an annual rate but reduced starting with the latest quarter

p—initial dividend, or the first time this company has paid a dividend

r—declared or paid in the preceding 12 months, plus a dividend paid in stock

t—paid in stock in the preceding 12 months. This figure is the estimated cash value of the stock dividend on the ex-dividend date.

y—ex-dividend and volume that are noted in full, not in hundreds

6. The yield is how much dividend you receive as a percentage of the stock price, rounded off to the nearest tenth of a point. In the example, it is 2.8 percent, which is the $1 dividend (column 5) divided by the $34.75 stock price. The higher the dividend yield, the less volatile the stock usually is, and the more appropriate it is for income-oriented investors.

7. *PE ratio* means price-earnings ratio, which is the stock's price divided by the company's earnings for the past four quarters, rounded to the nearest whole number. In the example, the PE ratio of 17 shows investors expect ExxonMobil Corporation to produce solid earnings gains over the next year. The higher the PE ratio, the more profit growth investors expect from the company. A PE ratio of 20 or more indicates a growth company. A PE ratio of less than 10 indicates the company's stock is not in great demand by investors. In two cases, a letter (or letters) follows the PE ratio. A *cc* means the PE ratio is 100 or more and therefore not meaningful. A *q* means that the stock is actually a closed-end fund, which has no PE ratio.

8. Vol 100s shows the stock's trading volume in yesterday's market in hundreds of shares. In the example, 3,000 means that 300,000 shares were traded. By watching the volume pattern over several days, you can tell whether the volume of trading is low or high. A *z* following the volume means that it is the total number of shares traded. An underlined *z* means that the volume on this day was particularly heavy, which might indicate that there were important corporate developments.

9. A stock's high is the highest price the shares traded during yesterday's session. In the example, that was $34.75 per share. A *u* following the high means that this price is a 52-week high as well.

10. A stock's low is the lowest price the shares traded during yesterday's session. In the example, that was $33 per share. A *d* following the low means that this price is a 52-week low as well.

11. The close (sometimes labeled last) is the price of the shares when trading stopped. In the example, ExxonMobil Corporation stock closed yesterday at $34.75 per share, which was also its highest price of the day. The high, low, and closing prices are all expressed in dollars and cents.

12. The net change is the amount the price of the shares moved up or down compared to the previous day's close. In the example, the shares rose one-half of a point, or 50 cents per share. A "+" change means that the shares rose in price, and a "–" means the shares fell. Net changes are expressed in minimums of one cent.

Dividend and Earnings Report Tables

The other two important tables you will see in many newspapers report both action on dividends and quarterly earnings.

Dividend report tables. These tell you whether a corporation's board of directors declared a higher, a lower, or the same dividend as the previous quarter or omitted the payout altogether.

Stock[1]	Period[2]	Amount[3]	Stock of Record[4]	Date Payable[5]
ExxonMobil Corp.	Q	.25	3–10	3–30

The following explanations correspond to the number above each column:

1. The first column states the name of the company declaring the dividend.

2. Period refers to the time in which the dividend will be paid, normally *Q,* for quarterly. *A* means annually; *M,* monthly; *S,* semiannually.

3. The per-share amount of the dividend. In the example, a $.25 quarterly dividend means an annual rate of $1. An *h* following the figure means that the amount is paid from earned income. A *k* signifies that it is paid from realized capital gains, usually taken by a closed-end mutual fund. An *n* means that it is an initial distribution or the first one ever paid by this stock. A *t* signals that it is the approximate dol-

lar amount of the dividend from a foreign company traded in the United States as an ADR.

4. The fourth column indicates that the dividend will be paid to shareholders of record on the date noted—in the example, March 10. The day after the record date, the stock goes ex-dividend, meaning that buyers will no longer receive the dividend. So if you buy the stock on March 11, in the example, you will not receive the $.25 dividend. However, the stock normally drops in price by the amount of the dividend when it enters the ex-dividend period.

5. The date payable is the date the dividend is actually paid.

Earnings report tables. Companies report their earnings on a quarterly basis, and newspapers usually run columns of reports that look like the following:

		This Year	Last Year
[1]	**ExxonMobil Corporation (N)**		
[2]	*Quar Dec. 31:*	*This Year*	*Last Year*
[3]	Revenues	$20,000,000	$18,000,000
[4]	Net income	1,000,000	800,000
[5]	Share earns	.10	.08
[6]	Avg. shares outstanding	10,000,000	9,000,000

The following explanations correspond to the number beside each line:

1. The first line notes the company that is reporting earnings. A letter will follow in parentheses.
   A—American Stock Exchange
   B—Boston Stock Exchange
   F—foreign stock exchange
   M—Midwest Stock Exchange
   Mo—Montreal Stock Exchange
   N—New York Stock Exchange
   O—over-the-counter market
   P—Philadelphia Stock Exchange
   Pa—Pacific Stock Exchange
   T—Toronto Stock Exchange
   In the example, ExxonMobil Corporation trades on the NYSE.

2. The quarter that is being reported ends on the date noted in line 2. In the example, the quarter ends on December 31.

3. *Revenues* is the gross sales figure for the company, comparing the latest quarter with the same quarter a year ago. In the example, sales rose from $18 million to $20 million.
4. The fourth line reports net income, the amount of profit earned in dollars during the quarter. This also is compared to the same quarter a year ago.
5. *Share earns* indicates how much of the profit noted in the previous line is attributable to each common share outstanding. This earnings-per-share number is used to compute the PE ratio. It also is compared to the same quarter a year ago.
6. Line 6 shows the number of common shares that were outstanding, on average, during the quarter. An increase in the number of shares means that the same amount of earnings would create a lower earnings-per-share figure. Fewer shares outstanding means that the same earnings would create a high earnings-per-share result.

Often, earnings report tables will use additional lines to account for special circumstances. Some of the most common abbreviations you will see include:

- *Acctg adj*—a significant accounting adjustment during the quarter
- *Extrd chg*—an extraordinary charge during the quarter, such as a losing business was sold or a division's assets were written down to a lower value
- *Extrd cred*—an extraordinary credit during the quarter, such as a business's value was upgraded or a large profit was made by selling securities
- *Inco cnt op*—income from continuing operations, or businesses that continue as part of the company
- *Inco dis op*—income from discontinued operations, which means the company received income during the quarter from a business that has since been sold or liquidated

Usually, earnings reports are released the trading day before you see them in the newspaper, so the stock market has already had time to react positively or negatively. Earnings report tables are only summaries of the most important aspects of the reports. As a shareholder, you will receive a more detailed quarterly earnings report in the mail a few weeks after it is released.

CHAPTER 2

Picking Winning Stocks

Before you buy any stocks, remember that they are vehicles that can be used to help you reach your financial goals. But stock investing does require patience and persistence. When you hear an exciting story about a hot growth stock, you may be tempted to put your life savings in it so you can become a quick millionaire. Resist the temptation. The best course is to try to build a balanced portfolio of outstanding stocks. You can use a number of techniques to pick winning stocks. What follows are a few general tips that should help you make profitable decisions.

PLAN TO INVEST FOR THE LONG TERM

Despite endless predictions by market gurus that stocks are about to soar or plunge, no one really knows what will happen to stock prices over the short term. So, for the most part, you should ignore such prognostications. The same advice holds for the economy, which is just as unpredictable as the stock market. Your emotions will probably get the best of you if you do a great deal of short-term trading. When prices are rising, you will tend to get caught up in the enthusiasm and buy more. When prices are falling, you will probably get depressed and sell out. Besides, excessive trading activity will generate hefty commissions for your broker and taxes on capital gains for Uncle Sam. Instead of trading for the short term, buy stocks that have good market positions, are financially strong, and offer products or services that seem sensible. If you can't explain what a company does in about two sentences, you probably shouldn't invest in it.

BUY STOCKS SYSTEMATICALLY

Instead of putting all your money into a stock in one lump sum, buy a fixed dollar amount of shares on a regular basis, whether that is monthly, quarterly, or annually. If you buy the same dollar amount of a stock, say $100 a month, you will automatically buy fewer shares when the price is high and more shares when the price is low, thereby assuring yourself of a low average price over time. This technique is known as *dollar cost averaging.* It's a lot safer and easier than trying to determine when a stock has hit its low or high point.

The following simple example demonstrates the value of dollar cost averaging (excluding the effect of commission costs).

Let's say you have $10,000 to invest in a stock. You could either invest it all at once or, using dollar cost averaging, you could buy $1,000 worth every month for ten months. The stock's price most surely will rise and fall over those ten months, so let's say the stock starts the year at $50 a share, steadily descends to $25 a share by June 1, then returns to $50 a share by November 1. If you were to put your entire $10,000 to work in January, your results would look like Figure 2.1.

Figure 2.1   Investing $10,000 All at the Same Time

Month	Amount Invested	Share Price	Shares Purchased	Cumulative Shares	Cumulative Market Value
January	$10,000	$50	200	200	$10,000
February	0	45	0	200	9,000
March	0	40	0	200	8,000
April	0	35	0	200	7,000
May	0	30	0	200	6,000
June	0	25	0	200	5,000
July	0	30	0	200	6,000
August	0	35	0	200	7,000
September	0	40	0	200	8,000
October	0	45	0	200	9,000
November	0	50	0	200	10,000
Total	$10,000	$50*	200	200	$10,000

*Average price

If, instead of investing all your money at once, you invested $1,000 on the first of every month, your results would look like Figure 2.2.

Notice that you would have ended up with $3,900 (or 39 percent) more if you had used the dollar-cost-averaging strategy than if you had bought all of your shares in January. The reason is that as the share price fell to a low of $25 on June 1, you kept buying more shares for your $1,000 each month. By the time the stock recovered back to the $50 level on November 1, you would have accumulated 78 more shares than if you had bought 200 shares in January. However, by buying ten times instead of once, you would incur ten commission charges, which would greatly reduce your gains. To avoid this problem, you can execute dollar cost averaging using a no-load mutual fund, or enroll in a company's dividend reinvestment plan (see later in this chapter), which allows you to buy shares commission free and in fractional share amounts.

Figures 2.1 and 2.2 present a best-case scenario for dollar cost averaging because the price of the shares fell and then rebounded. Even in a less optimal case, where share prices rose and then dropped, you would still come out ahead with dollar cost averaging compared to investing all your money at once. That's the power of systematic investing!

Figure 2.2   Investing $10,000 by Dollar-Cost-Averaging Strategy

Month	Amount Invested	Share Price	Shares Purchased	Cumulative Shares	Cumulative Market Value
January	$ 1,000	$50	20	20	$ 1,000
February	1,000	45	22.2	42.2	1,899
March	1,000	40	25	67.2	2,688
April	1,000	35	28.5	95.7	3,350
May	1,000	30	33.3	129	3,870
June	1,000	25	40	169	4,225
July	1,000	30	33.3	202.3	6,069
August	1,000	35	28.5	230.8	8,078
September	1,000	40	25	255.8	10,232
October	1,000	45	22.2	278	12,510
November	0	50	0	278	13,900
Total	$10,000	$37.5*	278	278	$13,900

*Average price

NARROWING THE FIELD

There are several other important steps to follow to help you develop a successful stock investment program for the long term.

Invest in stocks that you know well. Use your professional knowledge to spot companies that seem to be up and coming. For example, if you are a doctor, you may know what new drugs seem to be particularly effective, and who manufactured the new medical equipment that your hospital just installed. If you are a car mechanic, you may know which company is making the best components for new cars. If you are a homemaker, you may know which new stores seem to be crowded, and what new products seem to be hot sellers at the supermarket. You have many stock tips at your disposal. Use them to profit.

Research your choices carefully. For some reason, people will spend weeks investigating every feature of a car costing $20,000, but when it comes to stocks, they will spend $20,000 based on a hot tip, a broker's recommendation, or a mention in a newspaper story. Before you invest any money, know exactly what business the company is in, how profitable it is, whether it has much debt, which companies are competing with it, and what new products or services the company intends to introduce. Then look at who is running the company. Firms can have great plans, but they need top-quality management to transform those plans into profitable reality. The best way to judge management is by looking at its track record. If the management team has succeeded in the past, chances are that the team can do it again.

Monitor the company after you've bought shares. Read the quarterly and annual reports to see whether your projections are, in fact, coming to pass. Was the new product line successful? Did the company pay down its debt as you thought it would? Keep an eye on the company's stock price. You don't need to check it every day—maybe once a week or at least once a month. If the stock price rises or falls dramatically, someone knows something about the stock that you will probably find out later. You shouldn't own so many stocks that you don't have time to track them all. It's possible to be overdiversified as well as underdiversified.

Don't be pressured to buy or sell just because everyone else is doing so. In fact, if everyone else is doing it, it's probably the wrong time to be joining in. It takes courage, but you will most likely make the majority of your money by buying stocks when they are down and everyone dislikes them and by selling them when they are rising and every taxi cab driver lets you in on this latest "hot" tip.

Don't worry about missing out on a good stock. The best ones rise in value for years at a time, so you have plenty of opportunity to get in on them. If you had bought Wal-Mart stock any time in the early 1970s, you would have made more than 30 times your money if you had held until the 1990s. Just because a good stock moves up a few dollars doesn't mean it's not too late to invest.

Have a selling target price in mind when you buy a stock. If the stock reaches that price, either you can sell some or all of it, or you can reconsider your position based on the company's situation at that time. You should also know the price at which you would sell the stock at a loss. This might be between 25 percent and 50 percent less than you paid for it. One of the worst things you can do is to watch your stock's price melt away as you hope it will recover. Remember, your stock does not know or care what price you paid for it, so it has no obligation to return to that price.

Consider transaction costs before you buy. If you have only enough money to buy a few shares, the commission you will pay might not be worth the investment. Determine in advance whether you will buy the stock through a full-service broker, who offers advice but charges higher fees, or a discount broker, who only executes your order but at much lower commission rates. There are many online discount brokers to choose from, some of whom offer trades for as little as $5 a trade (although most are in the $10 to $25 range). For details about dozens of online brokers, go to <www.sonic.net/donaldj>.

UNDERSTANDING KEY FINANCIAL RATIOS

With these general rules in mind, let's look at the key financial ratios you must understand in order to pick a winning stock.

Price-earnings (PE) ratio. The most common way to compare how investors value one stock against another is to measure how much they will pay for a dollar of earnings. This is the most important ratio on Wall Street for analysts who want to determine the relative value of a stock. To calculate the PE ratio, divide the stock's latest price by its earnings for the latest four quarters. For example, if a stock is selling for $10 a share and it earned $1 a share last year, it has a PE ratio of 10.

$$\frac{\$10 \text{ Current stock price}}{\$1 \text{ Past earnings per share}} = 10 \text{ PE}$$

This PE ratio, called the *trailing PE ratio* because it is based on the past, is the figure shown in the newspaper listing under the heading PE.

An even more useful PE ratio is based on estimates of future earnings. Investors value stocks not only on what the stocks have done in the past but even more for what they think a firm's profits will be in the future. Stock analysts specialize in projecting earnings per share for the next two years, and even if they are not right on the button, you can get a sense of how the stock is valued based on analysts' expectations. In addition to looking at analysts' reports, which you can get from a broker, you can study estimates of future earnings from the *Value Line Investment Survey,* Standard & Poor's stock reports (available in libraries, by subscription, or on many Web sites), and most newsletters' commentary about individual stocks. To calculate a *future,* or *forward, PE ratio,* as it is known, divide the current stock price by analysts' estimates of next year's profits.

$$\frac{\$10 \text{ Current stock price}}{\$2 \text{ Projected earnings per share}} = 5 \text{ PE}$$

Once you've calculated the PE ratio, you must put it in proper context. The higher the PE ratio, the more earnings growth investors expect from the company. Any PE ratio over 20, for instance, means that investors have high expectations that the company's profits will grow rapidly in the next year. A PE ratio between 10 and 20 signals that investors expect solid growth. However, a PE ratio below 10 is a sign that investors do not anticipate much growth from the firm.

Compare the stock you are investigating to both the overall market and its industry peers to determine whether the stock is in or out of favor. The best benchmark for the overall market is the PE ratio of the Standard & Poor's 500 Index, which is published in *Barron's* and in most analysts' reports. Over the years, that PE ratio has ranged from a low of about 8 in the valleys of bear markets to around 25 at the peaks of bull markets. Because each industry has its own dynamics, you should also compare your stock to similar stocks' PE ratios. For example, if you are looking into a major city bank's stock, compare it to other big-city bank stocks. Do the same for airlines, oil firms, retailers, semiconductor chip makers, or any other industry. If your stock's PE ratio is higher than its peers, investors expect even better results from it than from its competitors. If your stock's PE ratio is lower than its peers, investors expect less than industry-average results.

You might be thinking that investing in stocks is easy because all you have to do is choose the stock with the highest PE ratio and, therefore, the brightest future. This is the essence of growth stock investing, described in more detail with the worksheet in Figure 2.4. Unfortunately, this strategy hardly ensures success—in fact, it almost guarantees disappointment. While stocks with high PE ratios do indeed have promising futures, they are also the most subject to disappointment. Let us assure you, one of the last places you want to have your money is in a stock with high expectations that, for whatever reason, lets down investors. The moment the bad news hits the streets, the stock's price will plummet.

Some investors use the opposite strategy: They purchase stocks with low PE ratios that they think have good prospects to improve. The thinking behind this approach is that a stock with a low PE ratio already has low investor expectations built into its price; therefore, if the company reports poor profits, the stock has little room to fall. If, however, the company reports better than expected profits, the stock has much room to rise. All of this sounds good in theory, but not every low-PE-ratio stock will spring to life some day. Some have low valuations for good reasons, and they will stay that way indefinitely. The kind of low-PE-ratio stock you want to buy is the one with a turnaround already underway that has not been perceived by most investors. For more on how to find such stocks, refer to the discussions with the worksheets in Figure 2.6 (out-of-favor stocks) and Figure 2.7 (value stocks).

Price-book value ratio. Instead of comparing a stock's current price to the company's earnings, you can compare the price to the worth of the company's assets, or what is known as the company's book value. This includes the company's real estate, patents, brand names, and all other assets, minus debts and other liabilities. To compute the ratio, divide the stock's price by the book value per share, which you can get from the annual report, Standard & Poor's company reports, or the *Value Line Investment Survey.*

$$\frac{\$10 \text{ Current stock price}}{\$5 \text{ Book value per share}} = 200\% \text{ Price-book ratio}$$

A company selling over its book value indicates that investors think highly of the company and therefore have put a high value on its assets. A company selling at or below its book value indicates that investors have low expectations for the company and do not prize its assets. Investors who specialize in buying undervalued stocks look for stocks selling at or below book value because they think they are getting a bargain if they can buy the stock for less than the company's assets are worth. Such stocks might also be takeover bait because another company or a raider may smell the same bargain, acquire the company, and sell off its pieces for more than their current price. For more on finding undervalued stocks, see the discussion with the worksheet on value stocks in Figure 2.7.

Measures of profitability. Another method used to size up a company is to analyze its level of profitability. In general, the more profitable a company is, the better its stock performs over the long term. Firms with high profitability usually have some proprietary niche product or a large and growing market share, and strong finances that enable them to invest in research and development to improve their products or services. The more profitable a company is, the more it tends to attract competitors that want to replicate its success. So a company that is able to ward off imitators and retain a high level of profitability is probably a good company to invest in over the long run.

The most commonly used measure of profitability is called *return on equity* (ROE). It is calculated by dividing a company's earnings by total shareholders' equity.

$$\frac{\$20 \text{ million earnings}}{\$100 \text{ million shareholders' equity}} = 20\% \text{ ROE}$$

In general, a return on equity of more than 15 percent is considered excellent, so the company in this example is extremely profitable.

As with PE ratios and price-book value ratios, return on equity varies greatly by industry, so it is important to compare a company against its peers.

Another way to determine profitability is by looking at a company's net profit margin. This measure shows a company's overall success not only in managing operations, but also in terms of borrowing money at a favorable rate, investing cash wisely, and taking advantage of tax benefits. To calculate it, divide net income by net sales.

$$\frac{\$20 \text{ million net income}}{\$200 \text{ million net sales}} = 10\% \text{ Net profit margin}$$

Profit margins also vary widely by industry. Supermarkets are happy with 2 percent margins, while newspaper publishers expect 20 percent margins. Therefore, compare the company you're investigating to similar firms.

Measures of debt. Just as it is in your personal life, debt can be either beneficial or detrimental to a company's financial health, depending on what the company does with the borrowed money and how easily it is able to make the interest and principal payments. In general, the more debt a company owes, the riskier it is as an investment because if its profits sag, it may be overly burdened by interest payments.

When you investigate a stock, look for its debt-equity ratio—the most common measure of indebtedness. The ratio is calculated by dividing a company's total liabilities (debts) by total shareholders' equity.

$$\frac{\$20 \text{ million total liabilities}}{\$100 \text{ million total shareholders' equity}} = 20\% \text{ Debt-equity ratio}$$

In this case, the company has a debt-equity ratio of 20 percent, which is usually very manageable. As with all other ratios discussed so far, the amount of debt companies owe differs greatly by industry. Electric utilities frequently have a debt-equity ratio of more than 50 percent because they constantly borrow to upgrade their generating plants. Small high-tech companies might have high debt levels because they fund new product research, which will pay off in the future but creates little revenue in the present. On the other hand, a well-established food manufacturer might have little or no debt because it has a steady flow of cash coming in from sales of its products. In general, a debt-equity ratio of more than 50 percent means the company has a high level of debt.

Dividend payout ratio. This measure tells you how much of a company's profits is being paid out in dividends. To calculate it, divide the dividends per share by the earnings per share.

$$\frac{\$1 \text{ Dividends per share}}{\$2 \text{ Earnings per share}} = 50\% \text{ Dividend payout ratio}$$

In this case, 50 percent of the company's profits are going directly to the shareholders in the form of a cash dividend. In general, the more established a company, the higher its payout ratio. Electric utilities, which investors buy for their dividends, probably have the highest payout ratio of any industry, typically around 50 percent. Other manufacturers might pay 30 percent to 40 percent of their profits as dividends and reinvest the rest in their businesses.

A high dividend payout ratio—more than 70 percent—can signal that the dividend is about to be cut. If a company is paying out nearly all of its profits in dividends, it has little money left to reinvest in its business, which ultimately makes it less competitive. Therefore, don't search for companies with very high payout ratios because you're likely to find stocks about to slice their dividends. For more on how the dividend payout ratio is used, see Figure 2.5.

CATEGORIES OF STOCK

Armed with an understanding of basic financial ratios, you are now equipped to choose individual stocks. There are many kinds of stocks, and some are more appropriate for you than others, depending on your risk profile and financial objectives. I will concentrate here on five categories of stocks (cyclical, growth, income, out-of-favor, and value) and provide worksheets, adapted with permission from worksheets I developed for *Money* magazine, that will tell you whether a stock you are interested in passes the test.

Cyclical Stocks

Luck, as they say, is being ready for the chance. By understanding the economic cycles and the effect they have on stocks, you may be able to help your luck along. Certain types of investments tend to do better during specific stages of the economy. You wouldn't want to make all your buying decisions based on the economic cycles, but you might improve your performance by shifting the weighting of your portfolio as the economy shifts.

Cyclical stocks, so called because they ride the economic cycle, are typically found in such heavy industries as auto manufacturing, paper, chemicals, steel, and aluminum. These companies all have relatively large fixed costs to run their factories. As a result, if the volume of the product they sell is high and the prices they receive are rising because of strong demand, they stand to cover those costs easily and earn enormous profits. However, when demand is weak and prices are falling, they are still burdened by the same costs, so their earnings plummet.

Cyclical stock prices are even more volatile than the company's earnings. Investors are constantly trying to determine whether the cycle is turning up or down because it has a tremendous impact on the company's bottom line. While all stock prices reflect investors' expectations of future profits, cyclical stocks are even more sensitive to perceptions about the future.

The best time to buy cyclical stocks, as hard as it may be to do, is when they are still losing money in the bottom of a recession but their situation is no longer deteriorating. The moment that investors sense a turnaround, the stock will shoot up. Conversely, the time to sell a cyclical stock is when the company is earning record profits and everything seems to be going well. When investors sense that the rate of improvement is slowing or growth is stalling, the stock will decline rapidly.

Following are the five phases of a typical business cycle, and the types of investments that tend to perform the best in each cycle.

1. *Recession.* Characterized by falling production, peaking inflation, and weakened consumer confidence, recessions are usually a good time to buy cyclical stocks (such as automakers, paper companies, and other heavy manufacturers). Their earnings may look anemic, and their stock prices may be floundering, but they are among the first stocks to take off when the economy turns around. Long-term bonds are also a good bet in a recession because the government tends to lower interest rates to help spur the economy. As interest rates go down, bond prices go up.

2. *Recovery.* Marked by stimulatory economic polices, falling inflation, and increasing consumer confidence, recovery is a good time to buy stocks, precious metals, and commodities. Smaller emerging growth stocks may do especially well during a recovery, and cyclical stocks should still have some growth left. Real estate is also a good bet.

3. *Early upswing.* The recovery period is past, confidence is up, and the economy is gaining some momentum. This is the healthiest period of the cycle in a sense, because economic growth can continue without any signs of overheating or sharply higher inflation. Consumers are prepared to borrow and spend more, and businesses—facing increased

capacity use—begin investing in plant or office expansion. Unemployment falls, but inflation may pick up. Higher operating levels allow many businesses to cut unit costs and increase profit margins and profits. The stock market should remain strong, while commodity prices continue to rise modestly. The early upswing stage could last for several years. Real estate should continue to do well. Unload the cyclical stocks, whose growth is probably over.

4. *Late upswing.* The economic boom is in full swing. Manufacturing capacity utilization nears a peak—prompting an investment rally—and unemployment continues to fall. Property prices and rents move up strongly, prompting a construction boom. Inflation picks up, as wages increase in the wake of labor shortages. With interest rates rising, bonds and financial services stocks like bank stocks become less attractive. In fact, the overall stock market may hit a lull. But commodity prices should continue to rise, bolstered by a huge demand for raw goods to feed the boom in manufacturing.

5. *Economic slowdown.* The economy begins to decline. Short term interest rates move up sharply, peaking as confidence drops. The slowdown is exacerbated by the inventory correction as companies, suddenly fearing recession, try to reduce their inventory levels. Manufacturing capacity utilization begins to drop, hurting profits, while wages continue to rise, resulting in increasing inflation. In the markets, bond yields top out and start to fall. The stock market may fall, perhaps significantly, with interest sensitive stocks such as utilities and banks faring the best. Commodity prices may also begin to decline. Long-term bonds, for which prices rise as interest rates drop, may be your best investment at that point in the economic cycle.

The worksheet in Figure 2.3 will help you evaluate where a cyclical stock is in its cycle and therefore whether now is a good time to buy it. All the numbers needed to complete this worksheet are available from Standard & Poor's company profiles or the *Value Line Investment Survey.* We have provided sample numbers for a cyclical stock.

Growth Stocks

The easiest way for most people to make money in stocks over the long term is to buy and hold shares in high-quality growth companies. If it is a true growth stock, its earnings will tend to compound at about 15 percent or more no matter what the overall economy is doing. Growth stocks can perform so admirably because their companies offer proprietary niche products or services and have well-known brand names, strong finances, and topflight management. As long as these factors remain constant, growth can

Figure 2.3   Cyclical Stock Worksheet

	Sample Stock Points	Your Stock Points

Sample Stock

$$\frac{\text{Current stock price} \qquad = \quad \$40}{\text{Stock price at last cyclical peak} \quad = \quad \$60} = 66\%$$

Your Stock

$$\frac{\text{Current stock price} \qquad = \quad \$}{\text{Stock price at last cyclical peak} \quad = \quad \$} = \quad \%$$

(If less than 75%, give your stock 2 points; if between 75% and 100%, 1 point; if more than 100%, 0 points.)   2   _____

Sample Stock

$$\frac{\text{PE ratio at last cyclical peak} \quad = \quad 20}{\text{PE ratio now} \qquad\qquad = \quad 25} = 80\%$$

Your Stock

$$\frac{\text{PE ratio at last cyclical peak} \quad = }{\text{PE ratio now} \qquad\qquad = } = \quad \%$$

(If less than 50%, give your stock 2 points; if between 50% and 80%, 1 point; if more than 80%, 0 points.)   1   _____

Sample Stock

$$\frac{\text{Estimated sales gain for next quarter} \quad = \quad 20\%}{\text{Gain for same quarter a year ago} \quad = \quad 10\%} = 200\%$$

Your Stock

$$\frac{\text{Estimated sales gain for next quarter} \quad = \quad \%}{\text{Gain for same quarter a year ago} \quad = \quad \%} = \quad \%$$

(If more than 125%, give your stock 2 points; if between 100% and 125%, 1 point; if less than 100%, 0 points.)   2   _____

Sample Stock

$$\frac{\text{Next year's estimated profit margin} \quad = \quad 10\%}{\text{This year's estimated profit margin} \quad = \quad 7\%} = 143\%$$

Figure 2.3   (continued)

	Sample Stock Points	Your Stock Points

Your Stock

$$\frac{\text{Next year's estimated profit margin} \quad = \quad \%}{\text{This year's estimated profit margin} \quad = \quad \%} = \%$$

(If more than 125%, give your stock 2 points; if between 100% and 125%, 1 point; if less than 100%, 0 points.)   2   _____

Sample Stock

$$\frac{\text{Next year's estimated return on equity} \quad = \quad 15\%}{\text{This year's return on equity} \quad = \quad 10\%} = 150\%$$

Your Stock

$$\frac{\text{Next year's estimated return on equity} \quad = \quad \%}{\text{This year's return on equity} \quad = \quad \%} = \%$$

(If more than 125%, give your stock 2 points; if between 100% and 125%, 1 point; if less than 100%, 0 points.)   2   _____

Total Points   9   _____

If your stock scores 6 points or more, you have probably found a cyclical stock about to take off. The example here is clearly a good investment.

continue indefinitely. At a certain point, though, once a company becomes very large, it becomes increasingly difficult to generate the same percentage profit increases. However, some companies, such as General Electric, Johnson & Johnson, Fannie Mae, and Microsoft, seem to keep the increases coming, despite the odds.

Investing in growth stocks may sound like a breeze, but it isn't quite that easy. The better the record a growth company establishes, the higher investors' expectations soar and the higher the stock's PE ratio climbs. As long as the growth continues unabated, no problem occurs. But the moment such a company reports a slight slip in its upward trajectory, the stock can take a seemingly senseless pounding. One of the last investments you want to own is a growth stock about to disappoint investors' earnings expectations.

Also, successful companies attract imitators, which usually try to copy the original company's products or services and sell them cheaper. Sometimes that can slow the company's profit growth.

Growth stock investing is also plagued by fads. In the 1960s and early 1970s, stocks like Avon, Polaroid, and Xerox were Wall Street darlings, until they plummeted by 50 percent or more in 1973. In the late 1970s, gambling stocks were the rage as Atlantic City casinos began to open. In the 1990s and 2000s, biotechnology, computer, software, and Internet stocks all had their day, only to fade after expectations got too high. Whenever you invest in a growth stock that seems like a fad, sell your shares the moment you think the fad is fading.

Growth in three sizes. Growth stocks come in three sizes. The largest, with annual sales of at least $5 billion, are known as blue chip growth companies. Medium-sized growth companies, with sales of $1 billion to $5 billion, are called mid-cap (*cap* for capitalization, which is the market value of the outstanding shares) growth stocks. Small companies, with sales of less than $1 billion, are known as emerging growth companies or small-cap stocks. In general, the smaller the company, the bigger the growth potential, because it is easier to grow quickly from a small base than from a large one. However, investing in stocks of smaller companies also entails more risk because they do not have market positions as established as those of larger companies.

One of the biggest mistakes people make when buying growth stocks is to get too excited by their prospects and pay too much for the stocks. An easy way to judge whether you are overpaying is to look at the stock's PE ratio. The higher the PE ratio, the more enthusiastic investors are about the company. Compare the PE ratio of your stock with that of similar companies in the same industry. If your stock's PE ratio is considerably higher, you could be paying too much.

The other key indicator growth stock investors look for is the earnings growth rate, or the rate at which profits grow from year to year. In general, the higher the growth rate, the higher the stock's PE ratio. The ideal growth stock is one selling at a PE ratio below its growth rate. For example, if Go-Go Computer's profits are growing at 30 percent a year, its stock would be considered a bargain if it were selling for a PE ratio of 20. While producing a solid growth rate is important, consistent growth is also highly prized. A company with profits up 40 percent one year and down 20 percent the next will not earn as high a PE ratio as one that grows 20 percent year after year.

The worksheet in Figure 2.4 will help you evaluate your own growth stock. All the numbers needed to complete this worksheet are available from Standard & Poor's company profiles or the *Value Line Investment Survey*. We have provided sample numbers for a growth stock.

Income Stocks

Most people think of stocks as vehicles to achieve capital appreciation, but they can also provide steady income. Good-quality income stocks have an advantage over bonds for income investors. While the interest that a bond

---

Figure 2.4   Growth Stock Worksheet

	Sample Stock Points	Your Stock Points
Sample Stock		
Projected five-year annual growth rate = 22%		
Your Stock		
Projected five-year annual growth rate = %		
(If more than 20%, give your stock 2 points; if between 10% and 20%, 1 point; if less than 10%, 0 points.)	2	
Sample Stock		
Earnings growth rate for past five years = 25%		
Your Stock		
Earnings growth rate for past five years = %		
(If more than 20%, give your stock 2 points; if between 10% and 20%, 1 point; if less than 10%, 0 points.)	2	
Sample Stock		
Average return on equity for past three years = 18%		
Your Stock		
Average return on equity for past three years = %		
(If more than 20%, give your stock 2 points; if between 10% and 20%, 1 point; if less than 10%, 0 points.)	1	

Sample Stock

$$\frac{\text{Projected five-year earnings growth rate} \ = \ 22\%}{\text{Stock's current PE ratio} \ = \ 16\%} = 137\%$$

Your Stock

$$\frac{\text{Projected five-year earnings growth rate} \ = \ \%}{\text{Stock's current PE ratio} \ = \ \%} = \ \%$$

(If more than 160%, give your stock 2 points; if between 125% and 160%, 1 point; if less than 125%, 0 points.)   1

Figure 2.4   Growth Stock Worksheet (continued)

	Sample Stock Points	Your Stock Points
Sample Stock		
Earnings consistency = Up 7% in each of past five years		
Your Stock		
Earnings consistency = Up % in each of past five years		
(If up 10% or more for each of the past five years, give your stock 2 points; if up for each of the past five years, 1 point; if down in any of the past five years, 0 points.)	1	
Total Points	7	

If your stock scores 6 points or more, it has long-term growth potential. The example here looks like an attractive growth stock.

pays is fixed until the bond matures, a stock's dividend can rise year after year. Although a bond usually provides a higher current yield, a stock with a solid record of dividend increases can actually pay more over time. Because those higher dividends are paid out of ever-increasing profits, the stock price should climb over time as well.

Consider Johnson & Johnson, for example. If you had purchased the stock in 1991, and held it for 10 years through 2001, your dividend would have grown 268 percent, from 19 cents (split-adjusted) to 70 cents. Although that 70-cent dividend represented only a 1.5 percent yield based on its 2001 price of about $50, it represents a 7 percent yield based on your original purchase price in 1991 of about $10 a share. On top of that, the stock price increased about 400 percent during that 10-year period, which means that a Johnson & Johnson shareholder would have seen his or her original investment increase 400 percent in addition to receiving a growing stream of annual dividend payouts. By comparison, with a 10-year bond, you would have received exactly the same yield all 10 years, with no increase in the value of the bond.

Companies that pay high dividends usually are well-established, profitable firms. Some businesses that offer high-paying stocks include banking firms, real estate investment trusts, and electric, gas, telephone, and water utilities. Unlike faster growing, younger companies, which reinvest profits in their own businesses, such firms traditionally pay out at least half their profits to shareholders in the form of dividends.

Even more than prices of other stocks, high-yield stock prices are greatly influenced by the direction of interest rates. When rates on Treasury bonds fall, high-yield stock prices tend to rise because that stock's dividends are more competitive with bonds. Conversely, when interest rates rise, high-yield stocks look less attractive, and their prices tend to drop.

To make sure an income stock you are considering can continue to raise its dividend, you should determine that the company is financially strong. You can do this examining three key items.

1. *The company's debt.* Debt that is more than 50 percent of the company's equity may be a sign of trouble.
2. *Credit rating.* Another quick way to gauge financial strength is to check the stock's rating with a reputable credit rating agency's ratings, such as Standard & Poor's or the *Value Line Investment Survey.* Any rating over B+ means that the company is financially solid.
3. *Payout ratio.* The final ratio to inspect before you buy a stock for income is the payout ratio, the percentage of earnings that is paid out in dividends. A payout ratio below 60 percent means that there is a sizable cushion for the company to fall back on before it has to cut its dividend. A low ratio also leaves room for the dividend to grow. On the other hand, a payout ratio above 80 percent might be a sign that the dividend may be cut.

Don't be entranced by a stock that sports an above-average yield, usually of more than 10 percent. There must be a reason why the yield is that high, and probably it is not positive. For example, the payout may be high because the stock price has fallen in anticipation of a dividend cut. Or it may be high because the company is in the process of liquidation, and the high payouts are actually a return of shareholders' capital. Whatever the reason, be suspicious of stocks with ultra-high yields.

All the numbers needed to complete the worksheet in Figure 2.5 are available from Standard & Poor's company profiles or the *Value Line Investment Survey.* We have provided sample numbers for an income stock.

Out-of-Favor Stocks

If the age-old way to make money in stocks is to buy low and sell high, then buying stocks when they are out of favor is a good way to buy low. Though this style of choosing stocks can be emotionally trying, it can be rewarding as well. Investors are not always rational. Just as they can bid up the price of a growth stock too high because they are so enthusiastic about its

Figure 2.5   Income Stock Worksheet

			Sample Stock Points	Your Stock Points

Sample Stock

Dividend yield   =   7%

Your Stock

Dividend yield   =   %

(If more than 6%, give your stock 2 points; if between
4% and 6%, 1 point; if less than 4%, 0 points.)   2   _____

Sample Stock

Dividend growth rate for the past five years   =   9%

Your Stock

Dividend growth rate for the past five years   =   %

(If more than 8%, give your stock 2 points; if between
5% and 8%, 1 point; if less than 5%, 0 points.)   2   _____

Sample Stock

Projected five-year earnings growth rate   =   10%

Your Stock

Projected five-year earnings growth rate   =   %

(If more than 8%, give your stock 2 points; if between
5% and 8%, 1 point; if less than 5%, 0 points.)   2   _____

Sample Stock

$$\frac{\text{Dividends per common share} \quad = \quad \$1}{\text{Earnings per common share} \quad = \quad \$2} = \text{Dividend payout ratio—50\%}$$

Your Stock

$$\frac{\text{Dividends per common share} \quad = \quad \$}{\text{Earnings per common share} \quad = \quad \$} = \text{Dividend payout ratio— \%}$$

(If less than 60%, give your stock 2 points; if between
60% and 70%, 1 point; if more than 70%, 0 points.)   2   _____

Figure 2.5   (continued)

	Sample Stock Points	Your Stock Points
Sample Stock		
Financial strength rating = A–		
Your Stock		
Financial strength rating =		
(If the credit rating agency's ratings is A or above, give your stock 2 points; if between B+ and A–, 1 point; if lower than B+, 0 points.)	1	
Total Points	9	

If your stock scores 6 points or more, it should provide steady, attractive income. The example here is a stock that any retiree could count on to pay uninterrupted dividends for years.

---

prospects, they can also pummel a stock that has momentarily slipped to unrealistically low prices. That's where bargain hunters swoop in. They sell out when the stock recovers.

The easiest way to spot neglected stocks is by looking for low PE ratios. A PE ratio of less than 10 signals that investors do not have much hope for the future of the company, which may, in fact, be an incorrect perception of the situation. The moment the company reports better-than-expected results, perceptions can change quickly, and the stock price can shoot up. Do your research first. Don't be tempted to buy a stock strictly because it has a low PE ratio, however. Some companies deserve their lowly valuation and, in fact, will not recover.

In addition to a low PE ratio, bargain hunters usually look for industries that are currently out of favor. They also look for several other signs, including:

- *Low price-book value ratios.* Out-of-favor stocks often have a low stock price-book value ratio. (Book value is the assessed value of a company's assets. Book value per share, which is frequently used in assessing the potential value of a company's stock, is defined as the per-share assessed value of a company's assets.) Stocks tend to trade at a multiple of their book value, so if you find a stock that is trading at or below its book value, that could be a bargain if other factors are positive.

- *Low institutional ownership.* Another sign of benign neglect in the market is if few of the shares are held by institutional investors, such as mutual funds or banks, because it is not fashionable to own such depressed stocks.
- *No interest by analysts.* If brokerage analysts do not pay attention to a stock, it is probably out of favor. Analysts are notoriously wrong in their evaluation of stocks, as the high-tech meltdown emphatically demonstrated, so you may be able to find some great gems that Wall Street's analysts have missed.

What you should look for is a stock with a fair chance at turnaround. You may infer that a recovery is on the way if sales and earnings are no longer deteriorating or if the company has a new product or service that has the potential to restart its growth. Another way to check for signs of life is to determine whether company executives are buying the stock themselves and whether they are increasing capital expenditures. If the people who know the company best are investing in it heavily, that could be a tip-off that recovery is at hand.

Not every ugly duckling turns into a swan, however. If your stock remains depressed after a year or more, you probably should turn it in for another one. It takes only one or two dramatic recoveries for this strategy to pay off.

All the numbers needed to complete the worksheet in Figure 2.6 are available from Standard & Poor's company profiles or the *Value Line Investment Survey.* We have provided sample numbers for an out-of-favor stock.

If your stock scores 6 points or more, you might have uncovered a worthy out-of-favor stock. The example here is a stock that has been neglected yet shows signs of a rebound. That means that its stock price should recover soon.

Value Stocks

If you could buy a stock worth $10 for $8, would you do it? Most people would because they know they are buying something for less than it is worth. In the stock market, this style of choosing stocks is known as value investing.

The key to value investing is being able to perceive when a stock's current price does not fully reflect the value of its assets. Those assets might include real estate, brand names, oil reserves, patented technology, or even cash or stocks in other companies. Value investors make money by buying when the stock's assets are worth more than the stock's price and selling when the value of the assets has been realized.

Shareholders can be paid for the true value of their company's assets in one of several ways. A company can be taken over by another company or by a raider at a premium price because the acquirer thinks it can sell the assets for even more. The company can by broken into pieces, leaving share-

---

Figure 2.6   Out-of-Favor Stock Worksheet

	Sample Stock Points	Your Stock Points

Sample Stock

$$\frac{\text{Current stock price} \quad = \$40}{\text{Book value per share} \quad = \$90} = 44\%$$

Your Stock

$$\frac{\text{Current stock price} \quad = \$}{\text{Book value per share} \quad = \$} = \quad \%$$

(If less than 25%, give your stock 2 points; if between 25% and 50%, 1 point; if more than 50%, 0 points.)   1   _____

Sample Stock

$$\frac{\text{Stock PE ratio} \quad = \quad 10}{\text{S\&P 500 PE ratio} \quad = \quad 15} = 66\%$$

Your Stock

$$\frac{\text{Stock PE ratio} \quad =}{\text{S\&P 500 PE ratio} \quad =} = \quad \%$$

(If less than 80%, give your stock 2 points; if between 80% and 100%, 1 point; if more than 100%, 0 points.)   2   _____

Sample Stock

Estimated five-year earnings growth rate   =   6%

Your Stock

Estimated five-year earnings growth rate   =   %

(If more than 7%, give your stock 2 points; if between 2% and 7%, 1 point; if less than 2%, 0 points.)   1   _____

Sample Stock

$$\frac{\text{Estimated capital expenditures for this year} \quad = \$50 \text{ million}}{\text{Capital expenditures for last year} \quad = \$20 \text{ million}} = 250\%$$

Figure 2.6   Out-of-Favor Stock Worksheet (continued)

	Sample Stock Points	Your Stock Points
Your Stock		

Estimated capital expenditures = $
      for this year   million

$$\frac{\text{Estimated capital expenditures for this year} = \$ \text{ million}}{\text{Capital expenditures for last year} = \$ \text{ million}} = \quad \%$$

Capital expenditures for last year = $
               million

(If more than 150%, give your stock 2 points; if between 100% and 150%, 1 point; if less than 100%, 0 points.)   2

Sample Stock

Percentage of outstanding stock held by institutions = 30%

Your Stock

Percentage of outstanding stock held by institutions = %

(If less than 25%, give your stock 2 points; if between 25% and 50%, 1 point; if more than 50%, 0 points.)   1

Total Points   7

If your stock scores 6 points or more, you might have uncovered a worthy out-of-favor stock. The example here is a stock that has been neglected yet shows signs of a rebound. That means that its stock price should recover soon.

---

holders with several stocks worth more separately than they were worth as a whole. The company's management can derive a way to make the formerly underused asset more productive, which would produce profits to boost the stock price. Or investors can finally realize the value of the company's assets, and the stock price will rise to reflect that changed perception.

Trying to determine the true value of assets is tricky and subjective. A valuable asset to one analyst may have far less worth to another. Still, you can get a sense of whether a stock is selling for less than its breakup value by looking at several factors, including:

- The company's book value per share
- Its tangible assets per share, such as land or oil reserves
- Its financial assets, including cash and securities

- Net net working capital. A particularly stringent test is to compare the stock's price to so-called net net working capital; that is, the amount of cash a company could raise in a hurry if it were liquidated today. To calculate it, subtract short-term and long-term debts from such current assets as cash, securities, receivables, and inventory. If the net net working capital of the stock you are looking at is 25 percent or more than the current price, you have found an undervalued stock.

The other way to identify a value stock is to see how much it would be worth if it continued in business. Take a look at the firm's cash flow (profits plus depreciation) per share, and divide it by the current stock price. The lower the price-cash flow ratio, the cheaper the stock is. At a certain point, the cash the company is throwing off could finance an acquisition of the company, making it a likely takeover target.

All the numbers needed to fill out the worksheet in Figure 2.7 are available from Standard & Poor's company profiles or the *Value Line Investment Survey.* We have provided sample numbers for a value stock.

USING TECHNICAL ANALYSIS TO CHOOSE STOCKS

Instead of concentrating on a company's earnings, book value, or products, some analysts look only at its stock's trading action to see whether the stock is worth buying or selling. This method of choosing stocks is called *technical analysis,* in contrast to *fundamental analysis,* which we have focused on so far.

For the novice, technical analysis can be mysterious and intimidating. Instead of understanding a company's products, you must interpret charts and graphs. However, even if you want to concentrate mostly on fundamentals, it is still a good idea to glance at the charts and graphs to see what the market action can tell you about the stock. The two key indicators that technical analysts use to determine whether a stock is headed up or down are price action and volume of trading.

Price action. Technicians look at a stock's price history and draw many conclusions from it. For example, a stock's low point is often called its support level, meaning that it is likely to find support from stock buyers when it hits that price. Conversely, a stock's high is called its resistance level, meaning that in order to lock in their profits, shareholders will tend to sell when the stock reaches that price. In general, technicians recommend buying when a stock is near its support level and selling as it approaches resistance.

Figure 2.7 Value Stock Worksheet

	Sample Stock Points	Your Stock Points

Sample Stock

$$\frac{\text{Current stock price} \quad = \$40}{\text{Book value per share} \quad = \$45} = 89\%$$

Your Stock

$$\frac{\text{Current stock price} \quad = \$}{\text{Book value per share} \quad = \$} = \quad \%$$

(If less than 100%, give your stock 2 points; if between 100% and 140%, 1 point; if more than 140%, 0 points.)   2   _____

Sample Stock

$$\frac{\text{Cash per share} \quad = \$\ 5}{\text{Current stock price} \quad = \$40} = 12.5\%$$

Your Stock

$$\frac{\text{Cash per share} \quad = \$}{\text{Current stock price} \quad = \$} = \quad \%$$

(If more than 25%, give your stock 2 points; if between 10% and 25%, 1 point; if less than 10%, 0 points.)   1   _____

Sample Stock

$$\frac{\text{Net net working capital per share} \quad = \$\ 6}{\text{Current stock price} \quad = \$40} = 15\%$$

Your Stock

$$\frac{\text{Net net working capital per share} \quad = \$}{\text{Current stock price} \quad = \$} = \quad \%$$

(If more than 25%, give your stock 2 points; if between 0% and 25%, 1 point; if less than 0%, 0 points.)   1   _____

Sample Stock

$$\frac{\text{Current stock price} \quad = \$40}{\text{Cash flow per share} \quad = \$10} = 4$$

Figure 2.7 (continued)

	Sample Stock Points	Your Stock Points

Your Stock

$$\frac{\text{Current stock price} \quad = \$}{\text{Cash flow per share} \quad = \$} =$$

(If less than 5, give your stock 2 points; if between 5 and 7, give it 1 point; if more than 7, 0 points.)   **2** _____

Sample Stock

$$\frac{\text{Outstanding debt} \quad = \begin{array}{c}\$19\\ \text{million}\end{array}}{\text{Total capital} \quad = \begin{array}{c}\$100\\ \text{million}\end{array}} = 19\%$$

Your Stock

$$\frac{\text{Outstanding debt} \quad = \begin{array}{c}\$\\ \text{million}\end{array}}{\text{Total capital} \quad = \begin{array}{c}\$\\ \text{million}\end{array}} = \%$$

(If less than 20%, give your stock 2 points; if between 20% and 30%, 1 point; if more than 30%, 0 points.)   **2** _____

Total Points   **8** _____

If your stock scores 4 points or more, you might be looking at an undervalued stock. The example here is a real bargain.

Volume of trading. The number of shares that a stock trades over a particular period gives technicians many clues about its future direction. High volume in a stock that is rising in price is considered bullish, and low volume in a stock that is falling in price is considered bearish.

People can dedicate their lives to analyzing each latest wrinkle in a stock's trading action. If you want to learn more about technical analysis, consult the following classics in the field:

- *Technical Analysis Explained: The Successful Investor's Guide to Spotting Investment Trends and Turning Points,* by Martin J. Pring. McGraw-Hill, PO Box 543, Blacklick, OH 43004; 800-634-3961; <www.mcgraw-hill.com>

- *Technical Analysis of Stock Trends,* by Robert E. Edwards and John Magee. Prentice Hall Professional Publishing, One Lake Street, Upper Saddle River, NJ 07458; 201-236-7156; 800-382-3419; <www.prenticehall.com>.
- *Mastering Technical Analysis,* by Michael C. Thomsett. Dearborn Trade Publishing; Chicago, IL; 800-245-2665; <www.dearborntrade.com>.

You can get current charts to use for technical analysis from all major full-service and discount brokers when you open an account.

Here are some Web sites that also deal with technical analysis.

- *Forex news.* Offers a wide range of charts, articles, and other information geared to the serious technical investor. <www.forexnews.com>
- *Jadco Stock Charts.* Provides tips, charts, and other tools for technical analysis. <www.jadco.com>
- *StockCharts.com.* Offers a wealth of information on stocks and the market, along with a variety of tools for stock analysis and access to stock movement charts. <www.stockcharts.com>
- *TheStreet.com.* This popular investment site includes a special section geared to technical analysis. <www.thestreet.com>
- *Traders.com.* Offers a variety of articles and investment tools to help investors with technical analysis. <www.traders.com>

CHAPTER 3

Beyond the Blue Chips

The vast majority of Americans who buy stocks invest almost exclusively in established common stocks, but there's a whole universe of other options available on the market, including brand new stocks (known as *initial public offerings* or IPOs), socially responsible stocks, and index shares that basically mirror an entire market index. While each type of investment carries its own unique risks and rewards, investing in these other types of stocks can spice up your portfolio and bolster your diversification.

The key for relatively conservative investors is to exercise moderation. Invest just a small portion of your assets in IPOs and index shares. There's an art to investing successfully in each of these specialized stocks.

NEW ISSUES

One of the most exciting yet dangerous opportunities in the stock market is IPOs, which are new stock issues in a company that had been privately held. Such companies usually "go public" with great fanfare and hype, which can make their stock prices soar immediately after they begin trading. In the most famous case, when Genentech, the first biotechnology company to go public, made its offering at $35 a share in the early 1980s, its stock soared to more than $80 a share by the end of the first day of trading. During the Internet IPO craze of the late 1990s, such stories of stocks that doubled or tripled after their IPO were almost a weekly occurrence.

The new issues market is extremely sensitive to the general direction of the stock market. When stock prices are high and rising and investors are enthusiastic, many new issues go public. When prices are low and depressed and no one wants to hear about stocks, it is almost impossible to sell a new issue.

Companies are most likely to launch an IPO when their industries are popular with investors. What's hot goes in and out of fashion quite frequently. One year, semiconductor company stocks are popular; next, it can be environmental stocks. Biotech stocks have had their day, and specialty retailer stocks were the rage among new issues at one point. In the 1990s, stocks of companies that had been taken private in the leveraged buyout craze of the 1980s started going public again, making the hottest new issue a "reverse leveraged buyout." Who knows what Wall Street will think of next?

By their nature, new issues are speculative because they usually have no history of performance as public corporations. Some might have very promising-sounding products or services, but they may not be able to produce results when they finally get the money to bring the products or services to market. Several studies have shown that in the long term, about a third of all new issues do well, a third don't move much from the price at which they go public, and a third go bankrupt.

Another study found that IPOs jump an average of 15 percent on their first day of trading—*then underperform the market by 44 percent over the ensuing three years!*

In deciding whether to buy a particular new issue, use the standard analysis tools discussed in the previous chapter. Also, you can get an offering statement, usually known as the *red herring,* from a broker, with all the company's financial history and plans. Other criteria to analyze include:

- How are the company's earnings affected by the issuance of millions of new shares in the IPO?
- What unique product or service does this company have that will allow it to compete with more established firms?
- How will the IPOs PE ratio compare with that of other companies in the same industry at the proposed initial offering price?
- Are company executives and other insiders on the board of directors using the IPO as a chance to unload their shares?
- What is the record of the brokerage firm underwriting the offering? How have other issues the firm has sold performed in the past year?

If a new issue with exciting prospects is coming to market, chances are that you will not be able to obtain many shares—if any at all. That's because hot IPOs are parceled out to brokers' best customers, almost as a favor. If the issue is so hot that its price soars immediately after it begins trading, many investors will "flip" the stock back into the market and pocket an instant profit. Don't expect to be a flipper, though, unless you are a steady customer of a broker with a great deal of pull at his or her firm.

Another way to invest in a new company involves direct investing through the Internet. Many start-up companies now elect to bypass the underwriting broker and offer shares directly to the public through the Internet. The Internet company that handles the offering will provide all the information on the start-up company to potential investors. The risk is probably higher with this approach, because it is unlikely that the Internet company will perform the same level of investigation and due diligence on the start-up company as the underwriting broker in a conventional IPO will provide.

In many cases, the best strategy for dealing with the new issues market is to wait for all the hype to calm down and buy the stock three months or so after the offering. By then, Wall Street will have moved on to other new issues, and these stocks tend to sink back to more reasonable levels.

For more information on new issues, consult the following:

- IPO Financial Network (10 East Willow Street, Millburn, NJ 07041; 973-379-5100; www.ipofinancial.com).
- Red Herring (Suite 450, 1550 Bryant Street, San Francisco, CA 94013; 415-865-2277; www.redherring.com). This magazine profiles new issues and helps investors profit from the new issues market.

You can also use the Internet to find out the latest information about initial public offerings. By retrieving information about coming offerings online, you will be able to find out and act on the best deals sooner than if you had to wait for a mailed newsletter. Here is a sampling of the most prominent IPO Web sites:

- Bloomberg IPO Center <www.bloomberg.com/markets/ipocenter.html>
- Capital Markets Financial Center <www.capmarkets.com>
- CNET Investor <www.investor.cnet.com>
- IPO Alert <www.alertipo.com>
- IBChannel.com <www.ibchannel.com>
- InvestorGuide <www.investorguide.com>
- IPO Central (go to <www.hoovers.com> then click on IPO Central)
- IPO.com <www.ipo.com>
- IPOfn Online <www.ipofinancial.com>
- IPO Home.com <ipohome.com>
- IPO Monitor <www.ipomonitor.com>
- IPOnder <cbs.marketwatch.com/news/current/iponder/>
- IPO Pros <www.ipopros.com>

- IPOs <www.tradingday.com/c/ipos>
- IPO Spotlight <www.ipospotlight.com>
- IPOwebwatch.com <www.ipowebwatch.com>
- 123Jump <www.123jump.com/ipomaven.htm>
- The Syndicate <moneypages.com/syndicate/stocks/ipo.html>

Internet companies and Web sites are now appearing that use the vast reach of the Internet to bring small but qualified investors together with cash-needy start-up companies before or in lieu of the company going public with an IPO. A qualified investor, according to the SEC, is one with at least $1 million in assets (including a home), or someone whose individual income exceeded $200,000 in each of the two most recent years or whose joint income with a spouse exceeded $300,000. Typically, the minimum investment required by these companies is $25,000. The Internet company will in most cases offer a group of investors (known as *angels*) the opportunity to invest in a start-up company and will arrange meetings with the start-up company and the interested investors for company tours and presentations.

There is always an element of risk investing in a start-up company, but if the investor is careful with his or her choice, this method may offer less risk than waiting for IPO shares to become available on the market at a higher price than company friends and suppliers were able to purchase them.

The following are Internet companies that provide this service:

- Garage.com <www.garage.com>
- Offroad Capital <www.offroadcapital.com>

INDEX SHARES: SPIDERS AND DIAMONDS

The American Stock Exchange, which is owned by Nasdaq, offers a fairly extensive array of index shares, which combine all the opportunities of indexes with the advantages of stock trading. The best-known among these index shares are *Spiders,* technically called Standard & Poor's Depositary Receipts, or SPDRs, and *Diamonds,* or the Dow Jones index shares. The index shares can be bought and sold through regular, discount, or online brokers just like other securities. Like an index fund, the shares mimic the markets they represent. The Spider, for example, is a unit investment trust that holds shares of all the companies in the S&P 500 and closely tracks the price performance and dividend yield of the index. Slight misalignments occur when the trust must be rebalanced and must adjust for an inflow of dividends. Diamonds are set up the same way, only they use the 30 stocks of the Dow Jones Industrial Average. The ticker symbol for Spiders is SPY, and the symbol for Diamonds is DIA.

Although an investor pays the typical brokerage fee when buying or sell-ing, neither of these instruments involves a sales load, unlike a load mutual fund. Unless a stock is added to or deleted from an index, generally there is little trading within a fund, so capital gains distributions are kept at a mini-mum. However, owners of Spiders and Diamonds are subject to taxes on the investor's share of dividends as they are granted. In most cases, expenses for Spiders and other index products are lower than those on a mutual fund or even an index fund. Annual expenses for Spiders are 0.18 percent, or put an-other way, for an investment of $10,000 the annual expense would be $18. There are no 12b-1 fees or hidden costs that are sometimes charged by mu-tual funds. As for performance, index products historically have outper-formed actively managed mutual funds over the long term.

At times when the markets are down, for those who have faith that they will revive given time, but feel unsure about which stocks will lead in the recovery, index-based investments offer a conservative, easy-to-understand way to participate in the next bull market. To learn more about Spiders, Di-amonds, and their strangely named relatives, visit <www.nasdaq.com> or telephone the American Stock Exchange at 800-843-2639.

SOCIALLY CONSCIOUS INVESTING

If you are one of the growing number of people who not only want their investments to do well, but to do good as well, you might be interested in so-cially conscious investing. This is the practice of seeking out companies that meet standards of social performance in addition to normal financial criteria. Most social criteria are positive; that is, they are attributes that people look for in a company. However, some criteria are negative; meaning they are as-pects of a company that would keep people from investing in it.

The most common positive social criteria are clean environmental records; widespread advancement of women and minority employees; action on child care and AIDS for workers; safe, nonpolluting products; active in-vestment in community and social projects; promoting alternative energy sources, such as solar and geothermal power; commitment to worker safety; and fair bargaining with unions.

The most common negative social criteria are dealing with the military or arms business, operating nuclear power facilities, testing products on ani-mals in a way that is considered cruel, selling tobacco or liquor, fostering gambling, and creating water or air pollution.

The financial idea behind socially conscious investing is that if a company does not pollute and treats its workers well, in addition to promoting other pro-gressive policies, it will probably be able to stay out of trouble with government agencies and the public. That will be good for business and, in the long run, the firm's stock price. Conversely, a company that is constantly fined by the government for polluting, suffers strikes by oppressed workers, and experiences nuclear meltdowns is probably not going to offer profitable stock.

One group that monitors corporate performance on a broad range of social issues is the Council on Economic Priorities (30 Irving Place, New York, NY 10003; 212-420-1133; 800-729-4237; www.cepnyse.org). Another company that issues social and financial reports on individual stocks is Trillium Asset Management Corp. (711 Atlantic Avenue, Boston, MA 02111; 617-423-6655; www.trilliuminvest.com). It has a newsletter on the subject titled *Investing for a Better World* that is published on its Web site. Two books on the topic are *Investing with Your Conscience,* by John C. Harrington (John Wiley & Sons, 605 Third Avenue, New York, NY 10158; 212-850-6000; www.wiley.com), and *Socially Responsible Investing,* by Amy Domini (Dearborn Trade, Chicago, IL; 312-836-4400; 800-245-2665; www.dearborntrade.com).

If you want a fund manager to make these sometimes tricky social screening decisions for you, there are about ten mutual funds that use ethical screens. Some of the better known funds include Calvert Income Fund (800-368-2748; www.calvertgroup.com), Dreyfus Third Century (800-645-6561; www.dreyfus.com), Parnassus (800-999-3505; www.parnassusfund.com), and Pax World (800-767-1729; www.paxfund.com).

Most socially responsible funds screen companies in tobacco, alcohol, and gambling. Some, like those below, also tackle heated issues, such as gay rights, abortion, and workplace equality, often handpicking companies with exemplary records.

- Citizens Emerging Growth <www.efund.com>
- Citizen Funds <www.citizensfund.com>
- Domini Social Equity <www.domini.com>
- Dreyfus Premier Third Century <www.dreyfus.com>
- Friends Ivory Social Awareness <www.friendsivoryfunds.com>
- Green Century Balanced <www.greencentury.com>
- Noah Fund <www.noahfund.com>
- Pax World Fund <www.paxfund.com>
- Portfolio 21 <www.portfolio21.com>
- Women's Equity <www.womens-equity.com>

CHAPTER 4

Buying Stocks
without a Broker

Although many investors prefer to work with a broker or financial advisor to build a successful investment portfolio, others enjoy making their own investment decisions, buying and selling stocks on their own. By making your own trading decisions, you can greatly reduce or even eliminate commission costs on most of your stock trades.

There are several options available for the do-it-yourself investor. You can set up an account with a traditional discount broker who will charge you considerably less than a full-service broker. By comparison, for a small purchase, a full-service broker would charge a commission of about $75 to $100 per trade, while a discounter would charge about $30 to $50.

The Internet has made stock trades even cheaper. Online brokerage companies such as E*Trade and Ameritrade typically charge $5 to $25 per trade, though a few are even cheaper. Another online investment company, FOLIOfn .com, charges just $149 for all of your trades for an entire year (as long as you don't exceed 500 trades per month). For a review of dozens of online brokers, go to <www.sonic.net/donaldj>.

You can also save on commissions with some stocks by buying shares directly from the company. A growing number of companies have begun to offer a direct stock purchase plan for new investors and a dividend reinvestment and stock purchase plan for existing customers. Most of those plans offer commission-free stock purchases.

DIVIDEND REINVESTMENT PLANS (DRIPS)

If you own a stock that is paying a dividend, chances are that the company offers a terrific benefit called a *dividend reinvestment plan,* commonly known as a DRIP. If you don't need the cash from your dividends to live on, you can reinvest the payment with the company and buy more shares of stock. About 1,000 companies offer a DRIP.

Enrolling in a DRIP offers several advantages. You put the magic of compounding to work for you. The shares that you buy with reinvested dividends earn more dividends, which buy more shares, and so on. Over time, the number of shares you own in the company grows steadily, without your having to contribute more cash.

Essentially, you are practicing dollar cost averaging. For example, say you receive $100 in dividends each quarter. When the share price is high, like $50, your dividends buy fewer shares—in this case, two shares. When the share price is low, like $20, the same dividends buy more shares—in this case, five. This counteracts your normal emotional inclination to buy more shares when the price is high and rising and fewer when the price is low and falling. Over time, your average cost of buying shares most likely will be lower than if you tried to time your purchases.

Most DRIPs are free of brokerage commissions and other charges. Because the company offering the plan wants to encourage shareholders to use it, the firm normally absorbs all brokerage commissions for buying the stock and the administrative costs of the program.

More than 100 companies offer a sweetened version of the DRIP, called a *discount DRIP.* To encourage shareholder participation, the company gives up to an additional 5 percent discount on reinvested dividends. So, if you reinvest $100 worth of dividends, you receive $105 worth of stock. This makes your holdings in the company grow even faster.

A list of companies that offer a 1 percent to 5 percent discount on reinvested dividends can be found in Charles Carlson's *Buying Stocks without a Broker* (McGraw-Hill, PO Box 543, Blacklick, OH 43004; 800-722-4726; www.mcgraw-hill.com). That book explains how DRIPs work and provides a directory of all plans, including a profile of each company with its address and telephone number, whether it offers optional cash purchase plans, and other details of its plans. Carlson also is editor of the monthly newsletter *The DRIP Investor* (Dow Theory Forecasts, 7412 Calumet Avenue, Hammond, IN 46324; 219-931-6480; www.dowtheory.com) which keeps the list of discount DRIPs up to date.

Several hundred companies not only allow you to reinvest your dividends, but offer optional cash purchase plans. These plans enable you to invest your own money, along with your dividends, in more shares at no cost. While that alone is a great deal, some firms even offer optional cash purchases at a discount. The companies that offer a 5 percent DRIP discount also extend the discount to any additional money you invest. Most of these programs, however, put limits on optional cash purchases, usually of about $25,000 a year. (They don't want to give away too much free money, after all.)

Several companies not only allow you to reinvest dividends and optional cash at no charge, but also make it easy to buy your original shares directly from the companies themselves, without commissions. Theoretically, you could buy shares in these firms, enroll in their DRIPs and optional cash programs, and build up a stake of hundreds of shares without ever paying a commission! (Don't tell your broker that you know about this one, or he or she may not return your calls!)

Another resource to keep you up to date on which companies are offering dividend reinvestment plans is the *DRP Authority* newsletter (The Moneypaper, Inc., 1010 Mamaroneck Avenue, Mamaroneck, NY 10543; 800-388-9993; www.moneypaper.com). In addition to the monthly newsletter listing new developments in the DRIP world, Moneypaper publishes a complete fact-filled *Guide to Dividend Reinvestment Plans* that has all the information you will ever need to get started with this sensible form of investing.

DIRECT INVESTING IN STOCKS

Another way to avoid brokerage commissions as you invest in individual stocks is by enrolling in the direct investment option at a growing number of companies. Charles Carlson, editor of the *No-Load Stock Insider* newsletter (7412 Calumet Avenue, Suite 200, Hammond, IN 46324; 219-852-3230) maintains a current list of such plans. Carlson refers to such stocks obtained through these plans as no-load stocks. The companies using the phone number 800-774-4117 are participating in the Direct Stock Purchase Plan Clearinghouse, which offers direct enrollment for many stocks around the world.

The number of companies with such plans is always expanding, because companies increasingly want to attract shareholders to buy their stock directly. In addition to Carlson's newsletter, you may be interested in the *Direct Investing* newsletter (The Moneypaper, Inc., 1010 Mamaroneck Avenue, Mamaroneck, NY 10543; 800-388-9993; www.moneypaper.com), which also tracks developments in the field.

You also can get a current list of direct purchase stocks online at Net-Stock Direct <www.netstockdirect.com>.

To enroll in a company's dividend reinvestment plan, you must have the stock registered in your own name. Normally, if you buy stock through a brokerage firm, the broker holds it in its street name; that is, under a consolidated name for all of its accounts. A company offering a DRIP, however, must know the name of the participating shareholder so it can set up a reinvestment account. Therefore, if you have your stock with a broker, you must reregister it with the company, which the company will gladly take care of for you. After you're enrolled in the plan, you will receive quarterly statements from the company disclosing how many shares your dividends purchased and how many total shares you now own.

SECURITIES PURCHASE PROGRAM

Another way to enroll in dividend reinvestment plans without paying brokerage commissions is to enroll in the First Share Program (305 Mitchell Mountain Road, Westcliffe, CO 81252-0222; 719-783-2929; www.firstshare .com). For a $30 enrollment fee, First Share allows you to buy one share of about 250 blue chip companies and sign up for direct purchase and dividend reinvestment programs.

CHOOSING STOCKS WITH AN INVESTMENT CLUB

If you don't want to choose stocks on your own, you have another alternative—starting an investment club or joining one that is already up and running. An investment club is a group of people, usually between 5 and 30, who pool their money and decide on stocks to buy or sell. Club members usually start the club by contributing $100 each, then make a monthly deposit of $25 or $50.

Advantages of investing through such a club include:

- You will hear about stocks you probably never would have discovered on your own. Because members of the club come from all walks of life, they often have insights into companies that are doing well in industries in which they work.
- You can gain valuable experience from other members that you can apply to your own portfolio.
- Through the club, you can be part of a more diversified portfolio than you could probably afford on your own.
- The club will probably pay lower commissions than you would because it is buying more shares in each transaction.
- You may make social or business contacts that are important beyond the investment club's scope.

You might think that putting a group of amateur investors together would be a recipe for disaster. In fact, just the opposite is true. The National Association of Investors Corporation (NAIC), the trade group for investment clubs, says that more than half of all clubs beat the Standard & Poor's 500 Index every year—a feat many investment pros fail to achieve. There seems to be some magic in the consensus-style stock selection process that makes many investment clubs successful. Most clubs would not agree to invest in the ideas of an eccentric member who recommends risky stocks.

Most successful investment clubs have a strategy that guides their stock selection. Some might concentrate on local stocks, while others look for growth stocks or undervalued companies. Whatever the style, it provides a framework for club members to research companies that might be of interest to the club.

If you want to set up a club, connect with a good broker who likes working with clubs. Though a broker can provide investment ideas and analysts' reports, do not let him or her dominate the club. Remember, the idea of the club is not only to make money, it is also to learn about choosing stocks by doing the research yourself. A good broker should offer the club attractive discounts on commissions not only because he or she wants to keep the club's business, but also because the broker wants to capture club members as individual clients.

Another way to keep commission costs under control is to enroll in the NAIC's Low-Cost Investment Plan. This allows clubs to buy as little as one share of many blue chip companies at a minimal fee. It also allows dividends to be reinvested automatically at no charge.

The easiest way to get your club started is to send for the step-by-step manual published by the NAIC (PO Box 220, Royal Oak, MI 48068; 248-583-6242; 877-275-6242; www.better-investing.org). The guide will tell you how to get a federal tax identification number, open a brokerage account, and set up a record-keeping system so the club's treasurer can track deposits and withdrawals.

Club members are required to report realized gains or losses, as well as dividend income, from the club's portfolio on their personal tax returns every year. On the other hand, your portion of the club's expenses, such as subscriptions to newsletters or accounting fees, will earn you deductions if you qualify.

Most people enjoy their investment club experiences as both a way to learn about and profit from investing and as a way to have fun.

CHAPTER 5

Using Your Computer and Other Resources to Pick Your Portfolio

P erhaps in no other area of personal finance is the computer better suited to help you make money than in picking and tracking a stock portfolio. The computer's ability to store and analyze data, get you online to find the latest news, and execute trades with lightning speed is perfectly suited to investing in individual stocks.

The first step in buying stocks, of course, is analyzing which individual securities are worth buying at current prices. By using a combination of analysis software and Web sites, you can get the data you need and the tools to crunch numbers to produce the result you want. Some software does fundamental analysis, screening stocks for price-earnings ratios, earnings growth rates, yields, book values, and the like. Other programs specialize in technical analysis, trying to predict future price movements based on trading patterns. There are online versions of both fundamental and technical analysis programs available at the Web sites listed in the Resources section of this chapter.

Web sites also allow you to keep up with news developments as they affect individual stocks. You can either search out stocks that have announced major developments on a particular day, or look up a company's history and see all the news stories about that company for the past few months. In either case, it is a good idea for you to be familiar with a company's financial, management, and operational history before you invest in it. The online world is loaded with financial advisors recommending individual stock trades. Before you take any of their counsel, you should know what you are getting into.

Once you have bought several stocks, software and Web sites will allow you to track your portfolio's value. You also can place price alerts so that the computer will signal you when a stock hits a certain price at which you want to buy or sell shares. Alerts can tell you when there is unusually heavy trading activity in a stock, which is often a signal that major news is about to break.

Of course, there are thousands of Web sites on the Internet offering help in picking individual stocks. For the following Resources section, I have chosen the best, easiest-to-use, and most comprehensive sites to help you put the power of your computer to work for you picking winning stocks.

First, let's look at some of the factors you can examine using online resources.

- *Track history.* Many online sites offer financial histories, including quarterly earnings and revenue figures that go back several years. You can look through those financial histories to see if a company consistently delivers rising earnings and revenue.
- *Stock price history.* How has the stock price fluctuated from year to year? Many sites provide stock histories, some with graphs, others with the actual numbers. This can give you a good idea of the stock's long-term stability.
- *Quarterly and annual balance sheet.* Check out every detail of the company's most recent reports for recent quarters and years at many online financial sites. You can look at revenue, cash flow, net income, and a wealth of other key items on the balance sheet.
- *Annual and 10k reports.* Dig deep into the companies operations by looking through its annual and 10k reports, which can be found at many financial Web sites, including Edgar Online <www.sec.gov>, a site operated by the Securities and Exchange Commission to release corporate reports from thousands of companies. You can also find annual and 10k reports at the Web sites of most publicly traded companies.
- *News reports.* Learn the latest news on any company by searching through its press reports available at dozens of financial sites.
- *Analysts' recommendations.* View analysts' recommendations and earnings projections on thousands of stocks at most of the leading investment sites.
- *Stock screening.* Want to find a computer maker that has posted at least 15 percent revenue growth the past five years? Many investment sites give you the ability to do many different types of screens to find exactly the stock that meets your criteria.

Here are some of the leading investment sites on the Web:

Allstarstocks.com. <www.allstarstocks.com> Offers stock quotes, financial information, news, market updates, stock screening, educational articles and model portfolios.

BigCharts.com. <www.bigcharts.marketwatch.com> Offers three-month stock price history charts for any company you choose. Companies are listed by industry, best and worst performers, or all companies in that industry. You can access charts and latest quotes by entering the stock symbol.

Bloomberg.com. <www.bloomberg.com> A comprehensive site offering current stock quotes, financial news, stock market update, after-hours trading data, chart data for a one-year history of stocks, and an S&P snapshot. Also has an IPO center with current information on initial public offerings.

Briefing.com. <www.briefing.com> This site is strong on currency analysis, foreign exchange, and fixed-income markets. Offers free live market coverage and three-times-a-day bond coverage. For a fee, you can have access to the IPO calendar, stock analysis, live bond coverage, and Fed policy analysis.

BusinessWeek Online/Investing (in partnership with Standard & Poor's). <www.businessweek.com/investor> This site, produced by *Business Week* and Standard & Poor's, offers up-to-the-minute market information. If you join as a member, you gain access to U.S. and global stock quotes. Members can set up a personal portfolio and track it. You have free access to IPO information and stock market news and commentary.

BUYandHOLD.com. <www.buyandhold.com> Allows you to buy individual stocks with monthly investments as low as $10. Charges $2.99 per trade.

CBS MarketWatch. <www.cbs.marketwatch.com> Offers stock quotes, stock interactive charting, broker research, IPO watch, industry analysis, stock alerts, and a stock tracker. Offers free links to Market Guide, Hoover's, Multex, Annual Reports Club, Zacks, Investools.com, NetStock Direct, Investment Data, and eSignal for free company reports, newsletters, analyses, direct stock buying, and other services.

CNBC Online. <moneycentral.msn.com> CNBC's financial information is offered through Microsoft's MSN.com. The CNBC portion of the site is full of information on stocks, mutual funds, and bonds. It has a Loan Center where you can research your loan and use calculators, and a Small Business Center, a Tax Center, and an Account Tracker you can set up to track your portfolio. There are good search, screening, and calculating tools.

CNNMoney. <www.money.cnn.com> From the editors of CNN and *Money* magazine, this site provides a wealth of information on the markets and individual companies. It also provides access to articles in *Money,* and offers a number of tools for investors.

DRIP Central. <www.dripcentral.com> DRIP Central offers a comprehensive collection of links, articles, tutorials, and other resources, from all across the World Wide Web regarding dividend reinvestment and stock purchase plans. Also offers a complete online book on DRIP investing.

Drip Investor. <www.dripinvestor.com> The site for *The Drip Investor* newsletter. You can join the site and subscribe to the newsletter. There are a few links to other DRIP sites and descriptions of Charles B. Carlson's (the Letter's Editor) books, and you can set up and track your own portfolio.

EarningsWhispers.com. <www.earningswhispers.com> Offers expert estimates of earnings by industry or company, and has an earnings warning program that monitors companies that issue warnings that earnings are not going to meet analysts' expectations.

eSignal. (3955 Point Eden Way, Hayward, CA 94545; 510-266-6000; www.esignal.com) The company's flagship product, eSignal, is a leading real-time quote service that delivers continuously updating, time-sensitive financial data over the Internet to active traders' and individual investors' PCs or laptops. The software provides market quotes for stocks, options, and futures, among others, as well as charts, news, research and alerts, to the growing base of online investors.

FOLIOfn. <www.foliofn.com> This site provides the ability to make up to 500 trades a month for a monthly fee of as little as $14.95. Also offers more than 100 pre-selected portfolios.

GainsKeeper. <www.gainskeeper.com> Track your portfolio and include events such as splits, spin-offs, mergers, distributions, liquidations, and wash sale trading activity that affect your portfolio but are not usually included in portfolio trackers. You can register for this service for $35/year, if you keep your activity under 100 trades per year.

Hoover's Online. <www.hoovers.com> Extensive data on over 10,000 public and private companies, including financial performance, news, Web addresses, and corporate profiles.

Investools.com. <www.investools.com> You can read articles from different investment newsletters for a fee. Has stock research and charting capability and offers current stock market status. Set up and track your own portfolio.

Investorama. <www.investorama.com> Full of investment information with links to some 12,000 Internet sites. Has directory of and links to discount and full-service brokers, day traders, money managers, and online brokerages. Set up and track your own portfolio on this site. Lots of educational materials for adults and children.

InvestorGuide.com. <www.investorguide.com> A massive site with links to thousands of other investment-related sites. Also has a great deal of

Figure 5.1 Hoover's Online

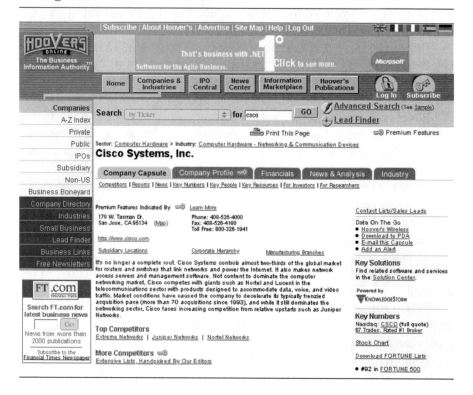

basic information on the principles of finance and investing, and what to watch for when you take others' advice. The site links you to articles of interest in the major personal finance magazines, as well.

InvestorPlace.com. <www.investorplace.com> This is a free portfolio tracking service, but registration is required. The site will send you daily e-mails with current information and news updates about the investments in your portfolio, plus a market overview of that day's market activity.

Investors Edge. <www.investorsedge.cibc.com> One of the best sites around to track your portfolio and research stocks. Investors Edge will constantly update the value of your portfolio at the end of each day, so that you can see your net worth rising and falling with every market fluctuation. The site is also linked to IPO Online, allowing you to see monthly calendars of new stock issues. Also offers access to Nelson's Company Research Summaries, which provide the latest research on stocks from major brokerage firms.

Figure 5.2   InvestorGuide.com

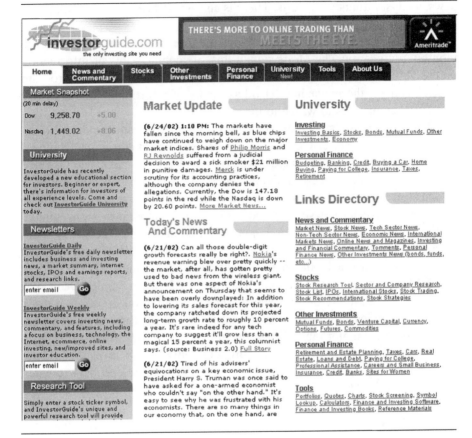

IPO.com. <www.ipo.com> Packed with worldwide initial public offering information. Shows the status of the current week's IPOs, new IPO filings, current prices of recent IPOs, and news and commentary on IPOs in general.

IPO Central. <www.ipocentral.com> This is a Hoover's site listing each day's IPO debuts, latest IPO filings, pricings, news, scorecard, and statistics. Includes links to a Hoover's capsule description of each IPO company, describing their operations and market, and including address, phone numbers, and Web site.

Lycos Finance. <www.finance.lycos.com> Offers a broad range of financial information and investment tools, including real-time quotes, news, and financial histories.

Money Central. <www.moneycentral.msn.com> At this Microsoft MSN site you can get stock quotes, market reports, stock research, charts, news, analyst ratings, and alerts. There is also an IPO center and a link to the Charles Schwab site.

The Moneypaper. <www.moneypaper.com> Associated with the monthly publication *The Moneypaper,* this site contains lots of information on DRIPs. Subscribe and you can join their Dividend Reinvestment Program (DRIP) and get the magazine. Also has plenty of information about DRIPs and DRIP companies in which to invest.

The Motley Fools. <www.fool.com> A popular investment site, also accessible through America Online, provides a great deal of educational material based on the Foolish theory popularized by founders Tom and David Gardner. The idea is that the average individual investor, usually considered "foolish" by the Wall Street establishment, can do better on their own than with advice from most financial newsletters and brokers, and outperform many mutual funds, based on the commonsense approach used in the site. The site includes Fool's School for novice investors and several forums in which investors can communicate with each other about stocks and mutual funds.

MSCI.com. <www.msci.com> Operated by Morgan Stanley Dean Witter, this is the best site on the Web to get information on the foreign stock markets. Includes up-to-date performance data on all foreign markets, including both the major markets and the emerging markets.

Multex Investor. <www.multexinvestor.com> Allows investors to order copies of reports from a range of brokerage houses and independent research firms over the Internet. Some of the reports are free, but most are available on a pay-per-view basis.

Netstock.com. <www.netstock.com> Includes a Sharebuilder plan that allows you to buy stocks from an inventory of 2,000 stocks at $2 per stock. You can pay for these using automatic monthly withdrawal from your checking account of say $100/month. Normal trades are $19.95 each.

The Online Investor. <www.theonlineinvestor.com> Offers investment education and advice and focuses on stock research and data, articles on investment, and daily investment tips.

Quicken.com. <www.quicken.com> Comprehensive financial site with lots of information for the investor. Get real-time stock quotes, look at company financial statements, read analyst estimates and research, look at insider trading activity, look at SEC 10-Q and 10-K filings (which include company management discussions), and look at charts of the stock's historical activity. You can set up and track your portfolio on this site—all for free.

Raging Bull. <www.ragingbull.com> Provides investors with stock quotes, news, and access to discussions and information on over 15,000 discussion boards.

Figure 5.3   Multex Investor

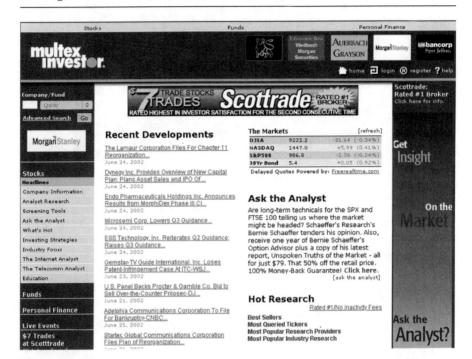

Reuters Money Network on the Web. <www.moneynet.com> A Web version of the Reuters Money Network, offering portfolio tracking, stock and bond price quotes, corporate and economic news, and price charts. The network also offers extensive research and annual reports.

SchwabNOW. <www.schwabnow.com> Includes current stock quotes, research and analyst reports, and investor education, and covers mutual funds. Lots of investor information on this site, and of course the ability to trade online through Charles Schwab. Gives you access to stock quotes from Quote.com, charts from BigCharts, and company information from Hoover's Online.

Securities and Exchange Commission. <www.sec.gov/edgarhp> Has 10-K reports of company financial data as reported to the Securities and Exchange Commission (SEC). This information will help you understand the financial condition of any company you are considering for investment.

ShareBuilder. <www.sharebuilder.com> Specializes in dollar-based investing, which lets you buy shares of stock in dollar amounts on a regular

Figure 5.4   SmartMoney.com

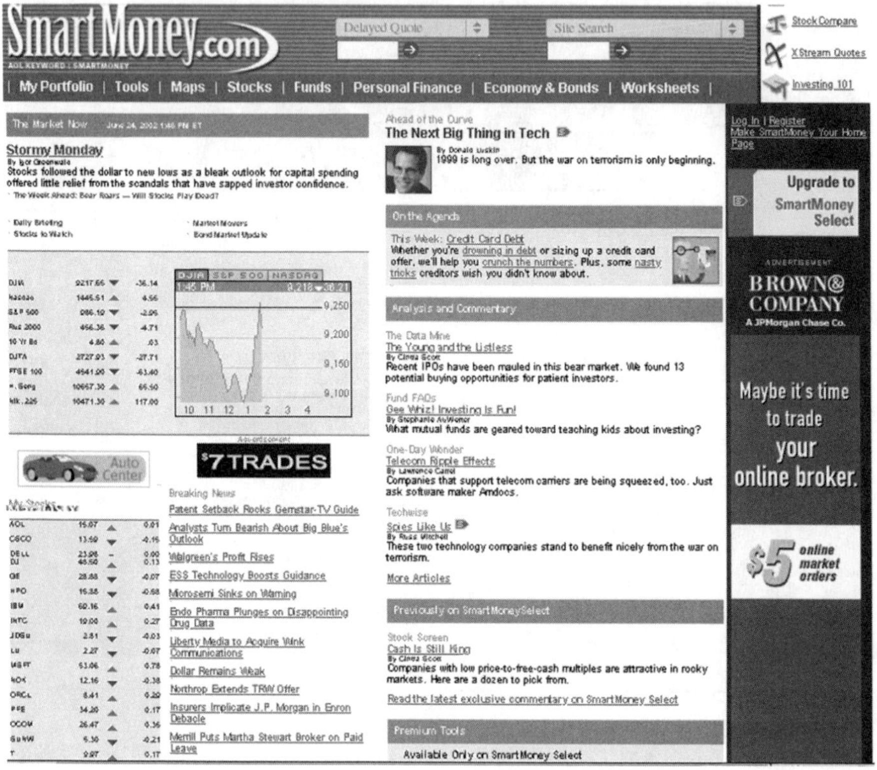

basis. For a fee, Sharebuilder purchases your choice of stock for you and consolidates the stock into a growth portfolio.

SiliconInvestor. <www.siliconinvestor.com> Offers stock quotes, market news, stock research, charts, screener, IPOs, and online trading. Set up and track your portfolio. Requires registration, but the services are free.

Smallcapcenter.com. <www.smallcapcenter.com> Offers in-depth coverage about the small-cap market segment. Find news, information, opinions, and in-depth analysis covering small-cap and micro-cap stocks on this site.

SmartMoney.com. <www.smartmoney.com> Offers hourly stock updates, market news, and stock screen, and will track your portfolio. Includes tools, calendar, asset allocator, broker meter, Dow tracker, and sector tracker. You have access to the Smart Money University, which offers one of the best investor primers available. You can access the interactive *Wall Street Journal* and *Barron's* sites from this one.

SPDRindex.com. <www.spdrindex.com> A Standard & Poor's site with information about SPDRs, which are index stocks that the Standard & Poor's 500 index. The S&P 500 is divided into nine sector index SPDR funds. You can customize your investments by picking the sectors that meet your investment goals. The nine sectors are: basic industries, consumer services, consumer staples, cyclical/transportation, energy, financials, industrials, technology, and utilities. You can buy or sell Select Sector SPDR shares on the American Stock Exchange throughout the trading day.

Standard & Poor's Index Services. <www.spglobal.com> Offers a snapshot of each global industry's performance. S&P global indexes are used by investors for investment performance measurement and as the basis for a wide range of financial instruments. Has links to the American Stock Exchange, Chicago Board Options Exchange, Chicago Mercantile Exchange, Montreal Exchange, Sydney Futures Exchange, Tokyo Stock Exchange, and Toronto and Montreal stock exchanges.

StockCharts.com. <www.stockcharts.com> On this site, you can conduct your own technical analysis using interactive tools offered there. These tools allow you to chart a stock's performance as far back as three years; you can then add trend lines and moving averages in search of a turning point in the stock's price.

StockSheet. <www.stocksheet.com> Provides company financial information for the past several years in an easy-to-view and easy-to-print format. A link to other businesses in the sector lets you see how the company stacks up against the competition.

TheStreet.com. <www.thestreet.com> Offers daily commentary on the market's highs and lows from well-known financial pundits. Includes analyst rankings of companies, a section on tech stocks, and a basic course on investing. A subscription-based site that offers a 30-day free trial.

Thomson Investors Network. <www.thomsoninvest.net> For a fee, will provide stock analysis, earnings estimates, research, and valuation. Tracks your portfolio.

ValueLine.com. <www.valueline.com> Online site for the well-respected *Value Line Investment Survey.* For a fee, members can access Value Line information and advice on approximately 1,700 stocks, more than 90 industries, the stock market, and the economy. The Ratings & Reports section contains one-page reports on the companies and industries; the Summary & Index section contains an index of all stocks in the publication as well as up-to-date statistics on the companies; and the Selection & Opinion section contains Value Line's latest economic and stock market forecasts.

Wall Street City. <www.wallstreetcity.com> A wealth of stock market information awaits you at this site. Includes market commentary, stock

Figure 5.5   Yahoo! Finance

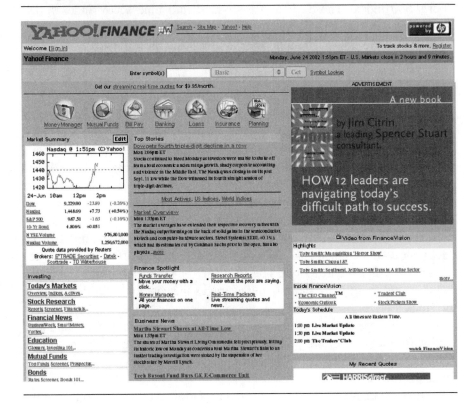

search capability, and reports on companies. You can even create your own stock ticker with the issues you want to follow most.

TheWhisperNumber.com. <www.thewhispernumber.com> Offers stock information, charts, stock analysis, and earnings estimates. Set up and track your portfolio on this site.

Yahoo! Finance. <finance.yahoo.com> Track stocks, read market news and research, scan the message boards for the latest whispers and rumors, listen to earnings calls, or create a custom portfolio.

Yardeni.com. <www.yardeni.com> The site of Dr. Yardeni, who is Prudential Financial's chief global economist and investment strategist. The site concentrates on new economy stocks, offering statistics, historical charts, and Dr. Yardeni's writings.

Zack's Analyst Watch. <www.zacks.com> Offers one of the best ways to track analysts' opinions and earnings estimates for publicly traded stocks.

Because stock prices react quickly to changes in analysts' opinions, this information can help improve your investment results significantly. The Web site can alert you to changes in opinion through daily e-mail. Also tracks positive and negative earnings surprises, and allows you to screen stocks based on earnings estimates.

RESOURCES

The Internet is not the only place to scout out information on the stock market. There are many books, publications, and newsletters devoted to helping you succeed in the market. Here are some of the top publications in the investment arena.

Books

All about Stocks: The Easy Way to Get Started, by Esme E. Faerber. (McGraw-Hill, PO Box 543, Blacklick, OH 43004; 800-634-3961; www.mcgraw-hill.com). Covers stock market basics for newcomers with concise and understandable answers to today's most-asked stock market questions.

Beating the Street, by Peter Lynch. (Simon & Schuster, 100 Front Street, Riverside, NJ 08075; 212-698-7000; 800-223-2348; www.simonandschuster.com). The legendary manager of the Fidelity Magellan Fund explains how he picks stocks, and details how he first heard about companies and where he found the information so critical to deciding whether to invest in them. Also offers advice on buying mutual funds and putting together an investment program.

Benjamin Graham on Value Investing: Lessons from the Dean of Wall Street, by Janet Lowe. (Penguin Putnam, 405 Murray Hill Parkway, East Rutherford, NJ 07073; 800-788-6262; www.penguinputnam.com). A book about the famous value investor Benjamin Graham that includes his successful investment philosophy and his investment record.

Buying Stocks without a Broker, by Charles B. Carlson. (McGraw-Hill, PO Box 543, Blacklick, OH 43004; 800-634-3961; www.mcgraw-hill.com). Shows how individual investors can avoid paying broker's commissions by buying stock directly from the issuing company.

Commonsense Global Investing: How to Successfully Navigate the International Marketplace, by Maurice K. Thompson. (Dearborn Trade, Chicago, IL; 312-836-4400; 800-245-2665; www.dearborntrade.com). Helps the investor diversify and profit from today's volatile international markets. Shows how to invest in the best countries for stability and profits.

The Complete Idiot's Guide to Online Investing, by Douglas Gerlach. (MacMillan Publishing Company, 866 Third Avenue, New York, NY 10022; 800-428-5331; www.macmillan.com). Provides users with an easy-to-understand book on the basics of investing and computing, researching options, and using the Internet for portfolio management.

Contrarian Investing: Buy and Sell When Others Won't and Make Money Doing It, by Anthony M. Gallea and William Patalon, III. (New York Institute of Finance, 1330 Avenue of the Americas, 16th Floor, New York, NY 10019; 212-641-6616; www.nyif.com). Describes contrarian strategy and explains how much of your portfolio to have in contrarian stocks.

Contrarian Investment Strategies: The Next Generation: Beat the Market by Going against the Crowd, by David N. Dreman. (Simon & Schuster, 1230 Avenue of the Americas, New York, NY 10020; 212-698-7000; 800-223-2348; www .simonandschuster.com). Combines proven techniques for selecting undervalued stocks with fresh insights on how to defy and thereby profit from the popular generally accepted fears or optimism of the moment.

The Craft of Investing: Growth and Value Stocks, Emerging Markets, Market Timing, Mutual Funds, Alternative Investments, Retirement and Estate Planning, Tax Savings, by John Train. (HarperBusiness, PO Box 588, Dunmore, PA 18512; 212-207-7000; 800-331-3761; www.harpercollins.com). Addresses everything from the psychology of the market to practical portfolio management tips. Explains growth investing, value investing, when to buy, and when to sell.

The Dictionary of Finance and Investment Terms, by John Downes and Jordan E. Goodman. (Barron's Educational Series, 250 Wireless Boulevard, Hauppauge, NY 11788; 631-434-3311; 800-645-3476; www.barronseduc.com). The standard reference work of finance and investment, defining more than 5,000 terms in simple language.

The Dividend Rich Investor: Building Wealth with High Quality, Dividend Paying Stocks, by Joseph Tigue and Joseph Lisanti. (McGraw-Hill, PO Box 543, Blacklick, OH 43004; 800-634-3961; www.mcgraw-hill.com). Learn why dividends are so important, what to look for in a dividend paying stock, and red-flag signals to avoid.

Divining the Dow: 100 of the World's Most Widely Followed Stock Market Prediction Systems, by Richard J. Maturi. (McGraw-Hill, PO Box 543, Blacklick, OH 43004; 800-634-3961; www.mcgraw-hill.com). Explains all of the major stock market prediction systems and how to use them to forecast stock price movements.

Eight Steps to Seven Figures, by Charles B. Carlson. (Bantam Books-Random House, 400 Hahn Road, Westminster, MD 21157; 800-733-3000; www.randomhouse .com). The author brings together in-depth interviews with over 200 everyday people whose investments have made them millionaires.

Electronic Trading: Day Trading Online, a Comprehensive Guide to One of Today's Hottest Forms of Trading, by Christopher A. Farrell (New York Institute of Finance, 1330 Avenue of the Americas, 16th Floor, New York, NY 10019; 212-641-6616; www.nyif.com). Overview of how to make a successful living, whether full time or part time, by trading over the Internet.

The Empowered Investor, by Robert E. Karoly. (Dearborn Trade, Chicago, IL; 312-836-4400; 800-245-2665; www.dearborntrade.com). Investors are shown how to practice safe investing and how to recognize "rogue" stockbrokers. Learn about the mysteries of brokerage firm statements, concealed losses, and firms' attitudes toward their clients.

The Finance and Investment Handbook, by John Downes and Jordan E. Goodman. (Barron's Educational Series, 250 Wireless Boulevard, Hauppauge, NY 11788; 631-434-3311; 800-645-3476; www.barronseduc.com). Everything you need to know about finance and investing. Contains explanations of investment alternatives and how to read the financial pages of newspapers and annual reports; a dictionary of 5,000 terms; and lists of stocks, mutual funds, futures and options, currencies, trade associations, government offices, and much more.

The First Time Investor: How to Start Safe, Invest Smart & Sleep Well, by Larry Chambers. (McGraw-Hill, PO Box 543, Blacklick, OH 43004; 800-634-3961; www.mcgraw-hill.com). Packed with easy-to-use information on every aspect of investing.

Getting Started in Online Investing, by David L. Brown and Kassandra Bentley. (John Wiley & Sons, 1 Wiley Drive, Somerset, NJ 08875-1272; 212-850-6000, 800-225-5945; www.wiley.com). Has current information on the best sites for research and trading news and has a well-informed up-to-date primer that helps investors navigate the information explosion connected with online investing.

Getting Started in Stocks, by Alvin Hall. (John Wiley & Sons, 1 Wiley Drive, Somerset, NJ 08875-1272; 212-850-6000; 800-225-5945; www.wiley.com). A primer on the basics of stock investing.

The Gorilla Game: Picking Winners in High Technology, by Geoffrey A. Moore, Paul Johnson, and Tom Kippola. (HarperBusiness, PO Box 588, Dunmore, PA 18512; 212-207-7000; 800-331-3761; www.harpercollins.com). Helps reader find high-tech stocks that dominate their market niches, looks at how the market values technology stocks, and provides case studies where "gorillas" have been born.

How the Stock Market Works, by John Dalton. (New York Institute of Finance, 1330 Avenue of the Americas, 16th Floor, New York, NY 10019; 212-641-6616; www.nyif.com). Explains the workings of the securities industry, including the mechanisms of the market, types of stocks, buy/sell and processing procedures, and the major theories of market analysis.

How to Be a Value Investor: Essential Guides to Today's Most Popular Investment Strategies, by Lisa Holton. (McGraw-Hill, PO Box 543, Blacklick, OH 43004; 800-634-3961; www.mcgraw-hill.com). Explains how to search for bargains, how to fit stocks into an overall financial strategy, how to establish a value portfolio, and how to gauge investment performance over time.

How to Buy Stocks, by Louis Engel and Henry R. Hecht. (Time Warner Trade Publications, 3 Center Plaza, Boston, MA 02108; 800-343-9204; www.timewarner.com). A readable book about the stock market that has become the classic in the field.

How to Buy Stocks the Smart Way, by Stephen Littauer. (Dearborn Trade, Chicago, IL; 312-836-4400; 800-245-2665; www.dearborntrade.com). A guide to reducing risk, spotting rising stocks, and getting the most from investments.

How to Invest $50–$5,000: The Small Investor's Step-by-Step, Dollar-by-Dollar Plan for Low-Risk, High-Value Investing, by Nancy Dunnan. (HarperBusiness, PO Box 588, Dunmore, PA 18512; 212-207-7000; 800-331-3761; www.harpercollins .com). Written with the beginning investor in mind; covers the full range of personal finance investments.

How to Invest the Smart Way: In Stocks, Bonds, and Mutual Funds, by Stephen L. Littauer. (Dearborn Trade, Chicago, IL; 312-836-4400; 800-245-2665; www .dearborntrade.com). How to achieve financial independence with as little as $50 a month to invest. Starts from basics and covers planning, strategies, techniques, and markets. Covers stocks, bonds, and mutual funds.

How to Profit from Reading Annual Reports, by Richard B. Loth. (Dearborn Trade, Chicago, IL; 312-836-4400; 800-245-2665; www.dearborntrade.com). Explains how to interpret the numbers and language of annual reports.

If You're Clueless about the Stock Market and Want to Know More, by Seth Godin. (Dearborn Trade, Chicago, IL; 312-836-4400; 800-245-2665; www.dearborntrade .com). Covers the basics of investing in the stock market.

InvestBeyond.com: A New Look at Investing in Today's Changing Markets, by Victoria Collins. (Dearborn Trade, Chicago, IL; 312-836-4400; 800-245-2665; www .dearborntrade.com).

Investing on a Shoestring, Barbara M. O'Neill. (Dearborn Trade, Chicago, IL; 312-836-4400; 800-245-2665; www.dearborntrade.com). Takes readers step by step through the process of putting together an investing plan, including investing with small dollar amounts, choosing the right financial advisor, and understanding the power of compound interest, and offers resources for shoestring investors.

Investing Online for Dummies, by Kathleen Sindell. (IDG Books, 919 E. Hillsdale Boulevard, Suite 400, Foster City, CA 94404; 650-653-7000; 800-434-3422; www.idg.com; www.dummies.com). Covers all the basics for the online investor, including setting up stock screens, selecting mutual funds, looking for IPOs, and online banking and trading.

Investment Clubs: A Team Approach to the Stock Market, by Kathryn Shaw. (Dearborn Trade, Chicago, IL; 312-836-4400; 800-245-2665; www.dearborntrade .com). A simple step-by-step guide that shows the investor how to start and run a successful money-making investment club.

Mastering Online Investing, by Michael C. Thomsett. (Dearborn Trade, Chicago, IL; 312-836-4400; 800-245-2665; www.dearborntrade.com). Offers readers a program and an approach to Internet investing that covers the basics within the framework of Internet tools and resources. Investors can find online sources about a company's fundamentals, analyze mutual fund performance, and use the Internet to track an options portfolio.

The Neatest Little Guide to Stock Market Investing, by Jason Kelly. (Penguin-Putnam, 405 Murray Hill Parkway, East Rutherford, NJ 07073; 800-788-6262; www.penguinputnam.com). Provides friendly guidance, sound financial expertise, and all the information needed to make smart stock choices.

The New Money Masters, by John Train (HarperCollins, PO Box 588, Dunmore, PA 18512; 800-331-3761; www.harpercollins.com). Profiles some of the most successful money managers of all time—people you can emulate.

The 100 Best Technology Companies to Own for the Long Run, by Gene Walden. (Dearborn Trade, Chicago, IL; 312-836-4400; 800-245-2665; www.dearborntrade .com). Includes a compilation of the top technology industries, an industry overview, analysis of key sectors, explanation of key technologies, market niches, the economic business model, and future prospects.

The 100 Best Stocks to Own for Under $25, by Gene Walden. (Dearborn Trade, Chicago, IL; 312-836-4400; 800-245-2665; www.dearborntrade.com). Profiles the top inexpensive stocks.

The 100 Best Stocks to Own in America, by Gene Walden. (Dearborn Trade, Chicago, IL; 312-836-4400; 800-245-2665; www.dearborntrade.com). Profiles 100 top-quality growth companies and reveals shareholders' perks each company offers.

One Up on Wall Street, by Peter Lynch. (Simon & Schuster, 200 Old Tappan Road, Old Tappan, NJ 07675; 800-223-2336; www.simonandschuster.com). A compendium of sensible advice from the former manager of Fidelity's legendary Magellan Fund.

Online Investing, by Jon D. Markman. (Microsoft Press, One Microsoft Way, Redmond, WA 98052-6399; 425-882-8080; www.microsoft.com). Learn how to find, evaluate, and use sites that offer the most comprehensive sets of fundamental data, technical-analysis charting tools, and corporate financial statements.

Online Investing: Become a Successful Internet Investor, by Reporters and Editors of *The Wall Street Journal.* (Random House, Order Dept., 400 Hahn Road, Westminster, MD 21157; 800-733-3000; www.randomhouse.com). This book is loaded with Web sites and information about online investing. Discusses regulator sites, calculators, screening, and charting, and sites where these can be found.

Online Investing the Smart Way, by Stephen L. Littauer. (Dearborn Trade, Chicago, IL; 312-836-4400; 800-245-2665; www.dearborntrade.com). Identifies the best Internet sites for investors, recommends online brokers, shows how to use computer programs to screen for investment selections, offers tips on online investing, and warns against scams.

Online Investing with Quicken, by Susan Price and Maria Langer. (McGraw-Hill, PO Box 543, Blacklick, OH 43004; 800-634-3961; www.mcgraw-hill.com). Along with the financial software package Quicken, this book shows the reader how to track a portfolio on the Web. Unique blend of investing book with Quicken coverage. Offers worksheets, charts, and sidebars.

The Online Trading Survival Guide, by Jack Guinan. (Dearborn Trade, Chicago, IL; 312-836-4400; 800-245-2665; www.dearborntrade.com). Insights from an insider. Includes tips on opening and managing an online account, and working with an online broker.

Profiting from Emerging Market Stocks, by Mitchell Posner. (New York Institute of Finance, 1330 Avenue of the Americas, 16th Floor, New York, NY 10019; 212-641-6616; www.nyif.com). Explains exactly how investors can realize big gains in the global market. Features a unique step-by-step approach to global investing.

Profiting from IPOs and Small Cap Stocks, by Norman H. Brown. (New York Institute of Finance, 1330 Avenue of the Americas, 16th Floor, New York, NY 10019; 212-641-6616; www.nyif.com). Advice on investing in small-cap stocks through initial public offerings.

A Random Walk Down Wall Street, by Burton G. Malkiel. (W.W. Norton & Co., Inc., 500 Fifth Avenue, New York, NY 10110; 212-354-5500; www.wwnorton.com). This comprehensive guide to investing in the stock market is an investment classic; it covers stock analysis and investment strategies.

Security Analysis: Principles and Techniques, by Benjamin Graham and David Dodd. (McGraw-Hill, PO Box 543, Blacklick, OH 43004; 800-634-3961; www .mcgraw-hill.com). Written by the fathers of fundamental stock analysis, this book is their seminal work on the subject. Might be too dense for first-time investors.

Six Secrets to Successful Technology Investing in the New Millennium, by Michael Murphy. (Technology Investing, Dept 40Q001, 7811 Montrose Road, Potomac, MD 20897-5961). The author suggests that using traditional methods to evaluate today's tech stocks will not work and will lead to losses. He describes a different method that he claims will provide good returns.

The Small Investor Goes to Market: A Beginner's Guide to Buying Stocks, by Jim Gard. (Ten Speed Press, PO Box 7123, Berkeley, CA 94707; 510-559-1600; 800-841-2665; www.tenspeedpress.com). This book takes the novice step by step through the process of evaluating a stock, working with a broker, and managing investments.

Socially Responsible Investing: Making a Difference and Making Money, by Amy L. Domini. (Dearborn Trade, Chicago, IL; 312-836-4400; 800-245-2665; www.dearborntrade.com). Select investments to meet specific social criteria, such as a clean environment, social justice, and treating workers fairly. Investors can profit and feel good about making a difference with their investments.

The Stock Market, by Dian Vujovich. (IDG Books, 919 E. Hillsdale Boulevard, Suite 400, Foster City, CA 94404; www.idg.com; www.dummies.com). Offers strategies on when to buy or when to sell stocks, tips on using discount brokers and online services, and descriptions of different stock categories.

Stock Picking: The 11 Best Tactics for Beating the Market, by Richard Maturi. (McGraw-Hill, PO Box 543, Blacklick, OH 43004; 800-634-3961; www.mcgraw-hill .com). Simple, time-tested techniques for choosing winning stocks in any market environment.

Take Stock: A Roadmap to Profiting from Your First Walk Down Wall Street, by Ellis Traub. (Dearborn Trade, Chicago, IL; 312-836-4400; 800-245-2665; www .dearborntrade.com). Beginning investors can invest in individual companies using the interactive, step-by-step process outlined in this book. Includes a CD-ROM to allow interactive use.

Teach Yourself Investing Online, by Thomas S. Gray and Claire Mencke. (IDG Books, 919 E. Hillsdale Boulevard, Suite 400, Foster City, CA 94404; 650-653-7000; 800-434-3422; www.idg.com; www.dummies.com). Step-by-step instructions on how to properly research, buy, sell, and manage investments.

24 Essential Lessons for Investment Success: Learn the Most Important Investment Techniques from the Founder of Investor's Business Daily, by William J. O'Neil. (McGraw-Hill, PO Box 543, Blacklick, OH 43004; 800-634-3961; www.mcgraw-hill.com). William O'Neil distills his 40 years of experience, study, and analysis of the market into a series of lessons about how to buy and sell stocks.

Understanding Wall Street, by Jeffrey Little and Lucian Rhodes. (Tab Books/ McGraw-Hill, PO Box 543, Blacklick, OH 43004; 800-634-3961; www.mcgraw-hill .com). An in-depth look at how to evaluate stocks and bonds and how the brokerage industry works.

The Unofficial Guide to Investing, by Lynn O'Shaughnessy. (IDG Books, 919 E. Hillsdale Boulevard, Suite 400, Foster City, CA 94404; 650-653-7000; 800-434-3422; www.idg.com; www.dummies.com). Demystifies the range of investment options available today and provides practical tools that will help readers make financially sound decisions.

Value Investing Made Easy, by Janet Lowe. (McGraw-Hill, PO Box 543, Blacklick, OH 43004; 800-634-3961; www.mcgraw-hill.com). Describes value investing methods as espoused and used by Benjamin Graham in an easy-to-read-and-understand format.

Value Investing Today, by Charles Brandes. (McGraw-Hill, PO Box 543, Blacklick, OH 43004; 800-634-3961; www.mcgraw-hill.com). International look at value investment approach from one of its most famed practitioners.

What You Need to Know before You Invest: An Introduction to the Stock Market and Other Investments, by Rod Davis. (Barron's Educational Series, 250 Wireless Boulevard, Hauppage, NY 11788; 516-434-3311; 800-645-3476; www.barronseduc .com). Explains the stock market, how it works, and the Dow Jones averages. Advises how to select a broker, open a brokerage account, invest in bonds, mutual funds, and how to read financial statements.

Winning on Wall Street, by Martin Zweig. (Time Warner Books, 3 Center Plaza, Boston, MA 02108; 800-343-9204; www.timewarner.com). A famous money manager explains how to choose winning stocks according to his theories on the economy and investor psychology.

Woman's Guide to Investing, by Virginia B. Morris (McGraw-Hill, PO Box 543, Blacklick, OH 43004; 800-634-3961; www.mcgraw-hill.com). This pocket-sized guide is a broad-based investing book that tackles all aspects of investing, based on research of women's issues.

The Worth Guide to Electronic Investing: Everything You Need to Know to Use Your Home Computer to Make More Money in the Stock Market, by Jim Jubak. (HarperBusiness, PO Box 588, Dunmore, PA 18512; 212-207-7000; 800-331-3761; www.harpercollins.com). Explains how to analyze stocks, choose mutual funds, and take advantage of the extensive financial resources available online.

Magazines

Weekly and monthly investment magazines usually give far more detail on individual stocks than do newspapers. Articles are also researched in more depth, providing a better basis to judge whether you are interested in a particular company. The best magazines are:

Business Week. (McGraw-Hill, 1221 Avenue of the Americas, 39th Floor, New York, NY 10020; 212-512-2511; www.businessweek.com). Although it concentrates more on the economy and business strategy, *Business Week* also has columns about Wall Street and personal investing.

Equities. (160 Madison Avenue, 3rd Floor, New York, NY 10016; 212-213-1300; 800-237-8400, ext. 21, for credit card orders and subscriptions only) Formerly known as OTC Review, focuses on the outlook for individual emerging growth stocks.

Forbes. (60 Fifth Avenue, New York, NY 10011; 212-620-2200; 800-888-9896; www.forbes.com). Known for its acerbic and witty style. Uncovers good stocks and exposes stocks it considers overpriced.

Fortune. (1271 Avenue of the Americas, New York, NY 10020; 212-522-1212; 800-541-1000; www.fortune.com). A business magazine with extensive coverage of Wall Street and stock selection. Fortune also publishes an annual Investor's Guide with many stock ideas.

Money. (Time and Life Building, Rockefeller Center, New York, NY 10020; 212-522-1212; 800-541-1000; www.money.cnn.com). A popular magazine that publishes several articles each month on individual stocks and mutual funds. It also covers all other areas of personal finance, including banking, taxes, real estate, and financing college education.

Newsletters

Hundreds of newsletters give stock advice. These letters usually reflect the personality and interests of the letter writer. Some use technical analysis and are therefore loaded with graphs and charts. Others rely on fundamental analysis and explain the prospects for a company's business. Still others focus on takeovers, foreign stocks, IPOs, or emerging growth stocks. Some newsletters provide solid advice, but many do not. To some extent, the success of a letter's recommendations depends on how the kinds of stocks it favors are doing at the moment.

The referee for this chaotic field is Mark Hulbert, who publishes the *Hulbert Financial Digest,* which ranks the monthly performance of recommendations in the most influential newsletters. To find out which letter has had a good record recently, you can subscribe to the digest at CBS Marketwatch <www.cbsmarketwatch.com>. Newsletter performance is also tracked by Timer Digest (PO Box 1688, Greenwich, CT 06836; 203-629-3503; 800-356-2527).

For more on what kind of stock information each letter contains, contact them at the phone numbers or addresses given below. In many cases, the newsletter will send you a free sample so you can see what the letter is like. You can also get at trial subscription to most of these newsletters through Select Information Exchange (244 W. 54th Street, New York, NY 10019; 212-247-7123; www.stockfocus.com). The following list of newsletters covers those tracked by Hulbert, which are the most widely followed publications:

The Aden Forecast. (PO Box 66710, St. Louis, MO 63166-9529, 888-ADEN-MKT)

All Star Asset Allocator and *All Star Fund Trader.* (PO Box 203427, Austin, TX 78720; 800-299-4223; allstarinvestor.com)

BI Research. (PO Box 133, Redding, CT 06875; 203-270-9244; www.biresearch .com)

Bernie Schaeffer's Option Advisor. (PO Box 46709, Cincinnati, OH 45246; 800-327-8833; www.optionsource.com)

The Blue Chip Investor. (575 Anton Boulevard, #510, Costa Mesa, CA 92626; 714-641-3579; www.checkcapital.com)

Bob Brinker's Marketimer. (PO Box 229, Irvington, NY 10533, 914-591-2655; www.bobbrinker.com)

Bob Carlson's Retirement Watch. (3700 Annandale Road, Annandale, VA 22033; 800-552-1152; www.retirementwatch.com/members)

The Bowser Report. (PO Box 6278, Newport News, VA 23606; 757-877-5979)

The Buy Low, Sell High! Small-Cap Canadian Stocks Review. (CanStock Information Services Corp. 35-750 Fortune Drive, Kamloops, BC, CANADA V2B-2L2; 250-554-3101; www.stockdepot.com)

The Buyback Letter and *The Buyback Premium Portfolio* (15415 Sunset Boulevard, Suite 200-D, Pacific Palisades, CA 90272; 800-567-2683; www.buybackletter.com)

The Cabot Market Letter. (176 North Street, PO Box 3067, Salem, MA 01970; 978-745-5532; www.cabot.net)

California Technology Stock Letter. (PO Box 308, Half Moon Bay, CA 94019; 650-726-8495; www.ctsl.com)

Charles M. LaLoggia's Superstock Invester. (PO Box 547, Rochester, NY 14603; 800-450-0551; www.superstockinvestor.com)

The Chartist and *The Chartist Mutual Fund Letter.* (PO Box 758, Seal Beach, CA 90740; 562-596-2385; www.thechartist.com)

Closed-End Country Fund Report. (725 15th Street, NW #50, Washington, DC 20005; 202-783-7051)

Closed-End Fund Digest & Real Estate Securities. (4521 Campus Drive PMB #283, Irvine, CA 92612; 949-737-5966; www.cefd.com)

The Contrarian's View. (132 Moreland Street, Worcester, MA 01609; 508-757-2881; www.nick.assumption.edu)

Coolcat Explosive Small Cap Growth Stock Report. (c/o El Sol, 2408 Tamarack, Sanger, CA 93657; 559-875-0613; www.coolcatreport.com)

Crawford Perspectives. (1382 Third Avenue, Suite 403, New York, NY 10021; 212-744-6973; www.astromoney.com)

Daily Premium Sound Sector Strategy. (1200 Westlake Avenue N., Suite 700, Seattle, WA 98109-3530; www.soundsectorstrategy.com)

Dennis Slothower's on the Money. (2230 N. University Parkway, Suite 9-D, Provo, UT 84604; 801-373-3381; www.onthemoney.com)

The Dines Letter. (PO Box 22, Belvedere, CA 94920; 800-84LUCKY; www.dinesletter.com)

Donoghue's Action Gram. (PO Box 309, Milford, MA 01757; 800-982-2455; www.donoghue.com)

Dow Theory Forecasts. (7412 Calumet Avenue, Hammond, IN 46324-2692; 800-233-5922; www.dowtheory.com)

Dow Theory Letters. (PO Box 1759, La Jolla, CA 92038; 619-454-0481; www.dowtheoryletters.com)

The Elliott Wave Financial Forecast. (PO Box 1618, Gainesville, GA 30503; 770-536-0309; www.elliottwave.com)

Equity Fund Outlook. (PO Box 76, Boston, MA 02117; 800-982-0055; www.efoutlook.com)

Eric Dany's Stock Prospector and *Mutual Fund Prospector.* (16 Thornwood Court, Moline, IL 61265; 309-736-9376; www.ericdany.com)

Eric Kobren's Fidelity Insight (Mutual Fund Investors Association, PO Box 9135, Wellesley Hills, MA 02481-9135; 800-444-6342; www.kobren.com)

Eric Kobren's FundsNet Insight. (20 William Street, PO Box 9131, Wellesley Hills, MA 02181-9131; 617-369-2500; www.kobren.com)

The F.X.C. Newsletter. (1268 Smithtown Avenue, Bohemia, NY 11716; 800-FXC-0992; www.fxcnewsletter.com)

Fabian's Sector Investing (2100 Main Street, Suite 300, Huntington Beach, CA 92648; 800-950-8765; www.fabian.com)

Fidelity Independent Advisor. (PO Box 387, Williamstown, MA 01267; 800-548-3797; www.fidelityadviser.com)

Fidelity Investor, Fidelity New Economy Investor, and *Fidelity Sector Investor.* (Phillips Publishing, 7811 Montrose Road, Potomac, MD 20859-0002; 800-718-8291; www.fidelityinvestor.com)

Fidelity Monitor and *Fidelity Sector Trader.* (PO Box 1270, Rocklin, CA 95677; 800-397-3094; www.fidelitymonitor.com)

Ford Investment Review. (11722 Sorrento Valley Road, Suite I, San Diego, CA 92121; 858-755-1327; www.fordinv.com)

Fredhager.com. (2000 Post Road, #200, Fairfield, CT 06430; 203-319-0114; www.fredhager.com)

FundAdvice.com. (1200 Westlake Avenue N., #700, Seattle, WA 98109; 800-423-4893; www.fundadvice.com)

Futures Hotline/Mutual Fund Timer. (PO Box 6275, Jacksonville, FL 32236; 904-693-0355)

Gerald Appel's Systems and Forecasts. (150 Great Neck Road, Great Neck, NY 11021; 516-829-6444; www.signalert.com)

Gerald Perritt's Mutual Fund Letter. (12514 Starkey Road, Largo, FL 33773; 800-326-6941; www.mutletter.com)

The Gilder Technology Report. (PO Box 660, Housatonic, MA 01236; 800-292-4380; www.gildertech.com/customerservice)

Global Investing. (1040 First Avenue, #305, New York, NY 10022; 800-388-4-ADR; wwwglobal-investing.com)

Global Markets Advisory. (PO Box 572494, 5049 Cottonwood Lane, Salt Lake City, UT 84157; 801-424-2385; www.creed.org)

Good Fortune. (PO Box 1500, Woodland, CA 95776; 530-661-7394; www.fundsystem.com)

The Granville Market Letter. (PO Box 413006, Kansas City, MO 64141; 816-474-5353)

Growth Fund Guide. (Growth Fund Research Building, Box 6600, Rapid City, SD 57709; 605-341-1971)

Growth Stock Outlook. (PO Box 15381, Chevy Chase, MD 20825; 301-654-5205)

Harry Newton's Technology Investor. (270 Madison Avenue, 13th floor, New York, NY 10016; 877-671-2840; www.technologyinvestor.com)

Independent Adviser for Vanguard Investors. (Fund Family Shareholder Association, 7811 Montrose Road, Potomac, MD 20854; 800-777-5005; www.adviseronline .com)

Index Rx. (PO Box 34452, San Antonio, TX 78265; www.invest@indexrx.com)

Individual Investor Special Situations Report. (125 Broad Street, 14th Floor, New York, NY 10004; 800-273-6890; www.iionline.com)

Individualinvestor.com. (212-742-2277; www.individualinvestor.com)

The International Harry Schultz Letter. (HSL, PO Box 622 CH-1001, Lausanne-Switzerland; (32)16-5336-84; www.hsletter.com)

InvesTech Market Analyst and *InvesTech Mutual Fund Advisor.* (2472 Birch Glen, Whitefish, MT 59937; 800-955-8500; www.investech.com)

Investment Quality Trends. (7440 Girard Avenue, Suite 4, La Jolla, CA 92037; 858-459-3818; www.iqtrends.com)

The Investment Reporter. (133 Richmond Street W, Suite 700, Toronto, Ontario, Canada M5H-3MB; 416-869-1177; www.idonline.ca)

Investor's Guide to Closed-End Funds. (PO Box 161465, Miami, FL 33116; 305-271-1900; www.herzfeld.com)

Investors Intelligence. (Chartcraft, Inc., PO Box 2046, 30 Church Street, New Rochelle, NY 10801; 914-632-0422; www.chartcraft.com)

Jack Adamo's Insiders Plus. (416 Hickory Highlands Drive, Antioch, TN 37013; www.jackadamo.com)

John Dessauer's Investor's World. (7811 Montrose Road, Potomac, MD 20854; 800-804-0942; www.dessauerinvestorsworld.com)

John Myers' Outstanding Investments. (1217 St. Paul Street, Baltimore, MD 21202; 800-433-1528; www.realasset.com)

Kenjol Alpha Timer. (4201 W Parmer Lane, Suite 250, Austin, TX 78727; 866-453-6565; allstarinvestor.com)

Listed Insight. (PO Box 5759, Walnut Creek, CA 94596; 800-955-9566)

Louis Navellier's Blue Chip Growth Letter. (Phillips Publishing, Inc., 7811 Montrose Road, Potomac, MD 20854-3394; 800-718-8289; www.navellier.com)

Louis Rukeyser's Mutual Funds and *Louis Rukeyser's Wall Street.* (1750 Old Meadow Road, 3rd Floor, McLean, VA 22102; 800-892-9702)

Lowry's Power & Velocity Ratings. (631 U.S. Highway One, #305, North Palm Beach, FL 33408; 561-842-3514)

MPT Review. (1 East Liberty, Third Floor, Reno, NV 89501; 800-861-5968; www.mptreview.com)

Maedel's Mini-Cap Analyst. (PO Box 28011, Harbour Centre, Vancouver, BC Canada V6B-5L8; 604-669-8270; www.maedels.com)

Mark Skousen's Forecasts & Strategies. (7811 Montrose Road, Potomac, MD 20854; 301-424-3700; www.forecasts-strategies.com)

The Market Radar. (PO Box 4142, Bayside, NY 11360; 800-365-5566; www.marketradar.com)

Martin Weiss' Safe Money Report. (4176 Burns Road, Palm Beach, FL 33410; 800-236-0407; www.safemoneyreport.com)

Maverick Advisor. (PO Box 2538, Huntington Beach, CA 92647; 800-950-8765; www.fabian.com)

Medical Technology Stock Letter. (PO Box 40460, Berkeley, CA 94704; 510-843-1857; www.bioinvest.com)

Minogue Stock Index Futures Hotline. (7630 Provinicial Drive, Suite 202, McLean, VA 22102; www.minogue.org)

Moneyflow. (PO Box 1076, Brookings, OR 97415; 541-412-0955; www.moneyflow.com)

Moneyletter. (360 Woodland Street, PO Box 6020, Holliston, MA 01746; 800-890-9670; www.moneyletter.com)

Morningstar Mutual Funds and *Morningstar Stock Investor.* (225 West Wacker Drive, Chicago, IL 60606; 312-424-4288; www.morningstar.com)

Motley Fool. (123 North Pitt Street, Alexandria, VA 22314; 703-838-3665; www.fool.com)

Mutual Fund Prospector. (16 Thornwood Court, Moline, IL 61265; 309-736-9376; www.ericdany.com)

The Mutual Fund Strategist. (PO Box 446, Burlington, VT 05402; 800-355-FUND; www.mutualfundstrategist.com)

Mutual Funds Magazine. (PO Box 60001, Tampa, FL 33660; 800-494-0129; www.mutual-funds.com)

NAIC Investor Advisory Service. (PO Box 220, Royal Oak, MI 48068; 810-583-6242)

Nate's Notes. (PO Box 667, Healdsburg, CA 95448; 707-433-7903; www .nates-notes.com)

The National Investor. (410 River Street, Spooner, WI 54801; www.nationalinvestor .com)

National Trendlines. (National Investment Advisors, 14001 Berryville Road, North Potomac, MD 20874; 800-521-1585)

Natural Contrarian. (7720B El Camino Real, #172, Rancho LaCosta, CA 92009; 858-495-9461)

NoLoad Fund*X. (235 Montgomery Street, Suite 662, San Francisco, CA 94104; 800-763-8639; www.fundx.com)

No-Load Fund Analyst. (4 Orinda Way, Suite 230-D, Orinda, CA 94563; 800-776-9555; www.nlfa.com)

The No-Load Fund Investor. (One Bridge Street, PO Box 318, Irvington-on-Hudson, NY 10533; 800-252-2042; www.sheldonjacobs.com)

No-Load Mutual Fund Selections & Timing Newsletter. (100 N. Central Expressway, Suite 1112, Richardson, TX 75080; 800-800-6563)

No-Load Portfolios. (8635 W. Sahara, Suite 420, The Lakes, NV 89117)

OTC Insight. (Insight Capital Management, Inc., PO Box 5759, Walnut Creek, CA 94596; 800-955-9566; www.icrm.com)

The Oberweis Report. (951 Ice Cream Drive, #200, North Aurora, IL 60542-1472; 800-323-6166; www.oberweis.net)

The Oxford Club. (105 W. Monument Street, Baltimore, MD 21201; 800-992-0205; www.oxfordclub.com)

P.Q. Wall Forecast. (PO Box 15558, New Orleans, LA 70175; 504-895-4891; www.pqwall.com)

The PAD System Report. (PO Box 43285, Cincinnati, OH 45243; 513-529-2863)

Paul Chapman's Hidden Value Stocks. (PO Box 22431; Minneapolis, MN 55422-0431; 763-533-0474)

Personal Finance. (1750 Old Meadow Road, Suite 301, McLean, VA 22102; 800-832-2330; www.pfnewsletter.com)

The Peter Dag Portfolio Strategy & Management. (65 Lakefront Drive, Akron, OH 44319; 800-833-2782; www.peterdag.com)

Peter Eliades' Stock Market Cycles. (PO Box 6873, Santa Rosa, CA 95406-0873; 707-769-4800)

Professional Timing Service. (PO Box 7483, Missoula, MT 59807; 406-543-4131; www.protiming.com)

The Prudent Speculator. (PO Box 1438, Laguna Beach, CA 92652; 800-258-7786; www.theprudentspeculator.com)

The Pure Fundamentalist. (7412 Calumet Avenue, Hammond, IN 46324; 219-852-3200; www.thepurefundamentalist.com)

Reminiscences. (PO Box 711, Westport, CT 06881; 203-341-0833, www.Ibirinyi.com)

Richard E. Band's Profitable Investing. (7811 Montrose Road; Potomac, MD 20854; 301-424-3700; www.rband.com)

Richard Geist's Strategic Investing. (1905 Beacon Street, Waban, MA 02168; 617-332-3323; www.investools.com)

Richard Schmidt's Stellar Stock Report. (7100 Peachtree-Dunwoody, #100, Atlanta, GA 30328; 800-728-2288)

Richard Young's Intelligence Report. (Phillips Publishing, 7811 Montrose Road, Potomac, MD 20854-3394; 301-424-3700; www.phillips.com)

Roger Conrad's Utility Forecaster. (1750 Old Meadow Road, 3rd Floor, McLean, VA 22102; 800-832-2330)

The Ruff Times. (PO Box 887, Springville, UT 84663; 801-489-8681; www.rufftimes.com)

Scientific Investing, Sector Fund Timer, Stock Market Leaders and *Ultimate Timing Service.* (12254 Nicollet Avenue S., Burnsville, MN 55337; www.timing.net, www.vital-info.com)

The Select Investor. (PMB 240, 15600 NE 8th Street, Suite B1, Bellevue, WA 98008; 425-821-9392; www.selectinvestor.com)

Short on Value. (2779 Clairmont Road, Suite F-9, Atlanta, GA 30329; 404-477-9092; www.shortonvalue.com)

Sound Advice. (156 Diablo Road, #200, Danville, CA 94526; 925-838-6710)

Sound Mind Investing. (2337 Glen Eagle Drive, Louisville, KY 40222; 502-426-7420; www.soundmindinvesting.com)

The Spear Report. (1224 Farmington Avenue, PO Box 271030; West Hartford, CT 06127-1030; 800-491-7119; www.spearreport.com)

Special Situations. (160 Madison Avenue, 3rd Floor, New York, NY 10016; 888-417-5400; www.equitesmagazine.com)

Standard & Poor's The Outlook. (Standard & Poor's Corp., 55 Water Street, New York, NY 10041; 800-852-1641; www.spoutlookonline.com)

Stock Trader's Almanac Investor. (The Hirsch Organization, 184 Central Avenue, PO Box 2069, Old Tappan, NJ 07675; 201-767-4100; www.hirschorganization.com)

Tech Stocks Insights. (600 University Street, Suite 2901, Seattle, WA 98101; 206-264-8442; www.techstockinsights.com)

Technology Investing. (Phillips Publishing, 7811 Montrose Road; Potomac, MD 20854-3394; 800-809-9612; www.techinvestingonline.com)

Timer Digest. (PO Box 1688, Greenwich, CT 06836-1688; 203-629-3503; www.timerdigest.com)

Todd Market Forecast. (26861 Trabuco Road, Suite E182, Mission Viejo, CA 92691; 949-581-2457; www.toddmarketforecast.com)

Top Down Market Forecast. (PO Box 33233, North Royalton, OH 44133; 440-877-1731; www.tdmresarch.com)

The Turnaround Letter. (New Generation Research, Inc., 225 Friend Street, Suite 801, Boston, MA 02114; 800-468-3810; www.turnarounds.com)

Two-for-One Stocksplit Newsletter. (140 O'Connor Street, Menlo Park, CA 94025; 888-775-4824; www.2-for-1.com)

U.S. Investment Report. (65 Chapel Road, New Hope, PA 18938; 215-862-1313)

Undiscovered Tech Stocks. (PO Box 109665, Palm Beach Gardens, FL 33410; 561-627-3300; www.undiscoveredstocks.com)

The Value Line Convertibles Survey, The Value Line Investment Survey, The Value Line Investment Survey—Expanded Edition, The Value Line Mutual Fund Survey, and *The Value Line Special Situations Service.* (220 East 42nd Street, New York, NY 10017, 800-634-3583; www.valueline.com)

Vantage Point: An Independent Report for Vanguard Investors. (300 Mt. Lebanon Boulevard, Suite 2218-A, Pittsburgh, PA 15234-1508; 412-594-4749)

Vickers Weekly Insider Report. (226 New York Avenue, Huntington, NY 11743; 800-645-5043; www.argusgroup.com)

The Wall Street Digest. (One Sarasota Tower, #602, Sarasota, FL 34236; 941-954-5500; www.wallstreetdigest.com)

Wall Street Winners. (1750 Old Meadow Road, Suite 301, McLean, VA 22102; 800-832-2330; www.wallstreetwinners.net)

Zacks Advisor. (155 North Wacker Drive, Chicago, IL 60606; 800-399-6659; www.aw.zacks.com)

Newspapers

While your local newspaper may have a few stories about companies in your region and a few general stock stories, it does not normally present enough information to expose you to a wide range of investment ideas. The best national newspapers aimed at investors are the following:

Barron's National Business and Financial Weekly. (200 Liberty Street, New York, NY 10281; 212-416-2700; 800-822-7229). Tabloid that features incisive articles on stocks and the stock market, and the best array of statistics around.

Investor's Business Daily. (12655 Beatrice Street, Los Angeles, CA 90066; 310-448-6000; 800-831-2525; www.investors.com). Daily paper with many short articles about individual companies, as well as many pages of statistics, graphs, and charts.

The New York Times, "Business Day" Section. (229 W. 43rd Street, New York, NY 10036; 212-556-1234; 800-631-2580; www.nytimes.com). An influential section that covers corporate news and features columns about individual stocks.

USA Today, "Money" section. (1000 Wilson Boulevard, Arlington, VA 22229; 703-276-3400; 800-872-8632; www.usatoday.com). A Gannett paper with many short articles on individual stocks and the stock market. Also carries a wide range of statistics on stock market activity.

The Wall Street Journal. (200 Liberty Street, New York, NY 10281; 212-416-2000; 800-228-3880; www.wsj.com). The most influential daily newspaper. Covers the stock market, particularly in the paper's third section, "Money and Investing."

Television and Radio

Several local TV and radio stations provide excellent coverage of the stock market. On radio, there are several all-business news stations, such as WBBR in New York City, which is run by *Bloomberg Financial Markets.* On a national level, several programs and cable channels can help you choose stocks. Among the best are the following:

CNBC. (Consumer News and Business Channel, 2200 Fletcher Avenue, Ft. Lee, NJ 07024; 201-585-2622; www.cnbc.com). The only round-the-clock cable channel devoted to business and financial news. During trading day, stock market ticker crawls at the bottom of the screen. Features interviews with prominent market analysts, fund managers, economists, and other stock gurus. Produces *Early Today,* aired on local stations nationwide in the morning, which highlights the day's financial news and offers interviews with investment experts.

CNN Business News. (Cable News Network, 5 Penn Plaza, New York, NY 10001; 212-714-7848; www.cnn.com). Airs two business news shows in the morning and one, called *Moneyline,* in the evening. Every hour while the market is open, updates what is happening to the stock market.

CNN Money. (Cable News Network Financial Network, 5 Penn Plaza, New York, NY 10001; 212-714-7848). A 24-hour financial news network using staff members from Cable News Network devoted to business and financial news. CNN Money provides in-depth coverage of the financial markets, interviews with newsmakers, opportunities for viewers to call in with questions and comments, and much more. The service also has a Web site <www.cnnmoney.com> that tracks the markets and offers information about programs on the channel.

Marketplace. (Minnesota Public Radio, 261 S. Figueroa Street, Suite 200, Los Angeles, CA 90012; 213-608-3500; www.marketplace.org). A daily radio show airing in the morning *(Marketplace Morning Report)* and the evening *(Marketplace)* on

Public Radio International stations. Jordan Goodman, author of this book, comments every Thursday morning on the "Road to Riches" personal finance segment. Covers the day's financial and economic news in more depth than is commonly found on radio.

Nightly Business Report. (14901 Northeast 20th Avenue, Miami, FL 33181; 305-949-8321; www.nightlybusiness.org). A daily TV show that airs on PBS stations. Covers the action in the stock market and features interviews with investment experts.

Sound Money. (45 E. 7th Street, St. Paul, MN 55101; 651-290-1212; 800-228-7123; www.mpr.org). A weekly call-in radio show produced by Minnesota Public Radio with host Chris Farrell and other investment experts, who answer listeners' questions.

Wall Street Week. (Maryland Public Television, 1167 Owings Mills Boulevard, Owings Mills, MD 21117; 410-356-5600; www.mpt.org). The granddaddy of TV shows about selecting stocks. This PBS offering airs on Friday nights, offering interviews with prominent stock analysts and money managers. You can call your local PBS station to find out when the show airs in your area.

Software

You can identify stocks of interest to you by using a software package designed to select stocks. These programs allow you to enter certain criteria, such as earnings growth rates, PE ratios, dividend yields, or debt levels, and screen for the stocks that fit your specifications. For a more detailed listing of software that chooses stocks, consult *Computerized Investing* (American Association of Individual Investors, 625 N. Michigan Avenue, Suite 1900, Chicago, IL 60611; 312-280-0170; www.aaii.com). The best ones follow:

Smarter Investing for Beginning Investors. (101 Montgomery Street, San Francisco, CA 94101; 800-4-SCHWAB; www.schwab.com). This product is an educational CD-ROM for beginning investors and is designed to introduce new customers to investing concepts, tools, and services available at Schwab.

Value Line Investment Survey. (220 E. 42nd Street, New York, NY 10017; 800-634-3583; www.valueline.com). Monthly, weekly, or quarterly, subscription to CD-ROMs with data on all the companies followed by Value Line. Allows you to screen stocks by many different criteria.

Trade Associations and Stock Exchanges

American Association of Individual Investors. (625 N. Michigan Avenue, Chicago, IL 60611; 312-280-0170). A nonprofit group that educates individual investors about the stock market through publications, conferences, and seminars. You also can contact them at their Web site <www.aaii.org>, which includes the *Information Guide,* a directory of regulatory agencies, exchanges, NASD offices, financial journals, data sources, and places to take complaints. The AAII Web site also provides extensive articles on the basics of investing, as well as a reference section allowing you to find information on a wide variety of topics, such as annuities, mutual funds, dividend reinvestment plans, and discount brokers.

American Stock Exchange. (86 Trinity Place, New York, NY 10006; 212-306-1000; www.amex.com). An exchange that lists mostly medium-sized and small-sized growth companies. Now part of Nasdaq-AMEX. Offers various pamphlets about investing in stocks.

Investment Counsel Association of America. (1050 17th Street, NW, Suite 725, Washington, DC 20036-5503; 202-293-4222; www.icaa.org). Represents money managers who select stocks for individual and institutional clients.

Investors Alliance. (707-571-2311). A nonprofit group formed to help individual investors become more capable and knowledgeable through diverse programs of investment education and research. Offers easy-to-use software for screening stocks by various criteria, as well as software to help users choose mutual funds. Publishes the monthly *IA Investor Journal* letter for members, which provides information on stock and mutual fund investing technique.

National Association of Investors Corporation. (PO Box 220, Royal Oak, MI 48068; 248-583-6242; 877-275-6242). Promotes the growth of investment clubs. The group's Web site <www.better-investing.org> provides a great amount of data for investors of all levels of sophistication. There are reprints from *NAIC's Better Investing* magazines, and you can download NAIC software programs to screen stocks based on fundamental factors. The site also makes it easy to find out about investment clubs near you, as well as investor fairs and other educational opportunities. You also can learn about NAIC's Low Cost Investment Plan, which allows you to purchase a single share of stock in many companies for a small fee over the purchase price. After that, you can buy additional shares of the stock directly from the company's dividend reinvestment plan at little or no commission.

National Association of Securities Dealers. (1735 K Street, NW, Washington, DC 20006-1500; 202-728-8000; 800-289-9999; www.nasd.com). Oversees the Nasdaq NMS and polices securities markets and brokers' actions. Offers the following publications: *NASD Disciplinary Procedures; NASD Manual; Basics of Saving & Investing Brochure; Investor Insight; Investor Protection Kit; Investor Series; NASD Backgrounder; Women & Investing: It's Your Money.*

New York Stock Exchange. (11 Wall Street, New York, NY 10005; 212-656-3000; www.nyse.com). The Big Board, where the largest and most well-known stocks trade. Offers many pamphlets and other literature about investing in stocks.

Securities Industry Association. (120 Broadway, New York, NY 10271; 212-608-1500; www.sia.com). Represents the securities industry in lobbying activities and educates the public about the stock market. Sponsors the Stock Market Game, which teaches students about the stock market.

Federal Government Regulators

Securities and Exchange Commission. (SEC, 450 5th Street, NW, Washington, DC 20549; 202-942-8088; 800-732-0330; www.sec.gov). The principal federal government agency that regulates the stock and bond markets. Offers the following free brochures: "Affinity Fraud: How to Avoid Investment Scams That Target Groups"; "Arbitration Procedures"; "Ask Questions"; "Broken Promises: Promissory Note Fraud"; "Bankruptcy"; "Certificates of Deposit: Tips for Investors"; "Cold Calling"; "Complaints and Inquiries: How the SEC Handles Them"; "Financial Facts Tool Kit"; "Internet Fraud: How to Avoid Internet Investment Scams"; "The Investor's Advocate"; "Microcap Stock: A Guide for Investors"; "Tips for Online Investing"; "Trade Execution: What Every Investor Should Know." Has 11 regional offices:

- California: 5670 Wilshire Boulevard, 11th Floor, Los Angeles 90036-3648; 323-965-3998
- California: 44 Montgomery Street, Suite 1100, San Francisco, 94104; 415-705-2500
- Colorado: 1801 California Street, Suite 4800, Denver 80202-2648; 303-391-6800
- Florida: 1401 Brickell Avenue, Suite 200, Miami 33131; 305-536-4700
- Georgia: 3475 Lenox Road, N.E., Suite 1000, Atlanta 30326-1232; 404-842-7600
- Illinois: Citicorp Center, 500 W. Madison Street, Suite 1400, Chicago 60661-2511; 312-353-7390
- Massachusetts: 73 Tremont Street, Suite 600, Boston 02108; 617-424-5900
- New York: 233 Broadway, New York, NY 10279, (646) 428-1500
- Pennsylvania: Curtis Center, 601 Walnut Street, Suite 1120 East, Philadelphia 19106-3322; 215-597-3100
- Texas: 801 Cherry Street, 19th Floor, Fort Worth 76102; 817-978-3821
- Utah: 500 Key Bank Tower, Suite 500, 50 South Main Street, Salt Lake City 84114-0402; 801-524-5796

The SEC's huge database of all filings is now accessible directly to the public over the EDGAR system <www.sec.gov/edgarhp.htm>. EDGAR stands for Electronic Data Gathering and Retrieval. The system offers all quarterly and annual reports, tender offers and takeovers, insider purchases and sales, and much more. The data are usually posted within 24 hours of being filed.

Securities Investor Protection Corporation. (SIPC, 805 15th Street, NW, Suite 800, Washington, DC 20005-2215; 202-371-8300; www.sipc.org). The agency that insures your brokerage account against loss due to the failure of the brokerage firm. Offers the free publication: "How SIPC Protects You."

State Securities Regulators

North American Securities Administrators Association. (10 G Street, NE, Suite 710, Washington, DC 20002; 202-737-0900; www.nasaa.org). A group representing state securities enforcement agencies. Offers several free pamphlets on avoiding scams, including those on blind pool offerings, dirt pile gold swindles, penny stock fraud, and unsuitable investments. Also offers the book, *Investor Alert! How to Protect Your Money from Schemes, Scams, and Frauds.* The following are the state offices of securities regulators:

- Alabama: 770 Washington Avenue, Suite 570, Montgomery 36130-4700; 334-242-2984
- Alaska: PO Box 110807, Juneau 99801; 907-465-2521
- Arizona: 1300 W. Washington, 3rd Floor, Phoenix 85040; 602-542-4242
- Arkansas: Heritage West Building, 201 E. Markham, 3rd Floor, Little Rock 72201-1692; 501-324-9260
- California: 320 W. 4th Street, Suite 750, Los Angeles 90013; 213-576-7500
- Colorado: Colorado Division of Securities, 1580 Lincoln Street, Suite 420, Denver 80203-1506; 303-894-2320
- Connecticut: 260 Constitution Plaza, Hartford 06103; 860-240-8299
- Delaware: State Office Building, 820 N. French Street, 5th Floor, Wilmington 19801; 302-577-8424
- District of Columbia: 717 14th Street, NW, Suite 200, Washington 20005; 202-626-9161
- Florida: 101 E. Gaines Street, Tallahassee 32399-0350; 850-410-9805
- Georgia: 2 Martin Luther King Drive, Suite 802, West Tower, Atlanta 30334; 404-656-3920
- Hawaii: 1010 Richards Street, Honolulu 96813; 808-586-2744
- Idaho: PO Box 83720, Boise 83720-0031; 208-332-8004
- Illinois: 520 South 2nd Street, Springfield 62701; 217-782-2256
- Indiana: 302 W. Washington, Suite E-111, Indianapolis 46204; 317-232-6681
- Iowa: Iowa Securities Bureau, 340 Maple Street, Des Moines 50325; 515-281-4441
- Kansas: 618 S. Kansas Avenue, 2nd Floor, Topeka 66603; 785-296-3307
- Kentucky: Department of Financial Institutions, 1025 Capitol Center Drive, Suite 200, Frankfort 40601-3868; 502-573-3390
- Louisiana: 8660 United Plaza Boulevard, 2nd Floor, Baton Rouge 70809; 222-925-4512
- Maine: 121 State House Station, Augusta 04333; 207-624-8551
- Maryland: 200 St. Paul Place, 20th Floor, Baltimore 21202-2020; 410-576-6360
- Massachusetts: One Ashburton Place, Room 1701, Boston 02108; 617-727-3548
- Michigan: The Michigan Department of Commerce, 6546 Mercantile Way, Lansing 48909; 517-241-6370
- Minnesota: 133 E. 7th Street, St. Paul 55101; 651-296-4026
- Mississippi: 202 N. Congress Street, Suite 506, Jackson 39202; 601-359-6371

- Missouri: PO Box 1276, Jefferson City 65102; 573-751-4136
- Montana: Mitchell Building, 840 Helena Avenue, Helena 59601; 406-444-2040
- Nebraska: The Atrium, 1200 N Street, Suite 311, Lincoln 68509; 402-471-3445
- Nevada: 555 E. Washington Avenue, Suite 5200, Las Vegas 89101; 702-486-2440
- New Hampshire: State House, Room 204, Concord 03301-4989; 603-271-1463
- New Jersey: 153 Halsey Street, Newark 07102; 201-504-3600
- New Mexico: PO Box 25101, 725 Saint Michaels Drive, Santa Fe 87505; 505-827-7140
- New York: 120 Broadway, 23rd Floor, New York City 10271
- North Carolina: Secretary of State Securities Division, 300 N. Salisbury Street, Suite 100, Raleigh 27603; 919-733-3924
- North Dakota: North Dakota Securities Commissioner, State Capitol, 600 E. Boulevard Avenue, 5th Floor, Bismarck 58505; 701-328-2910
- Ohio: 77 S. High Street, 22nd Floor, Columbus 43215; 614-644-7381
- Oklahoma: First National Center, 120 N. Robinson Street, Suite 860, Oklahoma City 73102; 405-280-7700
- Oregon: Department of Consumer and Business Services, Finance and Corporate Securities, 350 Winter Street Northeast, Room 21, Salem 97310; 503-378-4387
- Pennsylvania: 1010 N. Seventh Street, 2nd Floor, Harrisburg 17102-1410; 717-783-4689
- Rhode Island: 233 Richmond Street, Suite 232, Providence 02903-4232; 401-277-3048
- South Carolina: Office of the Attorney General, Securities Section, 1000 Assembly Street, Columbia 29211-1549; 803-734-0032
- South Dakota: 118 W. Capitol Avenue, Pierre 57501-2013; 605-773-4823
- Tennessee: Davy Crockett Building, 500 James Robertson Parkway, Suite 680, Nashville 37243-0575; 615-741-2947
- Texas: PO Box 13167, Austin 78711; 512-305-8300
- Utah: Box 146760, 160 E. 300 South, 2nd Floor, Salt Lake City 84114-6760; 801-530-6600
- Vermont: 89 Main Street, Drawer 20, Montpelier 05620-3101; 802-828-3420
- Virginia: PO Box 1197, Richmond, 23218; 804-371-9051
- Washington: PO Box 9033, Olympia 98507; 360-902-8760
- West Virginia: 106 Dee Drive, Charleston 25311; 304-558-2257
- Wisconsin: Division of Securities, PO Box 1768, Madison 53702; 608-266-3432
- Wyoming: State Capitol Building, Cheyenne 82002-0020; 307-777-7370

CHAPTER 6

Mutual Fund Basics

If the process of selecting individual stocks seems a bit overwhelming, there's another way to participate in the stock market without the complications of choosing stocks: mutual funds that invest in stocks.

Mutual funds have become the most commonly used vehicles for average Americans to invest in the stock market. They offer professional management and instant diversification at a very low cost to the individual investor. Mutual funds, which have been around since the 1920s, are easy to use and understand, and they provide some very convenient services.

Put simply, a stock mutual fund is a pool of money collected from investors that a fund manager invests in stocks to achieve a specific objective. The fund is sponsored by a mutual fund company, which may be an independent firm, such as Fidelity, T. Rowe Price, or Vanguard, or a division of a brokerage or insurance company, like Merrill Lynch, Salomon Smith Barney, or ZurichKemper.

LOAD VERSUS NO-LOAD FUNDS

There are two basic kinds of mutual funds, differentiated by the method by which they are sold. When you pay a commission to a salesperson, financial planner, or broker, that fee is called a load. One kind of fund therefore is called a *load mutual fund* because you have to pay a commission to buy it. The other kind of fund, called a *no-load fund,* is sold directly by the mutual fund company, with no salesperson involved. To buy no-load shares, you call the mutual fund company directly, usually at a toll-free number, and the company sends you the necessary prospectus and application forms. Sending them back with a check opens your account.

Both load and no-load funds have their roles in the marketplace, and you must decide which is best for your needs. The advantage of a load fund is that you receive professional advice on which fund to choose. Such advice may be well worthwhile because it might be difficult for you to isolate the few funds that are best for your situation among the more than 8,000 funds in existence. Ideally, the salesperson helping you will not only tell you when to buy the fund but also when to sell your shares and move your money into a better fund.

The disadvantage of a load fund is that the commission you must pay immediately reduces the amount of money you have at work in the fund. The load can amount to as much as 8.5 percent of your initial investment, though many funds today charge 3 or 4 percent. If you pay the full 8.5 percent load, for every dollar you sink into the fund, only 91.5 cents will earn money. In other words, if you invest $10,000 in a fund with an 8.5 percent load, $9,150 goes into your fund, and the other $850 goes to the fund company and salesperson. If you pay a 3 percent load, 97 cents of every dollar will be invested in stocks. In the short term, therefore, you are starting at a disadvantage over a no-load fund, where all of your dollars are at work from the beginning. Over a longer period, however, if the load fund performs better than the no-load fund, the up-front charge will pale in significance.

Clearly, the advantage of the no-load fund is that you have all of your money working for you from the moment you open your account. The disadvantage of a no-load fund is that you will not receive much, if any, guidance on which fund to buy. When you call a no-load company's toll-free number, the phone representative can explain the differences among all of the firm's offerings. He or she can describe each fund's investment objective, track record, dividend yield, size in assets, management style, and fees, and the stocks currently in its portfolio. But because the person does not know you or your situation, and chances are will never speak to you again, he or she may not be able to advise you on which fund to buy. (However, representatives at many no load fund companies often can be very helpful in guiding you through the selection process and suggesting top quality funds that meet your objectives.)

If you already have made up your mind based on information you have received about the fund from the fund company itself or reports in the press on the Internet, buying a fund is as easy as sending in your money to the fund company. Just realize that you are taking full responsibility for your investment decisions when you buy a no-load fund. No salesperson will call to sell you more of the fund, and no one will tell you when to sell your shares and move to a better performing fund.

People often wonder how no-load companies can offer mutual funds if they do not charge for the service. In fact, they charge plenty, but it is not in the form of an explicit fee for which you must write a check. Both no-load and load funds levy what is known as a management fee every year to compensate them for the services they render. The management fee ranges from as little as .2 percent of your assets to as much as 3 percent, although typically it falls between 1 and 2 percent. The fee is deducted from the value of the fund automatically. So, if a fund charges a 1 percent management fee, for example, and the fund's stock portfolio rose 10 percent over the past year, you will earn a 9 percent return. As long as you keep your money in a fund, you will pay the management fee, though you might never realize it. A management fee, listed in a fund's selling literature as part of the expense ratio, should not be much more than 1.25 percent of its (and therefore your) assets for it to be considered fair and reasonable.

THE ADVANTAGES OF MUTUAL FUNDS

Mutual funds offer several key advantages over individual stocks, which can make the management fee very worthwhile:

- *Professional management.* A professional skilled in choosing stocks does all of your work for you. Managers of stock mutual funds spend their entire day determining which stocks to buy and sell. They have instant access to information about every stock around the world at the push of a few computer keys. They work in companies where teams of research analysts pore over corporate quarterly and annual reports and managers and analysts visit company executives and factories to evaluate the firms' prospects firsthand. You have almost no opportunity to become as knowledgeable as these fund managers without quitting your job and taking up investing full time.
- *Instant diversification.* A mutual fund gives you instant diversification. If you have only $1,000 or $5,000 to invest, the money will not buy many shares of a single stock, and it will certainly not buy many different stocks. By putting your money in only two or three stocks, you are exposed to the possibility that one of them will plummet in price, wiping out much of your investment capital. Instead, when you put your $1,000 or $5,000 in a mutual fund, your money buys into a portfolio that may comprise 50 stocks, or maybe 500 different issues. If two or three stocks in the portfolio get hit hard, your losses will be

much more limited because the value of many of the other stocks will probably be holding their own or going up at the same time.

- *Broad selection.* A fund exists for every financial goal and risk tolerance level. Armed with your goals and risk level from the first chapter, you can find a fund that fits your situation. The different types of funds are described in more detail later in this section, but in broad terms, there are funds designed for various degrees of growth and for varying levels of income, as well as funds that combine both growth and income objectives.

- *Low transaction costs.* Transaction costs are much lower with mutual funds than they are when you invest in a variety of individual stocks. When you invest in a mutual fund, you benefit from the brokerage commission rates paid by the fund company, which are far lower than you would pay to make the same trades. Mutual funds are among the largest institutional investors on Wall Street, and because they buy and sell billions of dollars' worth of stock every day, they pay between $.02 and $.05 a share per trade. You would be lucky to pay $.10 a share at most brokerage firms, and if you trade in quantities of less than $1,000, you might have to pay as much as $.40 or $.50 a share. Over time, the lower transaction costs that the mutual fund pays will boost your return because you will have more money invested and less paid out in fees.

- *Easy access to funds.* You can get into and out of a mutual fund easily. All it takes is a phone call to your broker or the fund, or a visit to their Web site. By law, a fund must allow you to buy shares at the fund's closing price on the day the fund gets your money. The closing price, called net asset value (NAV), is the value of the stock portfolio at the end of the day divided by the number of shares in the fund. Conversely, if you want to sell, the fund must redeem your shares at the NAV on the day you give your instructions. This instant liquidity can be a big advantage when you want to buy or sell stocks quickly. For example, say stock prices are shooting up and you still haven't determined which stocks to buy, or you can't get your broker on the phone. Instead of watching helplessly on the sidelines, you can participate in the rally by buying a stock fund. On the other hand, if stock prices are plunging, it may be difficult to get decent prices if you have only a handful of shares to sell. When you sell the mutual fund, you know you will receive the fund's closing price that day, no matter what problems the fund manager has selling stocks.

- *Automatic investment option.* In addition to buying and selling fund shares on your request, mutual funds can set up automatic systems to add or subtract money from your account. Most mutual funds will automatically transfer a set amount—usually as little as $25—from your bank account or money-market mutual fund into the stock or bond fund of your choice on a regular basis, whether that be weekly, monthly, or annually. Many mutual funds actually waive their normal initial minimum investment amount (which often varies from about $500 to $3,000 depending on the mutual fund company) if you sign up for such a plan. This is a simple way to invest on autopilot. You probably won't even miss the money from your checking account, but over time, you will build up your capital in the mutual fund. On the other hand, if you are retired and want a regular income, most mutual funds will automatically withdraw a certain amount of money and send you a monthly check. This is called an automatic withdrawal program, which allows you to withdraw a regular amount of money from your funds every month. It is targeted mostly to retired people living off their funds.

- *Easy switching.* You can easily switch from one fund to another within a fund family. Most mutual fund companies offer a broad array of mutual funds so that as your views of the stock market or your needs change, you can simply switch from one fund to another. This is known as an exchange. For instance, you may have invested money in a growth stock fund for years to build capital for retirement. When you retire, you can exchange some of the shares in the growth fund for shares in a stock fund paying high dividends on a monthly basis, on which you will live. All fund families allow exchanges not only between stock funds but also from stock funds to bond funds and money-market funds, which may act as havens when stock prices are falling.

- *Automatic reinvestment.* The fund will reinvest dividends and capital gains automatically. If you want the power of compounding to work for you, you can instruct your mutual fund to reinvest in more fund shares all dividends it has earned from the stocks in its portfolio. In addition, as the fund captures capital gains by selling stocks at a profit, it disburses the proceeds as capital gains distributions. You can have the fund reinvest those distributions in more shares as well. Remember that you will have to pay taxes on both reinvested dividends and capital gains in the tax year you receive them even though you have reinvested the money, unless you hold shares in a tax-deferred retirement account. Over time, the shares you own from reinvestment produce more shares, and the compounding effect can dramatically increase your capital. For example, if you had invested $10,000 in the Denver-based Berger Growth Fund on September 30, 1974, you would have accumulated $371,479 by December 31, 2000, assuming you had reinvested all dividends and capital gains distributions. In contrast, your $10,000 would have grown to only $64,503 if you had taken the distributions. Figure 6.1 clearly illustrates the power of compounding.

THE DOWN SIDE OF FUNDS

While mutual funds offer many excellent advantages for individual investors, they do have some shortcomings when compared with individual stock investment:

- *Taxes.* If you buy an individual stock, you will never have to pay taxes on your gains until you sell the stock. Even if it grows 100-fold, you would owe no taxes on the gain until you sell. In fact, if you hold the stock in your portfolio and pass it onto your heirs, they won't ever have to pay taxes on the gains enjoyed while you owned the stock. With mutual funds, on the other hand, you will be forced to pay taxes each year on any of the gains made within the fund when the fund manager sells stocks at profit—even if you never sell a share of your mutual fund yourself.
- *Control.* When you invest in individual stocks, you have total control over the companies you own. You make the decisions based on your own research, your own strategies and your own personal preferences. If you don't want to own a tobacco stock or a stock of a company known to be a heavy polluter, that's your decision. When you buy a mutual fund, the fund manager makes all those decisions for you, and that person may invest in companies you would rather not own. There are, however, socially conscious mutual funds that invest in stocks of companies that the manager feels are solid corporate citizens. But, again, it is the fund manager—rather than you—who is making that decision on where to invest your money.
- *Annual fees.* Mutual funds charge an annual fee of about 1 to 2 percent of your total invested assets every year whether you make new investments or not. With individual stocks, once you own the stock, you don't have to pay any annual fees just to hold it.
- *Performance.* Although mutual funds are managed by professional investment specialists, they, too, can be prone to bad decisions. During the high tech crash of the 1999–2002, millions of mutual fund investors who thought they were invested in relatively conservative blue chip stock funds saw their portfolios drop dramatically because the fund managers had invested a large portion of assets in speculative technology and Internet stocks. In fact, only about 20 to 30 percent of mutual funds outperform the overall market over any two- to three-

Figure 6.1 The Effect of Compounding on a Berger Growth Fund Investment

BERGER GROWTH FUND

From Investment

From Capital Gains

From Dividends

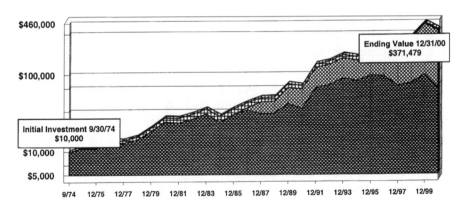

Dividends and Capital Gains Reinvested

Ending Value 12/31/00 $371,479

Initial Investment 9/30/74 $10,000

Past performance shows the fund's history and does not guarantee future results. The figures include changes in share price and reinvestment of dividends and capital gains, which will fluctuate so that shares, when redeemed, may be worth more or less than their original costs. The figures include the deduction of 12b-1 fees beginning in June 1990.

Source: Reprinted with permission of Berger Associates and TowersData.

year period. So just because a fund is professionally managed doesn't mean it will outperform the market, or even outperform a portfolio that you may have built yourself.

Despite these limitations, the positive aspects of mutual fund investing far outweigh the negatives. Mutual funds have generally proven to be outstanding investments for millions of Americans.

MAKING SENSE OF FUND FEES

In addition to the standard loads and annual management fees, some mutual funds levy additional charges, which you should be aware of before you invest. The funds cannot sneak these charges by you. They are all disclosed in a standardized fee table on the front of all mutual fund prospectuses. Prospectuses are the official legal documents describing funds. The section, titled Fund Expenses, appears in the example in Figure 6.2.

Note that funds are required to detail their expenses by category for the last year. In addition, they must project what that level of expenses would cost investors if they invested $1,000 over the next year, three years, five years, and ten years. You can use this section of the prospectus to compare one mutual fund with a similar fund in another fund family.

Here is an explanation of the most common fund fees.

Back-end loads. To compete with no-load funds, many broker-sold funds now waive a charge when you buy them but hit you with a fee if you sell the funds before a particular period of time elapses. This is also called a *contingent deferred sales charge.* Usually, the back-end load operates on a sliding scale, so you will pay 4 percent of the money you invested if you sell the fund in the first year you hold it, 3 percent in the second year, 2 percent in the third year, and 1 percent in the fourth year. If you hold the fund for at least four years, you will not pay the back-end load. A brokerage firm needs this system because it pays the broker his or her commission up front when you buy the fund even though the firm doesn't receive the money from you to pay the commission. If you sell the fund before the brokerage firm has had a chance to recoup that fee through management fees, it wants to be able to charge you. However, one fact that investors often do not realize is that back-end load funds almost always charge a higher annual fee than front-end load funds. So if you hold the fund for several years, you may not have to pay a load, but you will have to pay a higher-than-usual annual fee.

Dividend reinvestment loads. Although most mutual funds do not levy a sales commission on reinvested dividends, some fund groups do. This fee usually amounts to 4 percent of the reinvested funds. Because dividend rein-

Figure 6.2 Sample Charges That Funds Levy

Fund Expenses

The following table sets forth the fees that an investor in the Fund might pay and expenses paid by the Fund during its fiscal year ended December 31, 1991.

Shareholder Transaction Expenses

Maximum Sales Charge on Purchases (as a percentage of offering price)	5.75%
Sales Charge on Reinvested Dividends	None
Redemption Fee	None
Deferred Sales Load	None*
Exchange Fee	$ 5.00

Annual Fund Operating Expenses (as a percentage of average net assets)

Management Fees	.65%
12b-1 (Distribution Plan) Fees	.08%
Other Expenses	.22%
Total Fund Operating Expenses	.95%

*Certain purchases of $1 million or more are not subject to front-end sales charges but a contingent deferred sales charge of 1% is imposed on the proceeds of such shares redeemed within 18 months of the end of the calendar month of their purchase, subject to certain conditions. See "How to Buy Shares—Contingent Deferred Sales Charge," below.

The purpose of this table is to assist an investor in understanding the various costs and expenses that an investor in the Fund will bear directly (shareholder transaction expenses) or indirectly (annual fund operating expenses). The sales charge illustrated is the current maximum rate applicable to purchases of Fund shares. Investors may be entitled to reduced sales charges based on the amount purchased or the value of shares already owned and may be subject to a contingent deferred sales charge in limited circumstances (see "How to Buy Shares"). "Other Expenses" includes such expenses as custodial and transfer agent fees, audit, legal and other business operating expenses, but excludes extraordinary expenses.

The following example applies the above-stated expenses to a hypothetical $1,000 investment in shares of the Fund over the time periods shown below, assuming a 5% annual rate of return on the investment and also assuming that the shares were redeemed at the end of each stated period. The amounts below are the cumulative costs of such hypothetical $1,000 investment for the periods shown.

1 year	3 years	5 years	10 years
$67	$86	$107	$167

This example should not be considered a representation of past or future expenses or performance. Expenses are subject to change and actual performance and expenses may be less or greater than those illustrated above. For further details, see the Fund's Financial Statements included in the Additional Statement.

Source: Reprinted by permission of OppenheimerFunds[SM].

vestment is automatic and no sales advice is given, it is best to avoid funds that charge for counsel you are not receiving.

Exchange fees. Some fund groups charge a fee if you exchange one fund for another within a fund family. The fee covers administrative costs and usually amounts to about $5 per transaction.

12b-1 fees. These charges, like management fees, are deducted automatically from the fund's assets each year. They cover distribution costs, which include advertising, promotion, literature, and sales incentives to brokers, and range from .25 percent to as much as 1.25 percent of the fund's assets each year. The idea behind these fees is that if a mutual fund increases its assets through more promotion, fund shareholders will benefit because the fund's expenses will be spread over a wider customer base, thereby lowering each shareholder's cost. In many cases, however, expenses do not decrease as fund assets grow. In general, unless you invest in a fund that has a superb record or some other compelling reason to buy it, avoid funds that impose 12b-1 fees.

CHAPTER 7

Choosing the Best Fund for You

With about 8,000 mutual funds available in the investment market, narrowing the field to the best fund (or funds) for you is no easy task. There are stock funds for nearly every objective, from broad-based, long-term growth funds to the highly specialized sector funds that confine their holdings strictly to stocks of a single industry group. There are small stock funds, aggressive funds, international funds, and balanced funds that invest in both stocks and bonds. Before you decide which fund is right for you, you need to decide which type of fund (or funds) works best based on your financial goals and your risk tolerance level.

The following is a rundown of the different categories of stock funds, separated into the sectors of the investment pyramid.

HIGH-RISK APEX FUNDS

Aggressive growth funds. These funds buy stocks of fast-growing companies or of other companies that have great capital gains potential. They might buy stocks in bankrupt or depressed companies, anticipating a rebound. Such funds often trade stocks frequently in hope of catching small price gains. They are also known as *maximum capital gains funds.*

Foreign stock funds. These funds buy stocks of corporations based outside of the United States. In addition to the usual forces affecting stock prices, fluctuations in the value of the U.S. dollar against foreign currencies can dramatically affect the price of these funds' shares, particularly over the short term.

Sector funds. Sector funds buy stocks in just one industry or sector of the economy. Some examples would be environmental stocks, oil company shares, and stocks in automakers and gold-mining companies. Because these funds are not diversified, they soar or plummet on the fate of the industry in which they invest.

Small-company growth funds. Such growth funds invest in stocks of small companies, typically those having outstanding shares with a total market value of $1 billion or less. These companies have enormous growth potential, yet the stocks they invest in are much less established—and therefore riskier—than blue chip stocks.

Special situation funds. These funds often place large bets on a small number of stocks, anticipating a big payoff. The special situation the fund manager looks for might be a takeover or a liquidation of the company at a price higher than the shares currently sell for. Some funds offer venture capital financing for privately held firms, hoping to cash in when the companies offer shares to the public in the future.

MODERATE-RISK FUNDS

Growth funds. Growth funds invest in shares of well-known growth companies that usually have a long history of increasing earnings. Because the stock market fluctuates, growth funds rise and fall over time as well, though not as much as funds holding smaller, less proven stocks.

Equity-income funds. Such funds own shares in stocks that pay higher dividends than do growth funds. Whereas a growth fund's payout may be 1 percent or 2 percent, an equity-income fund might yield 4 percent or 5 percent. That higher yield tends to cushion the fund's price when stock prices fall. When stock prices rise, equity-income funds tend to increase less sharply than do pure growth funds. A slightly more aggressive version of an equity-income fund is called a *growth and income* fund or a *total return* fund because it strives for gains from both income and capital appreciation.

Index funds. These funds buy the stocks that make up a particular index to allow investors' returns to match the index. The most popular index used is the Standard & Poor's 500. Proponents of index funds argue that because many money managers fail to match or beat the S&P 500 each year, investors can come out ahead by just matching the index. The management fees of an index fund are much lower than those of a regular stock fund because the fund manager just replicates an index; he or she does not research or make decisions on which stocks to buy and sell.

Option-income funds. These funds buy stocks and write options on the shares, which generates more income for shareholders. This usually results in a higher dividend than growth funds offer. On the other hand, if stock prices rise, the funds lose their position in the stocks because the options are exercised. Therefore, these funds have limited appreciation potential.

Socially conscious funds. Such funds look for companies that meet certain criteria, such as advancing minority and female employees or helping clean up the environment. These funds screen out stocks of companies that are major polluters, defense contractors, or promoters of gambling or tobacco. See the section on socially conscious investing in Chapter 3 for more on these funds.

Low-Risk Sector Funds

Balanced funds. Balanced funds keep a fairly steady mix of high-yielding stocks and conservative bonds. This allows the funds to pay a fairly high rate of current income and still participate in the long-term growth of stocks.

Flexible portfolio funds. These funds have the latitude to invest in stocks, bonds, or cash instruments, depending on the fund manager's market outlook. If he or she thinks stock prices are about to fall, the manager can shift all the fund's assets into cash instruments, thereby avoiding losses. If he or she thinks stock prices are about to rise, the manager can move all the fund's assets into stocks. Usually, the fund will have some money in stocks, bonds, and cash, which tends to stabilize its performance. These funds are also known as *asset allocation funds*.

Utilities funds. Such funds buy shares in electric, gas, telephone, and water utilities. Because all these companies are regulated monopolies, they have steady earnings and pay high dividends. Utilities funds are subject to swings in interest rates, however. Nonetheless, for a high-yielding and relatively stable stock fund, it's hard to beat a utilities fund.

Another way to look at this trade-off between risk and return is illustrated in the dial in Figure 7.1.

Selecting a Fund within a Category

Once you have chosen the fund category that fits your needs, you must narrow your options further by looking at the best funds within the category.

Performance. The first criterion in selecting a particular fund is performance. You want to choose a fund that has established a solid long-term record of achieving its objectives. It is also preferable if the fund has had the

Figure 7.1   Trading Risk for Return: A Mutual Fund Dial

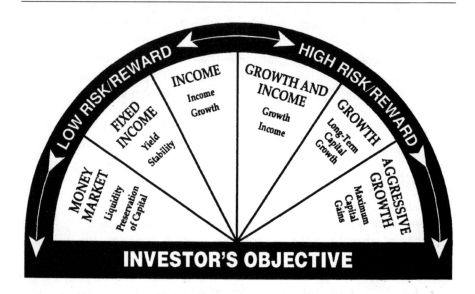

Source: *The Investor's Guide to Low-Cost Mutual Funds.* Reprinted by permission of The Mutual Fund Education Alliance.

same manager for a long time so that you can be assured that the fund's style will remain consistent.

Several independent fund-monitoring organizations rank fund performance. The two biggest and best known are Lipper Inc. (110 Wall Street, New York, NY 10005; 212-607-2259) and Morningstar (225 W. Wacker Drive, Chicago, IL 60606; 800-876-5005). Results from both are published regularly in *The Wall Street Journal, USA Today,* and *Investor's Business Daily,* as well as *Money* magazine and other reputable personal finance journals. You can also track fund performance in the many newsletters that follow this action. The names, addresses, and telephone numbers of these newsletters are listed in Chapter 8.

The best measure of fund performance is called *total return.* This combines all dividends and capital gains distributions with changes in a fund's price. It is a far better yardstick to use when comparing funds than just the change in a fund's price over time. The listings for total return you will see from the ratings services and in the media normally show a fund's results thus far in the current year, over the past 52 weeks and over the last three, five, and ten years. They will also refer to the average annual return, which is the averaging of returns over longer periods. Any average annual return of more than 15 percent for at least five years is considered exemplary.

In choosing a fund, you should feel comfortable with its style. What exactly is a fund's style? It is a methodology of selecting stocks that differentiates one fund from another. Some styles work well at certain points in a stock market cycle, while others take over as the stock market changes. The two broadest kinds of stock-choosing styles are growth and value. *Growth* refers to selecting stocks with ever-rising earnings, while value means buying stocks temporarily out of favor that the manager expects will become popular again. Therefore, you can often determine a fund's style by its name. For instance, the Kemper Growth Fund is a classic growth stock fund, while the T. Rowe Price Small Cap Value Fund looks for small stocks that are currently out of favor. In general, growth stocks shine when the economy is well into an economic recovery, while value stocks tend to outperform others when the economy is in recession or is just starting to emerge from a recession.

It is difficult for the average investor, as well as the Wall Street professional, to evaluate whether growth or value stock funds are on the upswing at any particular moment. For that reason, the best long-term strategy is to diversify among styles. If half your holdings are in growth stocks and the other half are in value stocks, you will perform better over time than if you invest all your money in one style of stock.

Another difference in investment styles is based on whether the fund manager makes market timing decisions. A fund run by a market timer, even though it is a stock fund, can sell most or all of its stocks if the manager senses the stock market is about to tumble. This fund is designed to protect shareholders' capital from huge losses. Funds operating under the other style maintain that it is impossible to time the stock market's ups and downs, so it is best to be nearly fully invested in stocks at all times. These funds will be more volatile than funds that try to time the market. This means that fully invested funds will rise faster when stocks rise but fall further when stocks tumble. The managers of such funds leave the market timing to you.

Convenience. The second criterion you should use to choose a fund is convenience. Though you might receive a higher return by having holdings in the top ten funds in ten different fund families, the record keeping and headaches in following so many funds are most likely not worth the higher return. It's probably best to find a top-quality fund family or two and keep most of your capital with them. Most families offer consolidated statements, meaning you can see all of your fund holdings on one statement. Also, you will be able to transfer money from one fund to another easily if you keep most of your assets in one place.

You have one way around this problem of proliferating fund families. Most discount brokers, including Charles Schwab, Fidelity, and TD Waterhouse, allow you to buy almost any mutual fund in any family and keep it in one account. Schwab calls its service the Mutual Fund Marketplace or One-

Source; Fidelity calls its equivalent FundsNetwork. For many funds, you pay no loads, transaction fees, or commissions. By consolidating all of your fund holdings under one custodian, you can save yourself much frustration and still participate in the best funds.

Quality of service. The quality of the service you receive is also important in choosing a fund family. While most fund complexes offer good service, there is variation. Following are a few services that top fund groups offer. You should have access to each of them.

- *Automated phone answering systems.* They can give you prices, yields, and other information about your funds, as well as allow you to make transactions. In many cases, these systems operate 24 hours a day, seven days a week.
- *Knowledgeable and helpful telephone service representatives.* Remember that phone reps at no-load funds will describe funds but will not advise you on which fund to buy. Some large fund companies have walk-in investor centers in large cities where you can discuss your investing needs with a fund representative in person.
- *Easy-to-read statements.* You should not have to be a lawyer or mutual fund expert to be able to make sense of your statement. It should clearly spell out how many shares you have, how many shares you bought or sold in your latest transactions, the yields on your funds, and other relevant data. Most funds will calculate your cost basis, which is the amount of money you spent to buy your shares. That can be quite complex to ascertain on your own if you have been buying shares with reinvested dividends and capital gains for years. You will need your cost basis to determine the amount of taxes you owe when you sell fund shares.

Once you have opened an account with a fund that meets your criteria, hold onto it unless its performance starts to deteriorate, its fees shoot up, its star manager leaves, its style changes dramatically, or you have some other major reason to sell the fund. That includes, of course, a change in your financial situation or your stage in the life cycle. Otherwise, continue to add to the fund and watch it grow!

CLOSED-END MUTUAL FUNDS

So far, all of our discussion of mutual funds has pertained to open-end funds. Another variety of fund is called a *closed-end fund,* which has its own advantages and disadvantages. Like open-end funds, closed-end funds offer the advantages of professional management, diversification, convenience, and automatic reinvestment of dividends and capital gains.

The difference between the two types of funds comes in the way they sell shares. Open-end funds create new shares continually, as more money is invested in them. When cash is taken out of the fund, the number of outstanding shares shrinks. The portfolio manager therefore is faced with an ever-changing pool of assets that can be small one month and huge the next. This can make it difficult to manage the fund because millions of dollars usually pour into the fund after it has had a hot record and stock prices are high, and millions leave the fund when it has underperformed the market and stock prices are falling. This pattern of volatile cash flow can severely harm the fund's performance because the manager is forced to buy stocks when prices are high and sell them when prices are low.

Closed-end funds are designed to avoid this problem. Instead of constantly creating and redeeming shares, these funds issue a limited number of shares, which trade on the New York or American Stock Exchange or on the Nasdaq National Market System. Instead of dealing with the fund company directly when you buy or sell shares, as you do with open-end funds, you trade closed-end shares with other investors, just as you do any publicly traded stock. You pay standard brokerage commissions to buy and sell them, and you can look up the fund's price in the stock tables of the newspaper every day.

From the closed-end fund manager's point of view, there is no need to worry about huge flows of cash into and out of the fund. The manager knows how much money he or she must invest and selects stocks based on the fund's investment objective. This allows the manager to concentrate on meeting long-term objectives because he or she does not have to keep a stash of cash around to meet redemptions.

Like an open-end fund, a closed-end fund always has a certain NAV (the worth of all the stocks in its portfolio divided by the number of shares). But unlike an open-end fund, a closed-ender can sell for more or less than the value of its portfolio, depending on demand for the shares.

When the fund sells for more than its portfolio is currently worth, that is called selling at a premium. This usually happens when the fund is extremely popular and it offers some unique style or investing niche, which make investors willing to pay a high price for it. For example, the Korea Fund, which at the time was the only fund granted permission to invest in fast-growing Korea by the Korean government, soared to a 100 percent premium at one point because investors had no other way of investing in Korea. That means that investors were willing to pay $20 a share—or double the $10 that the underlying portfolio of Korean stocks was worth. Another reason a fund might sell at a premium is that it is named after a famous money manager with a good track record, so brokers actively sell it. Funds that meet this description include the Gabelli Fund, the Templeton Emerging Markets Fund, and the Zweig Fund.

In general, closed-end funds tend to jump to premiums immediately after they first issue shares to the public because the brokerage firms that underwrite the issues actively promote them for a few months. Often, once the brokers have moved on to the next closed-end issue, the older funds drop to a discount. The moral of the story: It almost never pays to buy a new issue of a closed-end fund.

On the other hand, a fund investing in an unpopular category of stocks can fall to a steep discount. For example, the Brazil Fund dropped to a 35 percent discount when the country was suffering through a bout of political scandals and hyperinflation. That means a buyer paid only $6.50 per share, or 65 percent of the $10 value of the Brazilian stock portfolio. Closed-end funds can also drop to discounts because few people pay attention to them and, therefore, there is little demand for them. That can provide an opportunity to buy assets cheaply. In fact, if a fund's discount remains too deep for too long a time, raiders will often swoop in. Their game is to buy millions of shares at a discount, then force a vote to convert the fund from closed-end to open-end status. Because open-end funds always trade at the worth of their underlying portfolios, the raiders can walk off with huge profits.

Therefore, you should assess two factors when you buy a closed-end fund. The first is the fund manager's record in choosing winning stocks that allow the fund to achieve its investment objective. The second factor is whether you are buying the fund at a premium or a discount. Some investors' entire strategy with closed-end funds is to buy them at a discount and wait for them to rise to a premium, at which point they sell.

To determine whether a fund is selling at a premium or a discount, you can look in Monday's *Wall Street Journal* or in *Barron's*. A sample table, along with an explanation of each column, follows:

1. Column 1 lists the name of the fund. Funds are broken down alphabetically by categories, such as diversified funds, specialized equity funds, and bond funds.
2. The second column notes the exchange where the fund's shares are traded. In the example, both the General American shares and the China Fund trade on the New York Stock Exchange.
3. The NAV is the total per-share worth of the underlying portfolio of securities on this day. In the example, all of the stocks in General American, divided by the number of fund shares, are worth $9 per mutual fund share.
4. The stock price is the dollar amount that the fund currently sells for on the New York Stock Exchange.

Fund[1]	Stock Exchange[2]	Net Asset Value[3]	Stock Price[4]	% Difference[5]
General American Investors	NYSE	$ 9.00	$10.00	+11%
China Fund	NYSE	13.00	10.00	−23%

5. The difference is the percentage difference between the stock price and the NAV. In the example, General American is trading at an 11 percent premium, while the China Fund is selling at a 23 percent discount.

There are several kinds of closed-end funds, each with its own objective and risk characteristics. Some of the most common types follow.

Bond funds. These funds buy either taxable government or corporate bonds or tax-free municipal bonds and pass the income on to shareholders.

Diversified equity funds. These funds buy a portfolio of stocks in many industries. If the fund manager is bearish (the manager thinks that the stock prices are about to fall), though, the fund can hold cash or some bonds. The objective of diversified equity funds is usually growth.

International funds. International funds buy stocks in other countries. Their prices are therefore affected not only by changes in stock prices but also by fluctuations of foreign currencies against the U.S. dollar. Some international funds specialize in a particular area of the world, like Europe or Asia. Some specialize in stocks of developing countries. Some funds buy stocks in a particular industry, like health care or telecommunications, on a worldwide basis.

Sector and specialty funds. These funds specialize in the stocks of a particular industry, such as banking, media, natural resources, or health care. Such funds have more potential for gain if the selected industry does well but also have a higher risk of loss if the industry falls out of favor.

Single-country funds. Such funds invest in the stocks of a single country. This makes them more volatile than broadly diversified international funds. For example, on the euphoria about the possibilities of German reunification, the Germany Fund shot up sharply to a huge premium after the Berlin Wall fell. A few years later, when it was clear that reunification would take longer and be more costly than expected, shares in the Germany Fund fell to a deep discount.

USING YOUR COMPUTER TO PICK MUTUAL FUNDS

The World Wide Web provides a great resource to help you pick and monitor a mutual fund portfolio. By tapping into several of the Web sites listed in the Resources section of Chapter 8, you can screen databases of funds, such as the one maintained by Morningstar, to identify funds that meet your investment objectives. For example, you could search for funds with the highest long-term total return that take the lowest risk. Or, if you are an income investor, you can search for funds with the highest, safest yields. You also can identify funds with low expense ratios, which automatically gives you an advantage over buying high-expense funds. Once you have identified funds that sound promising, you can go to their Web sites to find out more detail and even ask for applications and prospectuses online. Many mutual funds, and discount brokers offering mutual funds, make it easy to buy shares right from your computer.

By participating in online discussions and chat groups, you may be able to pick up useful information on good mutual funds. Be careful, however, to know who is in these groups and what their hidden agendas and levels of expertise may be. Two good places to look for chat groups are the Mutual Funds section of America Online and the various discussion groups hosted by major personal finance magazines such as *Money, Mutual Funds Magazine, Smart Money,* and *Worth.*

Once you have opened an account with a mutual fund company, you can use its Web page to monitor the value of your holdings and receive information on how the fund is doing and what its current investment strategy is. Many mutual fund company Web sites also have extremely helpful tools to help you in all areas of personal finance, such as calculators to help you figure out your financial needs in retirement, or the pros and cons of rolling over money from a regular IRA to a Roth IRA. You also can ask your mutual fund questions online, such as how to calculate your cost basis if you have been reinvesting dividends and capital gains for years.

The profusion of thousands of mutual funds may at first make it seem more difficult than ever to pick the funds that are right for you. But adept use of your computer for research and portfolio monitoring may make your job of fund-picking significantly easier.

For both beginning and sophisticated investors, there is probably no better way to set up a diversified portfolio than through mutual funds. Both open and closed-end funds offer many services at reasonable cost. The wide array of choices of different types of funds means that there is a fund for every

investing need you may ever have, from the most aggressive to the most conservative. Millions of shareholders who have studied about and invested in
funds are satisfied with their holdings. With the explanation of mutual funds
provided in this chapter, you should now feel confident about choosing the
best fund for your situation.

CHAPTER 8

Buying Your Stock Mutual Fund

To invest successfully in mutual funds, it is helpful to know what to look for in a fund, and how to follow the performance of your fund on a regular basis. The fund company provides plenty of information on its fees and objectives in literature that is available to you from the fund at no charge—simply for the asking. And there are plenty of other places to track your fund, if you know where to look.

Mutual fund companies have made it as easy as possible to open an account, but there is still a certain amount of legal paperwork you must go through in the process. In protecting consumers and making sure they receive enough information about a fund, the Securities and Exchange Commission (SEC) requires that potential fund shareholders receive a prospectus and an application form from the fund.

THE PROSPECTUS

While you shouldn't expect the prospectus to compete with your favorite novel for light reading, it does contain several important facts you should understand before you give the fund any money.

- *The fund's investment objective.* The fund may be aiming for aggressive growth, steady income, or something in between.
- *The investment methods used to achieve the fund's goals.* The fund may restrict itself to certain kinds of stocks, or it may use complex hedging

strategies involving futures and options to prevent losses. The fund will also tell you what kinds of stocks it will not buy.

- *The fund's investment advisor.* The prospectus will outline the background of the fund company and usually tell you which portfolio manager makes the decisions about what stocks to buy and sell. Ultimately, the fund's performance is determined by the quality of the investment advisor. Some firms use a team approach, while others are run by an individual.

- *The amount of risk the fund will assume.* Depending on the type of fund, the prospectus will reveal how volatile the fund's price is. The more risks the fund takes, the more its price will jump around.

- *The tax consequences of holding the fund.* For example, the prospectus will mention that you must pay taxes on all dividend and capital gains distributions.

- *A list of services provided by the fund.* The prospectus will tell you whether the fund is suitable for individual retirement accounts (IRAs) and Keogh accounts, whether you can reinvest dividends and capital gains automatically, and whether you can set up an automatic investment or withdrawal program. The prospectus will also tell you the minimum initial investment to get into the fund, as well as the minimum amount to make subsequent investments.

- *A financial summary of the fund's performance for the past ten years* (if it has been around that long). A table will track the fund's price, dividends, and capital gains distributions that have been paid and expenses.

- *A listing of all fund fees.* This table will summarize the management fee, 12b-1 fees, sales charges, and any other fees charged to shareholders.

THE APPLICATION FORM

When you've decided that you want to invest in a particular fund, you must fill out the application and return it to the fund with a check. Once you've completed this form, you will not have to do so again for this fund group.

Your account should be established within a few days. You will receive a confirmation statement from the fund showing how much you invested, how many shares you received, and the current price per share. Unlike stocks, certificates are not usually issued as evidence of ownership of mutual fund shares. Some mutual fund companies will issue certificates, but only if requested.

RESOURCES

For further information on stock mutual funds, we recommend that you consult the following resources. They include the names, addresses, and telephone numbers, where applicable, of books, newsletters, software, major fund companies, ratings services, and trade associations. The fund companies will provide a list of their funds, along with such data as current performance and fees.

There are several ways to follow the action in closed-end funds. Some brokerage house analysts issue research reports on the funds, and you will spot occasional stories about closed-end funds in financial newspapers and magazines. For more in-depth coverage, consult those books and newsletters in the following list written specifically about closed-end funds.

Books about Stock Mutual Funds

The Art of Astute Investing: Building Wealth with No-Load Mutual Funds, by C. Todd Conover (AMACOM, 1601 Broadway, New York, NY 10019; 212-586-8100; 800-262-9699; www.amanet.org). This step-by-step commonsense book teaches readers how to use their investment dollars to their best advantage with no-load mutual funds.

Bogle on Mutual Funds: New Perspectives for the Intelligent Investor, by John C. Bogle (McGraw-Hill, PO Box 543, Blacklick, OH 43004; 800-634-3961; www. mcgraw-hill.com). Bogle, the founder and chairman of the Vanguard mutual funds group, gives sage advice on setting up a portfolio of funds to meet investment objectives, spotting excessive fees and false advertising claims, and interpreting mutual fund data.

Building Wealth with Mutual Funds, by John H. Taylor (Windsor Books, Box 280, Brightwaters, NY 11718; 516-321-7830; 800-321-5934; www.windsorbooks .com). Offers a step-by-step approach to investing in mutual funds. Covers, among other topics, international investing, index funds, variable annuity funds, and socially responsible investing.

Business Week Guide to Mutual Funds, by Jeffrey M. Laderman (McGraw-Hill, PO Box 548, Blacklick, OH 43004; 800-634-3961; www.mcgraw-hill.com). Explains the different types of funds in an easy-to-read format. Recommends investment strategies for all ages and explains why some funds may work better than others. Explains how loads and high expenses can ruin investment returns.

But Which Mutual Funds?: How to Pick the Right Ones to Achieve Your Financial Dreams, by Steven T. Goldberg (Kiplinger Washington Editors, 1729 H Street, Washington, DC 20006; 800-280-7165; www.kiplinger.com). Walks readers through the basics of mutual funds, helping decide how much they'll need to invest and for how long, and at what level of risk. Includes tables and worksheets.

Buying Mutual Funds for Free, by Kirk Kazanjian (Dearborn Trade, Chicago, IL; 312-836-4400; 800-245-2665; www.dearborntrade.com). How to put together a diversified portfolio of the world's finest funds by opening an account at one of the discount brokers and selecting from the list of no-load, no-transaction-fee offerings.

CDA Wiesenberger Mutual Funds Update (CDA Wiesenberger, 1455 Research Boulevard, Rockville, MD 20850; 800-232-2285). A detailed monthly compilation of mutual fund performance statistics.

Common Sense on Mutual Funds: New Imperatives for the Intelligent Investor, by John C. Bogle (John Wiley & Sons, 1 Wiley Drive, Somerset, NJ 08875; 212-850-6000; 800-225-5945; www.wiley.com). Teaches the basic principle that for investments in mutual funds to provide wealth in the long term, the reader must abandon the current popular gambling on the latest mutual fund fad and invest in solid, low-cost no-load funds.

The Complete Guide to Managing a Portfolio of Mutual Funds, by Ronald K. Rutherford (McGraw-Hill, PO Box 548, Blacklick, OH 43004; 800-634-3961; www.mcgraw-hill.com). Explains investment philosophy development techniques, explores all asset classes of mutual funds, and covers statistical and nonstatistical issues involved in selecting and managing a balanced portfolio of mutual funds.

Getting Started in Mutual Funds, by Alvin D. Hall (John Wiley & Sons, 1 Wiley Drive, Somerset, NJ 08875; 212-850-6000; 800-225-5945; www.wiley.com). Easy-to-follow commonsense guide for successful mutual fund investing. Suitable for novices; provides everything they need to know about mutual funds.

The Handbook for No-Load Fund Investors, by Sheldon Jacobs (McGraw-Hill, PO Box 543, Blacklick, OH 43004; 800-634-3961; www.mcgraw-hill.com). The definitive guide to mutual funds that do not levy sales commissions.

How to Buy Mutual Funds the Smart Way, by Stephen Littauer (Dearborn Trade, Chicago, IL; 312-836-4400; 800-245-2665; www.dearborntrade.com). A thorough introduction to mutual funds for the financial do-it-yourselfer who likes to be in control, reduce costs, and rely on his or her own judgment.

Kurt Brouwer's Guide to Mutual Funds: How to Invest with the Pros, by Kurt Brouwer (John Wiley & Sons, 605 Third Avenue, New York, NY 10158; 212-850-6000; www.wiley.com). A good book explaining how mutual funds work and the best strategies for buying and selling them.

Mutual Funds for Dummies, by Eric Tyson and James C. Collins (IDG Books, 919 E. Hillsdale Boulevard, Suite 400, Foster City, CA 94404; 650-653-7000; 800-434-3422; www.idg.com, www.dummies.com). Contains all new market data and analysis about the ever-changing world of mutual funds. Simplifies financial planning and points to the mutual fund investments best suited for you.

New York Institute of Finance Guide to Mutual Funds, 2000, by Kirk Kazanjian (Prentice Hall Press, One Lake Street, Upper Saddle River, NJ 07458; 201-236-7156; 800-382-3419; www.prenticehall.com). Performance data for 8,000 funds from *Value Line Mutual Fund Survey,* profiles of the year's 100 most-promising fund performers, 25 Web sites, model portfolios, and worksheets.

Smart Money Moves: Mutual Fund Investing from Scratch, by James Lowell (Penguin-Putnam, 405 Murray Hill Parkway, East Rutherford, NJ 07073; 800-788-6262; www.penguinputnam.com). Mutual fund investing guide, with strategies and information for investing online. Shows readers how to choose the right funds and how to explore online investing.

Straight Talk about Mutual Funds, by Dian Vujovich (McGraw-Hill, PO Box 543, Blacklick, OH 43004; 800-634-3961; www.mcgraw-hill.com). A primer on the basics of mutual funds.

The 100 Best Mutual Funds to Own in America, by Gene Walden (Dearborn Trade, Chicago, IL; 312-836-4400; 800-245-2665; www.dearborntrade.com). Presents profiles of 100 of the top performing stocks mutual funds of the past few years.

The Ultimate Mutual Fund Guide: 20 Experts Pick the 46 Top Funds You Should Own, by Warren Boroson (McGraw-Hill, PO Box 543, Blacklick, OH 43004; 800-634-3961; www.mcgraw-hill.com). Identifies the best mutual funds according to leading fund experts in all major categories, including money market, stock, bond, and sector funds. Presents performance data and an interview with the fund manager for each of the highlighted funds.

Well-Kept Secrets Every Vanguard Investor Should Know, by Dan Wiener (Fund Family Shareholder Association, Dept. 48F002, 7811 Montrose Road, Potomac, MD 20859-0014; 800-211-6359). Tips and ideas on how to avoid fees and lower costs, how to open two accounts for the price of one, how to get into closed-end funds, when to use Vanguard's variable annuity, how to sidestep taxable switches, and how to deal with other issues.

Books about Closed-End Mutual Funds

Herzfeld's Guide to Closed-End Funds, by Thomas J. Herzfeld (McGraw-Hill, PO Box 543, Blacklick, OH 43004; 800-634-3961; www. mcgraw-hill.com). A thorough review of everything you need to know to profit in closed-end funds. Profiles more than 300 fund portfolios and provides statistical analysis and rankings for most closed-end funds.

Investing in Closed-End Funds: Finding Value and Building Wealth, by Albert Freedman and George Cole Scott (Prentice Hall Press, One Lake Street, Upper Saddle River, NJ 07458; 201-236-7156; 800-382-3419; www.prenticehall.com). A more sophisticated overview of strategies for buying and selling closed-end funds.

The Thomas J. Herzfeld Encyclopedia of Closed-End Funds, by Thomas J. Herzfeld (Thomas J. Herzfeld & Co., PO Box 161465, Miami FL 33116; 305-271-1900). An annual book filled with detail on the performance of all closed-end funds, along with strategies for buying and selling funds.

Newsletters about Stock Mutual Funds

All Star Alpha Fund Timer (PO Box 203427, Austin, TX 78720; 800-299-4223)

CDA Mutual Fund Report (Thomson Financial, 1455 Research Boulevard, Rockville, MD 20850; 301-545-4000; www.cda.com)

The Chartist Mutual Fund Letter (PO Box 758, Seal Beach, CA 90740; 310-596-2385)

Closed-End Fund Digest (4521 Campus Drive, PMB #283, Irvine, CA 92612; 949-737-5966)

Equity Fund Outlook (PO Box 76, Boston, MA 02117; 617-397-6844)

Fidelity Independent Advisor (PO Box 387, Williamstown, MA 01267; 800-548-3797)

Fidelity Insight and *FundNet Insight* (Mutual Fund Investors Association, 20 William Street, PO Box 9135, Wellesley Hills, MA 02180; 617-369-2500; 800-444-6342; www.kobren.com)

Fidelity Monitor (PO Box 1270, Rocklin, CA 95677; 800-397-3094; www .fidelitymonitor.com)

Fund Advice and *Fund Kinetics Investor* (1200 Westlake Avenue, N., Suite 700, Seattle, WA 98109; 800-423-4893; www.paulmerriman.com)

Gerald Perritt's Mutual Fund Letter (12514 Starkey Road, Largo, FL 33773; 800-326-6941; www.mutletter.com)

Graphic Fund Forecaster (6 Pioneer Circle, PO Box 673, Andover, MA 01810; 800-532-2322; www.tysfred.com)

Growth Fund Guide (PO Box 6600, Rapid City, SD 57709: 605-341-1971)

Independent Adviser for Vanguard Investors (Fund Family Shareholder Association, 7811 Montrose Road, Potomac, MD 20854; 800-777-5005)

Investech Mutual Fund Advisor (2472 Birch Glen, Whitefish, MT 59937; 406-862-7777; 800-955-8500; www.investech.com)

Louis Rukeyser's Mutual Funds Newsletter (1750 Old Meadow Road, Suite 300, McLean, VA 22102; 800-892-9702)

Maverick Advisor (PO Box 2538, Huntington Beach, CA 92647; 800-950-8765)

Morningstar Mutual Funds (225 W. Wacker Drive, Chicago, IL 60606; 312-424-4288; www.morningstar.com)

Mutual Fund Forecaster (Institute for Econometric Research, 2200 SW 10th Street, Deerfield Beach, FL 33442; 954-421-1000; 800-442-9000; www.mfmag.com)

Mutual Fund Guide (Commerce Clearing House, 4025 W. Peterson Avenue, Chicago, IL 60646; 800-835-5224; www.cch.com)

Mutual Fund Investing (7811 Montrose Road, Potomac, MD 20854; 800-777-5005)

Mutual Fund Prospector (16 Thornwood Court, Moline, IL 61265; 309-736-9376)

Mutual Funds Magazine (1271 Avenue of the Americas, New York, NY 10020; 800-494-0129; www.mfmag.com)

Mutual Fund Strategist (PO Box 446, Burlington, VT 05402; 802-658-3513; 800-355-3863; www.mutualfundstrategist.com)

Mutual Fund Timer (PO Box 6275, Jacksonville, FL 32236; 904-693-0355)

Mutual Fund Trends (PO Box 6600, Rapid City, SD 57709; 605-341-1971)

No-Load Fund Analyst (4 Orinda Way, Suite 230D, Orinda, CA 94563; 925-254-9017)

No-Load Fund Investor (PO Box 318, Irvington-on-Hudson, NY 10533; 914-693-7420; 800-252-2042; www.sheldonjacobs.com)

NoLoad Fund*X (3705 Haven Avenue, Menlo Park, CA 94025; 650-482-3050; 800-567-2683; www.investools.com)

No-Load Mutual Fund Selections and Timing Newsletter (100 N. Central Expressway, Suite 1112, Richardson, TX 75080-5328; 800-800-6563)

No-Load Portfolios (8635 W. Sahara, Suite 420, The Lakes, NV 89117; 702-871-4710)

Sector Fund Timer (12254 Nicollet Avenue, South Burnsville, MN 55337; 612-808-0148)

Value Line Mutual Funds Survey (220 E. 42nd Street, New York, NY 10017; 800-634-3583)

Vantage Point Newsletter for Vanguard Investors (2927 W. Liberty Avenue, Suite 195, Pittsburgh, PA 15216; 412-594-4749)

Newsletters about Closed-End Mutual Funds

Closed-End Country Fund Report (725 15th Street, NW, Suite 501, Washington, DC 20005; 202-783-7051)

Investor's Guide to Closed-End Funds (Thomas J. Herzfeld Advisors, PO Box 161465, Miami, FL 33116; 305-271-1900)

Software and Web Sites

BusinessWeek Online: Mutual Fund Corner. Features articles, quotes, charts, quarterly and annual scoreboards, portfolio tracking, and excerpts from *Business Week's Guide to Mutual Funds.* Registration required. <www.businessweek.com /mutualfunds/index.html>

CBS MarketWatch: SuperStar Funds. Features articles, news headlines, top fund performers, quotes and charts, and a research directory. Includes links to fund families and a list of individual funds. <cbs.marketwatch.com/funds>

Charles Schwab Mutual Fund Marketplace. Includes more than 1,000 no-load mutual funds-all available without transaction fees. <www.schwab-online.com/mutual _funds.htm>

Closed-End Fund Investor. A comprehensive site focusing on closed-end funds. It provides profiles, charts, holdings, and reports on hundreds of funds. There is also a tutorial on how to invest in closed-end funds. <www.icefi.com>

CNN/Money.com. Has database of 7,500 funds to research. Includes day's best-performing fund, worst-performing fund, and overall top performers. <www.money .cnn.com>

Forbes Digital Tool: Mutual Fund Information Center. Forbes-Lipper has a database of some 5,500 funds, with closing performance updated daily. Lists the 25 largest stock and bond funds and provides fund performance rankings by investment objective. Includes articles on fund investing. <www.forbes.com/tool/toolbox/lipper /index.asp>

FundAlarm. Updated monthly, this site offers information and commentary to help you decide when to sell a mutual fund. Includes data for 1,200 funds and a list of recent fund manager changes. <www.fundalarm.com>

Fundscape. A service allowing you to update data about your mutual fund holdings. You can calculate the value of your portfolio and your rates of return in a series of customized reports. <www.fundscape.com>

Fund Spot. Links to mutual fund companies and investment sites. Includes a weekly list of links to the best mutual fund articles available on the Web. <www .fundspot.com/main.html>

ICI Mutual Fund Connection. Sponsored by the Investment Company Institute, this site offers information on mutual funds, closed-end funds, and unit investment trusts. Includes a mutual fund fact book, statistics, economic commentary, and retirement planning. Also includes full listing of member mutual funds and companies. <www.ici.org>

The Internet Closed-End Fund Investor. CDA/Wiesenberger presents information on 500 closed-end funds. Includes an investing guide, daily and weekly charts, fund profiles, and performance and market sentiment indicators. Most services by subscription only. <www icefi.com>

INVESTools. A large part of this comprehensive investing Web site is devoted to mutual funds. It offers access to the Morningstar OnDemand service, in which you can screen thousands of mutual funds by their track records, Morningstar star rating, investment objective, and other measures. <www.investools.com>

IClub Central: Mutual Funds. A directory of links to mutual fund analysis and information. Feature articles cover no-load funds, risk tolerance, and diversification. Includes links to mutual fund families. <www.iclub.com/investorama.htm>

InvestorGuide: Mutual Funds. Full explanations about mutual funds and how they work. Multiple links to other mutual fund sites, including Morningstar. <www.investorguide.com>

Manhattan Analytics. A sophisticated Web site to help pick mutual funds. The company offers Monocle software to help you track fund performance, screen for funds meeting your criteria, and keep track of tax liabilities in fund portfolios. <www.manhattanlink.com>

Mutual Fund Investor's Center. Sponsored by the Mutual Fund Education Alliance, a group of no-load fund families, this site is designed to educate you about how to invest in mutual funds. It also provides links to the Web sites of all the Alliance's member fund groups. <www.mfea.com>

Mutual Funds Central. Rates mutual funds with their performance numbers and lists the top 100 mutual funds with links to their Web sites, links to lots of mutual-fund-related Web sites. Has research capability and will deliver quotes. <www.fundz.com>

Mutual Funds Interactive. Full performance and other information available on any mutual fund. Lists and links to articles on mutual funds. <www.fundsinteractive.com>

Mutual Funds Magazine Online. The Institute for Econometric Research offers many tools to pick mutual funds. There is access to current and back issues of *Mutual Funds Magazine.* The site also features extensive performance rankings, fund profiles, and screening capability. <www.mfmag.com>

Quicken.com: Mutual Funds. Feature articles, commentary, top funds, Morningstar profiles, a retirement planner, and links to related sites. <www.quicken.com/investments /mutualfunds/>

Researchmag.com. Information on 10,000 stocks and 5,000 mutual funds. Includes quotes and charts. Registration required. <www.researchmag.com>

Smart Money.com. Information about fees and taxes, database of 6,000 funds that can be screened with your financial goals in mind, fund analyzer tools, and fund portfolio builder. <www.smartmoney.com>

Standard & Poor's. The site monitors more than 38,000 mutual funds in 20 countries. Includes a fund management group directory, performance tables, fund fact sheets, market reviews, and a searchable database. <www.funds-sp.com/win/en /Index.jsp>

Trade Associations

Closed-End Fund Association (PO Box 28037, Kansas City, MO 64188; 212-916-8400; www.closed-endfunds.com). Trade group representing closed-end funds. Offers a free brochure, "Understanding the Advantages of Closed-End Funds."

Investment Company Institute (1401 H Street, NW, Suite 1200, Washington, DC 20005; 202-326-5800; www.ici.org; www.msdc.com). The trade group for lobbying and public education on mutual fund issues. Will send you a copy of the following free pamphlets: "A Close Look at Closed-End Funds"; "Money Market Mutual Funds: A Part of Every Financial Plan"; "Planning for College? The Mutual Fund Advantage Becomes a Parent"; "Reading the Mutual Fund Prospectus"; "What Is a Mutual Fund?" To receive a copy of any of these brochures, write to the ICI at PO Box 66140, Washington, DC 20035-6140.

Mutual Fund Education Alliance (100 NW Englewood Road, Suite 130, Kansas City, MO 64118; 816-454-9422; www.mfea.com). An educational group composed mostly of no-load mutual funds. Some of its members charge low loads, back-end loads, or 12b-1 fees.

National Investment Company Services Association (850 Boylston Street, Suite 437, Chestnut Hill, MA 02167; 617-277-1855). Trade group specializing in mutual fund service issues.

Society of Asset Allocators and Fund Timers (165 S. Union Boulevard, Suite 415, Lakewood, CO 80228; 313-642-6640). A group of investment professionals who manage mutual fund assets for their clients through the use of dynamic asset allocation and market-timing strategies.

CHAPTER 9

Bond Basics

Although not as popular as stocks, bonds attract the interest of investors both for income and diversification. These interest-bearing vehicles are generally considered safer and more conservative than stocks, but they do not have same type of long-term growth potential. However, if you're looking for income or you need to add diversification to a portfolio that is already heavily weighted with stocks, bonds could be just the ticket.

When you invest in a bond, you are essentially loaning the issuer of that bond your money in return for a fixed rate of interest for a specific amount of time. Normally, you receive interest payments every six months, and when the bond matures, you receive your original principal, no matter how much the price of the bond had fluctuated since it was issued.

INVESTING IN BONDS

Bonds are one of the key investment vehicles available to help you achieve your financial goals. They allow you to lock in a set rate of income for a long period, which can give your financial plan a rock-solid foundation. In addition, if you want to trade bonds more actively, you can earn capital gains by buying them when their prices fall and selling them when their prices rise, just as you can do with stocks.

For many decades, bonds were quite simple. Interest rates remained remarkably stable at about 1 percent or 2 percent for years because inflation was low. Few, if any, bonds defaulted, meaning bond issuers failed to honor their pledge to pay interest or principal on time. Bond prices hardly budged.

Starting in the mid-1970s, when the Arab oil embargo and soaring government budget deficits ignited inflation, all of that changed. Interest rates jumped from 4 percent to 5 percent in the early 1970s to more than 20 percent in the early 1980s, giving rise to tremendous volatility in the bond market. Even as rates fell back from those heights during the 1990s and 2000s, bond yields remained higher than they had been in the 1950s, and bond prices continued to jump around. On top of gyrating rates, the number of bond defaults increased dramatically, as many companies, and a few municipalities, were unable to handle the increased interest payments required from higher yielding bonds.

The bond market was changed not only by increased volatility of interest rates, prices, and defaults, but also by an explosion in the variety of new bond types. For decades, the major issuers of bonds had been the federal government and its agencies, state and local governments and related agencies, foreign governments, and blue chip corporations. Starting in the 1980s, billions of dollars' worth of junk bonds were issued by small and risky growth companies or by raiders, who used the money to take over major corporations. Another new class of bond called *asset-backed securities,* which back the promise to repay the bond with interest from assets like mortgages, credit cards, and auto loans, was created and took in hundreds of billions of dollars.

Also, the bond market, which had formerly been the preserve of the rich, was democratized by the introduction of the bond mutual fund. Like stock funds, bond funds allowed average people access to the huge and complicated world of investing for a small amount of capital and reasonable fees. Bond funds became the haven for millions of income-oriented investors who had always kept their money in bank products like CDs and money-market funds.

With all these recent developments in the world of bonds, there is much to learn about the opportunities and pitfalls of today's bond market. There's a good chance that fixed-income securities will play an important role in your financial plan at some stage in your life, so it's important to understand the world of bonds.

THE BASICS OF HOLDING BONDS

When you buy bonds issued by a government agency or a company, you become a lender to that entity. This is very different from being a stockholder, which you become when you buy a company's stock. As a bondholder, you are entitled to receive the bond's stated interest rate when interest is due and your principal when the bond matures—nothing more. You do not receive quarterly or annual reports. You will not be invited to a firm's annual meeting. You do not earn dividends. If a company's earnings soar, you do not participate in that success.

On the other hand, the yield you receive from the bond typically is higher than the stock dividend yield because bondholders must be compensated for reduced purchasing power in the future because of inflation. (Of course, there is no way to buy stock in most government agencies, so bonds are the only way to invest in government securities.)

As with stocks, the money that you pay to buy bonds goes to the issuers only when the bonds are first sold to the public. After that, you buy bonds from the existing owners, or you sell bonds to other investors. Most bond trading is done automatically in a computer-driven system without specialists. In addition, bonds are bought and sold through competing dealers, who communicate with each other by computer and telephone.

Bonds are normally quoted on a price scale of 0 to 200, with 100 being the price at which the bond was issued, or what is known as *par*. Because bonds are sold in minimum denominations of $1,000, a price of 100 means that the bond is trading at $1,000 per bond. If the bond's price rises to 110, your holdings are worth $1,100.

Unlike stock transactions, bond buy-and-sell transactions normally occur without a separate commission charge. Instead, a broker makes money from a transaction by taking a piece of the spread between the buying and selling prices. For example, if a broker buys you a bond at a price of 100, he or she might charge you 102 for it and keep the two points as commission. If you try to sell the bond for a price of 100, you might get only 98 for it. Because the bond market is generally dominated by large institutions that trade millions of dollars' worth of bonds, you will pay a wider spread if you buy only a small number of bonds. Many bond dealers won't even execute a trade for fewer than 25 bonds, or $25,000, though some might go as low as five bonds, or $5,000. Because it is a competitive market, you should shop around among brokers to get the best deal.

Buying Direct

The only way you can avoid paying a large spread for small purchases, other than to buy bonds through a mutual fund, is to buy government bonds directly from the Treasury. You can buy bills, notes, and bonds whenever the Treasury auctions new issues. You can also buy U.S. savings bonds for only $25 through any bank or by payroll deduction. (Government bonds will be discussed in more detail later in this chapter.)

For decades, bondholders received fancy bond certificates with attached coupons entitling the coupon owners to the cash interest payment on the date due. These were known as *bearer bonds* because whoever bore a bond coupon would be paid the interest. Bearer bonds have not been issued since 1982; therefore, for the most part, the days of bearer bond certificates are long gone. Instead, bonds are now issued in either registered or book entry form. Registered bonds still have certificates, and the owner of the bond is named on the back of the certificate. To sell a registered bond, the owner must endorse it and have it changed to the new owner's name in the issuer's records. The more common form of bond issued today, however, is the book entry bond, for which interest payments are tracked by computers.

If you hold a bond in a brokerage account, interest and principal payments will be made automatically. Book entry bonds provide no certificate you can hold in your hands; the record exists only in the computer data banks of your brokerage firm. Because the bond is electronic, however, it is much easier to trade, because no endorsement is necessary for the bond to change hands.

✓ How Bond Prices Move

When you consider investing in bonds, you should understand that one cardinal rule about the movement of bond prices: Bond prices move in the opposite direction of interest rates. Normally, you might think that rising interest rates would be good for your bond, but nothing could be further from the truth. Even though it may sound illogical at first, it is true that when interest rates rise, bond prices fall. When interest rates fall, bond prices rise. The following example explains why.

Say you buy a bond yielding 10 percent at a price of 100 (the par price). If interest rates plummet to 5 percent over the next several years, your 10 percent bond would become very valuable, indeed. Its price would soar—maybe to a dollar value of 150—because people would be willing to pay a big premium to get their hands on a 10 percent bond in an environment where bonds pay only 5 percent. Notice that as interest rates fell, your bond's value rose.

Now let's take the opposite situation. You buy your 10 percent bond at 100, and instead of dropping, interest rates soar to 15 percent. Your bond won't be popular now because people would rather buy a new bond paying 15 percent than your old bond paying 10 percent. Therefore, if you want to sell your bond to buy a newer one at the higher current rate, you would suffer a loss. The price of your bond might drop to half, from 100 to 50. Notice that as interest rates rose, your bond's value fell.

Bond prices seem to move so perversely because bonds are a fixed-rate instrument. Because the bond's rate is locked in at whatever level it was when the bond was first issued, the bond becomes more or less valuable as interest rates fall or rise. Figure 9.1 might help you better understand the inverse relationship between interest rates and bond prices.

The longer the maturity of your bond, the more its price will react to the ups and downs of interest rates. A bond that locks in a high interest rate for 20 or 30 years is much more valuable to an investor if interest rates have fallen than a bond that matures in a year or two. Conversely, if interest rates have risen, the investor would rather get his or her money back quickly so he or she can reinvest at higher rates.

When calculating the effect of interest rates on an investor's holdings, analysts usually look at the total return; that is, the price change of the bond added to the income it is paying. Figure 9.2 shows how an interest rate increase of from one to four percentage points over one year would affect the total returns of several bond maturities, from 6 years to 30 years. This table assumes that 6-year bonds yield 6 percent, 10- and 20-year bonds yield 7 percent, and 30-year bonds yield 8 percent. Notice that the longer the bond maturity, the more the bond loses value as rates rise.

Figure 9.3 shows how much total returns on different bond maturities rise as interest rates fall over one year.

This bond volatility should always factor into your decision to buy bonds.

Figure 9.1   Relationship between Bond Prices and Interest Rates

When interest rates move up or down, the price of a bond usually moves in the opposite direction.

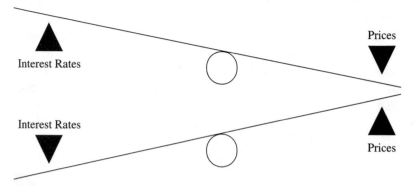

Short-term bonds (bonds that are close to maturity) are usually less affected by changes in interest rates than are long-term bonds.

Figure 9.2   Percentage Points Rate Increase in a Year

Maturity	Unchanged	+1%	+2%	+3%	+4%
6 years	+6%	+2%	−2%	−5%	−9%
10 years	+7	+1	−5	−10	−15
20 years	+7	+1	−7	−13	−19
30 years	+8	−3	−11	−19	−25

Source: Reprinted by permission of The Leuthold Group, an investment advisory firm in Minneapolis, Minnesota.

Figure 9.3   Percentage Points Rate Decrease in a Year

Maturity	Unchanged	−1%	−2%	−3%	−4%
6 years	+6%	+10%	+15%	+20%	+25%
10 years	+7	+13	+20	+28	+37
20 years	+7	+18	+28	+42	+57
30 years	+8	+20	+35	+51	+69

Source: Reprinted by permission of The Leuthold Group, an investment advisory firm in Minneapolis, Minnesota.

WHY INTEREST RATES FLUCTUATE

Many factors influence interest rate movements. In the long term, the outlook for inflation is the most important determinant of interest rates. If inflation is high and rising, investors demand a higher yield to protect the value of their money from erosion. If inflation is low and declining, investors settle for a lower yield because they are not as threatened by the loss of purchasing power. One way to measure investors' fear of inflation is to subtract the current inflation rate from a bond's yield. This produces what is known as the "real" interest rate. For example:

Current interest rate	10%
Consumer price index inflation rate	− 6%
Real interest rate	4%

If the resulting number is positive, it is known as a *positive real interest rate*. In the example, bondholders receive four percentage points more than the current inflation rate. Historically, positive real rates usually average around 3 percent, but they have stretched to 5 or 6 percent at times.

If bond rates are lower than inflation, it is known as a *negative interest rate*. For example:

Current interest rate	10%
Consumer price index inflation rate	−13%
Real interest rate	− 3%

In this example, which occurred during the late 1970s, bond investors actually lost money because their 10 percent yield did not compensate them for rampant inflation.

The 1970s lesson was so painful to bond investors that real interest rates have stayed positive since then and are likely to continue to do so because investors want a protective cushion over the current inflation rate. Still, there is no guarantee that yields won't shoot up sharply again in the future and investors will be stuck earning negative real interest rates again.

In addition to the outlook for inflation, supply and demand influence bond yields. If you think of an interest rate as the price of money, you will understand that as demand for money increases and supply decreases, the price, or interest rate, goes up. This situation might occur when the economy is picking up and businesses and consumers want to borrow money to expand and spend, while lenders—including banks and bond buyers—are reluctant to lend because they fear higher interest rates.

Interest rates tend to fall when the economy is declining or is in recession because there is little demand for borrowing, businesses are retrenching, and consumers are more interested in paying off existing debts than in taking on new loans. At the same time, a larger supply of money is available to lend because bond buyers want to lock in high interest rates.

Over the past two decades, a new factor has grown in influence on the interest rate level: the federal budget deficit. When the difference between what the government received in taxes and what it spent for programs each year was modest—less than $50 billion—the deficit was easy to cover with national savings. But as the size of the annual deficit grew—first to $100 billion, then to $200 billion, then to a staggering $300 billion in the early 1990s—the government consumed more and more of the supply of capital available in the United States. This enormous demand for money by the government as it sold billions of dollars' worth of new bonds, compounded by the fear of an ever-rising national debt, kept interest rates much higher than they normally would have been if the deficit had been controlled. By the late 1990s and 2000s, those huge federal budget deficits had disappeared and been replaced by growing budget surpluses. The Treasury started buying government bonds back and reducing the amount of national debt outstanding, bringing interest rates down sharply.

While these broad factors influence the general level of interest rates, more specific supply and demand issues affect the interest rates and prices of individual bonds. Whether a bond is issued by a corporation or a municipal agency, investors evaluate it by the strength of its financial condition. The better its financial shape, the more confident investors are that their interest and principal will be repaid on time and, therefore, the lower the bond's interest rate will be. One major factor influencing investors' perceptions of the bond is the rating it receives from one of the three big bond-rating agencies: Standard & Poor's, Moody's, and Fitch. Analysts at these agencies, using detailed financial information and judgment based on years of experience, assign a rating to each bond issuer. The ratings scales of the three services appear in Figure 9.4.

In addition to regular letter grades, Fitch and Standard & Poor's modify ratings with + or - signs. A corporate bond may be rated AA- or BBB+, for instance. Moody's uses numbers from 1 to 3 to signify gradations. The same corporate bonds might have a Moody's rating of Aa2 or Baa1, for example.

Although ratings agencies do not always agree on the risk of default by a particular issuer, their assessments are usually fairly similar. Therefore, such ratings, as well as the prospect for upgradings or downgradings in those ratings, can significantly affect a bond's interest rate and price.

Figure 9.4   Bond Rating Services' Rating System

| | Rating Service | | |
Explanation of Bond Rating	Standard & Poor's	Moody's	Fitch
Highest quality	AAA	Aaa	AAA
Very High quality	AA	Aa	AA
High quality	A	A	A
Medium quality	BBB	Baa	BBB
Predominantly speculative	BB	Ba	BB
Speculative, low grade	B	B	B
Poor to default	CCC	Caa	CCC
Highest speculation	CC	Ca	CC
Lowest quality, not paying interest	C	C	C
In default, in arrears, of questionable value	D		DDD
			DD
			D

Source: Reprinted by permission of Standard & Poor's Corporation, Moody's Investors Service, and Fitch Investors Service, Inc.

THE MEANING OF YIELD

While a bond has only one interest rate, there are four ways to calculate its yield; that is, your return at the bond's current price. They are as follows:

1. **Coupon rate.** The coupon rate is the interest the bond pays. It may equal the bond's yield when it is trading at its issue price of 100, or its $1,000 face value. A bond with a 10 percent coupon therefore would pay $100 a year in interest.
2. **Current yield.** This yield adjusts the bond's coupon rate for the bond's current price to determine what percentage you would receive if you bought the bond at its current price. In the example above, if the bond dropped in price from 100 to 90, for instance, the bond's value would fall from $1,000 to $900. At that price, the current yield would rise to 11.1 percent. Current yield is calculated as follows:

$$\frac{\$100 \text{ Annual interest payment of the bond}}{\$900 \text{ Current market price of the bond}} = 11.1\% \text{ Current yield}$$

Remember that rising interest rates cause bond prices to fall. Therefore, in the example, if the bond's price rose from 100 to 110, the bond's value would rise from $1,000 to $1,100. Current yield is calculated as follows:

$$\frac{\$100 \text{ Annual interest payment of the bond}}{\$1,100 \text{ Current market price of the bond}} = 9.09\% \text{ Current yield}$$

Don't worry about having to calculate the yield of every bond you consider buying. Current yields are displayed on your broker's computer screen and also in any newspaper's bond listings. (See "Reading the Bond Tables in Newspapers" later in this chapter.)

3. **Yield to maturity.** This yield takes into account the bond's coupon rate, its current price, and the years remaining until the bond matures. It is a more complicated calculation, but your broker should be able to tell you the yield to maturity on any bond you are considering. You can also consult a book with yield-to-maturity tables or figure it using a programmable calculator. If you want only to approximate the yield to maturity, you can use the following calculations. This example will use a bond with a 10 percent coupon (paying $100 a year) trading at a price of 85 (now worth $850) with ten years before it matures.

First, subtract the current bond value (in this case, $850) from par ($1,000) to arrive at the discount.

$$\begin{array}{lr} \text{Par} & \$1,000 \\ \text{Current bond value} & \underline{-850} \\ \text{Discount} & \$\ \ 150 \end{array}$$

Divide the discount ($150) by the number of years remaining until the bond matures (10) to calculate the annual gain in the bond's price as it moves from $850 currently to $1,000 at maturity.

$$\frac{\$150 \text{ Discount}}{10 \text{ Years to maturity}} = \$15 \text{ Annual gain}$$

Combine the annual gain ($15) with the bond's annual interest ($100) to get the bond's yearly total gain.

$$\begin{array}{rl} \$\ 15 & \text{Annual gain} \\ \underline{+\ 100} & \text{Annual interest} \\ \$115 & \text{Yearly total gain} \end{array}$$

Divide the yearly total gain ($115) by the bond's current price ($850) to calculate the yield to maturity.

$$\frac{\$115 \text{ Yearly total gain}}{\$850 \text{ Current price of the bond}} = 13.5\% \text{ Yield to maturity}$$

4. **Yield to call.** This is the yield up to the first potential date at which the issuer can call, or redeem, the bond—usually several years before the bond is scheduled to mature. You calculate the yield to call exactly the same way you calculate the yield to maturity, except that you replace the number of years to maturity with the number of years to the first call date.

   You should always assume that a corporation or municipality will put its shareholders' or constituents' interest ahead of bondholders'. Therefore, if interest rates have fallen sharply from the time the bond was issued to the first date that the bond can be called, you should assume the bond will be redeemed. The yield to call is the most realistic yield you can calculate for a bond because you can never assume the bond will remain outstanding between its first call date and its stated maturity.

EARLY REDEMPTION

A bond can be redeemed before it is scheduled to mature. That sounds illegal, but it isn't—as long as the issuer's ability to redeem the bond is written into the thick legal document that accompanies the original bond issue.

In that document, called the *indenture,* bondholders are guaranteed a certain number of years before which the bond cannot be redeemed. This can be as little as five years or as many as 15 to 20 years, although a 10-year call protection is more typical.

When the first date of a potential call arrives, the issuer decides whether it makes more sense to continue to pay interest on the bond or to pay off the bond and issue another one at a lower interest rate. For example, if the bond was issued at 10 percent and rates have dropped to 7 percent over the past few years, the issuer would probably refinance. If rates have dropped only to 9 percent, though, refinancing might not be worthwhile. In many cases, bondholders whose bonds are called before maturity will receive a slight premium over par for the bonds. Therefore, they might receive 102 per bond, or $1,020, at redemption. Otherwise, they would receive only par, or $1,000, per bond.

Whenever you consider buying a bond, find out how many years of call protection you have. The more years you know your bond will pay interest, the better.

THE YIELD CURVE

Because bonds mature in the future, the amount of time until the maturity point is key in determining the bond's yield and price. In general, the further off an event will occur, the less sure you are about exactly what will happen in the meantime. You might have a pretty good idea of what the next five minutes hold, but you're sure to be a lot fuzzier about what will happen 20 years from now. This uncertainty about the future, and the related risk, are normally built into bond prices.

As discussed earlier, the longer the maturity of a bond, the more its price fluctuates with any movement in interest rates. For example, if yields on 30-year Treasuries are 7.5 percent, a 1 percentage point rise in interest rates to 8.5 percent might make a 1-year bond's price fall by 5 percent, while a 30-year bond's price might plunge 30 percent. Conversely, a 1 percent drop in interest rates would translate into a 5 percent rise in a 1-year bond's price but a 40 percent rise in the price of a 30-year issue. Keep this extra volatility in mind if you plan to buy a longer-term bond. While you usually receive a higher yield, it comes at the cost of much more price fluctuation over the life of the bond.

The yield curve is a convenient chart allowing you to compare the current yields of short-term, medium-term, and long-term bonds. Though there are yield curves for many different kinds of bonds, the curve you will see most often is for Treasury securities. The Treasury curve is printed daily in

The Wall Street Journal and other newspapers and also appears in financial magazines. A typical yield curve looks like Figure 9.5.

Across the bottom of the chart are the various bond maturities, from the shortest maturity of three months to the longest maturity of 30 years. Down the side of the chart are the various yields on Treasury securities. This particular chart shows potential yields ranging from a high of 7.5 percent to a low 2.5 percent yield. The curve illustrates how much more interest a bond with a longer maturity earns. In this case, for instance, a 30-year bond pays nearly 7 percent, while a three-month bill pays only about 3.25 percent. The difference between the long and the short maturity—in this case, 4.25 percentage points—is the premium investors currently demand for committing their money for a long time. When long-term interest rates are much higher than short-term rates, as in this case, bond experts call the resulting curve a steeply sloped positive yield curve (see Figure 9.6).

At other times, the difference between short- and long-maturity bonds can be very slight, producing a yield curve that looks like Figure 9.7. Here, there is virtually no difference between 3-month Treasury bills and 20-year bonds; both yield about 7 percent. This is known as a flat yield curve.

Figure 9.5   Sample Treasury Yield Curve

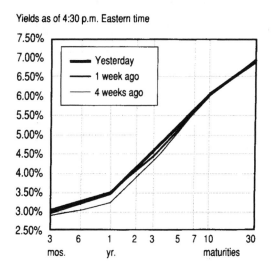

Yields as of 4:30 p.m. Eastern time

Figure 9.6   Sample Positive Yield Curve

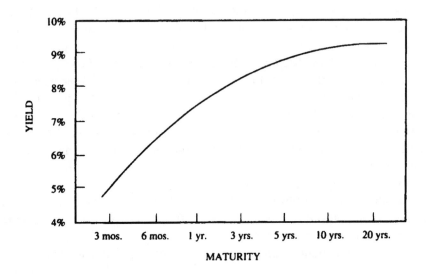

Figure 9.7   Sample Flat Yield Curve

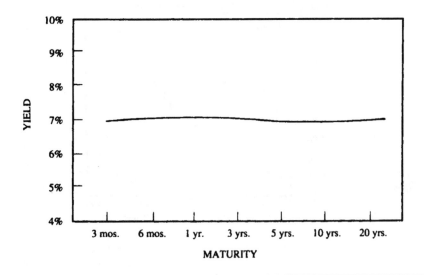

An abnormal yield curve occurs when short-term rates are actually higher than long-term rates, usually when the economy is about to head into a recession. In this case, yields on 3-month bills are 9.2 percent, while yields on 20-year bonds are 5 percent. This is known as a negative, or an inverted, yield curve (see Figure 9.8). An inverted curve occurred in the early 1980s and the early 2000s, for instance, when the Federal Reserve pushed up interest rates sharply to combat inflation, while long-term rates rose more gradually.

When choosing the maturity of a bond, you might look for the "sweet spot" on the yield curve. This is the maturity at which you receive the highest possible yield for the lowest possible risk. No definitive sweet spot exists; it varies according to the shape of the yield curve and your view of the direction of interest rates.

READING THE BOND TABLES IN NEWSPAPERS

Corporate bonds. The most complete corporate bond listings, which cover the most actively traded bonds, appear in *The Wall Street Journal, Investor's Business Daily,* and other financial newspapers, though your local newspaper may feature limited bond listings as well. Even the most complete listings, however, highlight just a fraction of the outstanding bonds traded

Figure 9.8   Sample Inverted Yield Curve

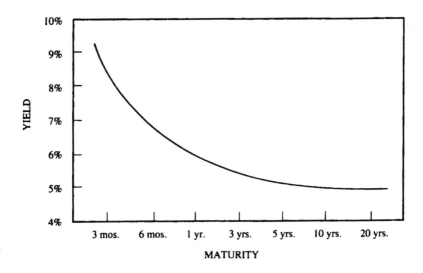

every day. Following is an example of the form most corporate bond tables take, along with an explanation of each column:

Bonds[1]	Current Yield[2]	Volume[3]	Close[4]	Net Change[5]
ATT 7½ 06	7.0	272	106	+2
General Electric 8½ 03	7.7	100	111	−½

1. Column 1 lists the issuer of the corporate bond. The corporate name is abbreviated, sometimes differently than you see in stock tables. After the company name are the coupon rate of the bond and the final two numbers of the year the bond is scheduled to mature. In the example, the first bond is issued by AT&T, has a 7½ percent coupon rate, and is scheduled to mature in 2006. The second bond is issued by General Electric, carries an 8½ percent coupon rate and is scheduled to mature in 2003.

2. The current yield column shows the annual interest payment as a percentage of the current bond price. You would receive this effective yield if you bought the bond at the current price. This column allows you to compare one bond's yield with those of competing issues. In the example, the AT&T bond yields 7 percent, while the General Electric bond pays 7.7 percent.

3. Volume means the number of trades in the bond in yesterday's trading. It is expressed in sales of $1,000 bonds. The trading volume will tell you how actively traded the bond is. In the example, 272 AT&T bonds traded yesterday, and 100 General Electric bonds changed hands.

4. Close means the closing price for the bond in yesterday's trading. The number is quoted in $100 units, so to calculate the value of the bond, multiply by ten. In the example, the AT&T bond, now selling at $106, would bring $1,060. The General Electric bond, trading at $111, would cost $1,110.

5. The net change column indicates whether the bond's price rose or fell from the previous day's closing price. In the example, the AT&T bond rose 2 in yesterday's trading, or $20 per bond. The General Electric bond fell ½, or $5 per bond. As the price on the AT&T bond rose, its current yield fell. As the price on the General Electric bond fell, its yield rose.

Corporate bond tables also contain various footnotes.

- *cf* Certificates, meaning the bond comes with certificates.
- *cld* Called, meaning the bond is in the process of being redeemed.
- *cv* Convertible, allowing the bond's owner to convert it into common shares at some point in the future.
- *dc* Deep discount, signifying the bond is selling far below its par value of 100. A deep discount bond may be selling at 20, for instance.
- *ec* Denominated in European currency units, not dollars.
- *f* Flat, signifying the bond is not paying interest. A bond that has defaulted is flat, for instance.
- *m* Matured, meaning it has limited trading potential because it is in the process of being paid off.
- *na* No accrual, signifying the bond is not accruing interest.
- *r* Registered, meaning the bond has a registration certificate.
- *t* Floating rate, signifying the bond's rate is tied to some index that changes over time, unlike most bonds, which are fixed at a certain rate when they are issued.
- *vj* An issuer currently in bankruptcy or receivership. In many cases this means the bond is not currently paying interest.
- *wd* When distributed, indicating the bond has not actually been distributed to investors yet.
- *ww* With warrants, meaning that when you buy this bond, you also get warrants (or rights) to buy more bonds.
- *x* Ex-interest, meaning the bond just made its interest payment. If you buy it now, you will receive the next interest payment, probably in six months.
- *xw* Without warrants attached.
- *zr* Zero-coupon, meaning the bond has a coupon of 0 but is sold at a deep discount. The bond gains value each year until it matures at a par price of 100.

Treasury bonds. Depending on how many years remain to maturity, federal government fixed-income securities are called *bills* (up to one year to maturity), *notes* (one to ten years), or *bonds* (ten years or more).

Treasury note and bond prices are listed in the same tables in *The Wall Street Journal, Investor's Business Daily,* and other financial newspapers. The tables present a long list of bonds in order of maturity, from the closest to maturity to the furthest from maturity. If there is a normal yield curve, you will notice that the yields rise as you look down the column because longer maturity bonds tend to pay higher yields.

Because the government bond market is run by dealers trading with each other and not by an exchange like the New York Stock Exchange, the prices you see in Treasury bond tables are the prices at which dealers are willing to buy and sell those maturity bonds on that particular day. The government bond market also uses denominations of 32nds rather than 100ths, so the decimal points do not mean what you might think. A price of 101.01 means 101$\frac{1}{32}$, for example.

Following is a typical Treasury bond table, plus an explanation of each column:

Rate[1]	Month/Year[2]	Bid[3]	Asked[4]	Change[5]	Asked Yield[6]
5½	Feb 04	99:24	99:26	−1	5.66
6¼	Feb 07	102:01	102:03	−6	5.77
8⅛	May 22	125:10	125:16	−25	6.07

1. The first column notes the bond's coupon rate. In this example, the first bond has a coupon of 5½ percent; the second, 6¼ percent; and the third, 8⅛ percent.
2. Column 2 lists the month and year the bond is scheduled to mature. The month is abbreviated, and only the final two numbers of the year are shown. In the example, the bonds listed will mature in February 2004, February 2007, and May 2022.
3. The bid price is the dollar amount dealers will pay for the bond. The decimal point refers to 32nds, not 10ths or 100ths. Each 32nd is worth 31¼ cents. In the example, the 99:24 price of the first bond equals 99 and $\frac{24}{32}$. If $\frac{24}{32}$ amounts to $7.68, the bond is worth $997.68. The price of the second bond, at 102:01, amounts to $1,020.31¼. The price of the third bond, at 125:10, equals $1,253.12½.
4. The asked price is the dollar amount for which dealers will sell the bond. The method of showing prices is exactly the same as in column 3. Note that the asked price is slightly higher than the bid price. The difference is the dealers' profit, or spread.
5. Column 5 notes the change in the bond's price from the previous day's closing price, based on the bid price.
6. *Asked yield* means the bond's yield to maturity. This yield combines the bond's current yield and the difference between the current price and the bond's value when it is redeemed.

Major newspapers such as *The Wall Street Journal* also list prices of government agency bonds, such as those issued by the Federal National Mortgage Association (Fannie Mae), the Federal Home Loan Bank (FHLB), and the Student Loan Marketing Association (Sallie Mae). The newspapers use exactly the same listing format as they do for Treasury bonds.

Municipal bond prices are generally not quoted in newspapers because thousands of such bonds exist, and many trade infrequently. The best way to obtain municipal bond prices is to contact a dealer, who can bring up current quotes on a computer. You can also look up prices of most actively traded municipals online at <www.investinginbonds.com> (see Figure 9.9) and on the Web sites of many online brokerage firms.

Figure 9.9   Investinginbonds.com

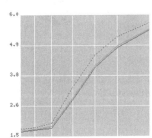

InvestingInBonds.com

THE BOND MARKET ASSOCIATION

Wall Street Comes to Main Street en Español

Ahorrando.org is a unique Spanish-language site offering basic information and step-by-step guidance. Personal finance issues covered include budgeting, the need to save, financial goal setting, and the characteristics of different saving and investing instruments. A separate section is a guide to making financial decisions in times of unexpected change, such as losing a spouse or a job.

Search:

Bond Prices
Municipal Bonds
Corporate Bonds
Treasurys

Features
Tax-Free vs.
  Taxable Yield
  Comparison
  Calculator
Planning for
  Retirement
Tomorrows
  Money . org
New:
  Ahorrando.org
Bond Glossary
Where Wall Street
  Meets Main
  Street
Investor's
  Checklist
Taxation of
  Municipals
Q&A on Buying and
  Selling Munis
Putting Compound
  Interest to Work

7 simple steps

Getting Started: Educate Yourself About Investing in Bonds!

1. Read "An Investor's Guide to Bond Basics," An overview of the concepts that investors should know about bonds.

2. Try the "Investor's Checklist" of questions to ask yourself when considering an investment in bonds.

3. Learn more about different types of bonds by reading some of our other Investor's Guides, such as those on Municipal Bonds, Zero-Coupon Munis and Corporate Bonds.

4. Read "How much of your portfolio should be in bonds?" It describes what factors you should consider in making a decision and provides

VITAL STATISTICS

The daily muni summary information has more listings than ever — now showing any bond that traded three or more times the previous day. And in addition to browsing yesterday's trades, you can now search the database to see past trades for bonds in which you may be interested. You can find also links to Thomson Financial's database of Official Statements. This information can be helpful in assessing relative value on bonds you own, or are thinking of buying or selling.

Investors can also get composite reports on US Treasurys, updated frequently throughout the day.

And visit our "Gateway," offering links to over 400 sites with market and price information for all segments of the bond market.

Current Treasury Yield Curve

CHAPTER 10

Choosing the Best Type of Bond for You

N ow that you understand the basics of bonds, it is time to discuss the advantages and disadvantages of the many kinds of bonds that exist. Selecting the best bond for you depends on the size of your assets, your financial goals, your risk tolerance, your tax situation, and your knowledge level. The following sections touch on each kind of bond, starting with the most conservative (Treasuries) and ending with the most speculative (junk bonds).

TREASURY BONDS

Bonds issued by the U.S. government are considered the safest around because Uncle Sam has a weapon to back these bonds that no other entity has: the printing press. If the government does not have enough funds to honor its debts, it can always print more money. When Congress raises the national debt ceiling every year or so, the government is, in effect, giving itself permission to borrow more money. This is known as the full faith and credit of the U.S. government, and it backs every Treasury security.

From a bond investor's point of view, Treasury bonds trade as though they are free from the risk of default. No one can even envision a default on Treasury bonds; the government must borrow money constantly in order to operate. It would be totally against the government's interest to default because the government would never again be able to sell bonds in the market, thus ensuring the government's instant collapse.

Because Treasuries are considered immune from default, they are the benchmark against which all other bonds are compared. Treasuries are to the bond world what diamonds are to the precious gem world: nothing is more secure than a Treasury, and no stone is harder than a diamond. Whenever you investigate another bond's default risk, yield, after-tax return, and ease of trading, compare it to what a Treasury offers. Treasury notes work just like bonds except that notes have shorter maturities.

Treasury bonds are issued in minimum denominations of $1,000 and also in $5,000, $10,000, $100,000, and $1 million sizes. To invest in Treasury bonds, you put up your $1,000 (or more) and receive interest checks every six months. Under a program called Treasury Direct, you can have your interest checks deposited electronically in any bank or financial institution you choose. For more information see <www.treasurydirect.gov>.

Treasury bills mature in a year or less and come in minimum denominations of $10,000. To invest in Treasury bills, you pay less than the $10,000 face amount but receive $10,000 when the bill matures. So, for example, you might pay $9,500 for a three-month Treasury bill, and in three months, you get $10,000. The $500 in interest you received means the bill yielded 5.26 percent. To calculate your yield on a Treasury bill, divide the interest by the amount you invested.

$$\frac{\$500 \text{ Interest earned}}{\$9,500 \text{ Capital invested}} = 5.26\% \text{ Yield on Treasury bill}$$

If you buy Treasury securities directly from a Federal Reserve bank or branch or the Bureau of Public Debt (1300 C Street, SW, Washington, DC 20239), you do not have to pay any fees. The easiest way to buy directly is to put in a so-called noncompetitive bid at one of the Treasury's quarterly auctions, which usually occur in February, May, August, and November. Entering such a bid means you will accept whatever average rate emerges for the securities you want to buy. If you buy a Treasury security through a regular bank or brokerage firm, it will charge a modest fee of between $50 and $60.

Because literally trillions of dollars' worth of outstanding Treasury securities exist, the market for them is huge, and it is extremely easy to buy or sell them. But remember, just because Treasuries are free from default risk does not mean you can't lose money on them. If you buy when rates are low and sell after rates have risen, the value of your Treasury bond will fall. On the other hand, if you buy when rates are high and sell after rates have fallen, you can capture a capital gain, on which you must pay a capital gains tax if you've held it for more than a year and regular income tax if held less than a year.

Treasuries have another feature quite unique in the bond world. Almost all Treasury bonds are noncallable. That means the Treasury cannot redeem them before maturity, as many corporations and municipalities can do with their bonds. In some rare cases, Treasuries may be redeemed early, but for the most part, you are able to lock in the current rate on a Treasury for much longer than you are with any other bond. Just ask any of those happy investors who, in the early 1980s, bought 30-year Treasury bonds with 13 percent yields. Despite the decade-long plunge in rates that followed, they are still collecting their 13 percent interest every six months.

U.S. government bonds have another advantage that many people do not realize: All the interest you earn is exempt from state and local taxes. As part of the U.S. Constitution, a separation of federal and state powers was set up so that states cannot tax federal securities. In addition, the federal government cannot tax state and local securities. This is why, for residents of the issuing state, municipal bonds are exempt from federal taxes. By avoiding state and local taxes on Treasury securities, your effective after-tax yield is actually a bit higher than you might think, particularly if you live in a high-tax city or state. For example, say you own a Treasury bond worth $10,000 that is yielding 10 percent, or $1,000, a year. If your combined city and state tax rate is 10 percent, you have avoided paying the $100 in local taxes that would have been due if Treasury interest were not exempt. You still must pay federal income tax on your Treasury bond interest, of course.

Treasuries have all these wonderful features, but what is their disadvantage? In return for the safety, liquidity, and tax advantages, you receive a lower yield than is available from other bonds. How much lower depends on the current market conditions and the bonds to which you compare Treasuries. But for conservative income-oriented investors, there's no match for Treasuries.

U.S. SAVINGS BONDS

Even though savings bonds are another form of Treasury security, they have several features that are worth discussing separately. Like other Treasuries, savings bonds have the backing of the full faith and credit of the U.S. government (see Figure 10.1), and the interest they pay is free from state and local taxes. Unlike other Treasuries, though, savings bonds have the following features.

- They are available in much smaller denominations. You can buy a savings bond at any bank, or through your company by payroll deduction, for as little as $25 apiece. They also come in denominations of $50, $75, $100, $200, $500, $1,000, $5,000, and $10,000. The government limits you to investing a maximum of $30,000 a year in savings bonds.

Figure 10.1 Savings Bond

Source: Courtesy of the United States Savings Bonds Division, Department of the Treasury.

- Series EE savings bonds are issued at half their face value. When you buy a $50 bond, for example, you pay $25 for it. They have no set maturity date and pay no current interest, but you can redeem them any time—from within six months of buying them to as long as 30 years later, according to a redemption schedule published by the Treasury Department. Depending on when the bond was issued, it has a different original maturity date, which is the maximum amount of time it takes for the bond to reach face value. This table shows the original term for Series EE bonds issued since 1980:

Issue Date	Original Term
1/80–10/80	11 years
11/80–4/81	9 years
5/81–10/82	8 years
11/82–10/86	10 years
11/86–2/93	12 years
3/93–4/95	18 years
5/95–Present	17 years

After a savings bond reaches its original maturity, it automatically enters one or more extension periods, usually of ten years duration. For bonds issued before May 1995, the interest is either based on a guaranteed yield or a market-based rate. If a guaranteed rate applies, it is the one in effect at the time the bond entered the extension period. If the bond was issued after April 1995, there is no guaranteed minimum yield, but instead a market rate of interest based on the rules applying to savings bonds at the time they enter the extension period. Savings bonds stop earning interest when they reach final maturity. For Series EE bonds, that is 30 years, and for Series HH bonds, it is 20 years.

- Savings bond interest is exempt from state and local income and personal property tax. You owe federal income tax on the interest earned when you redeem the bonds. When you cash in a savings bond at a bank, you will receive a Form 1099 INT from the bank telling you how much interest to report on your federal income tax return. Savings bond principal and interest are also subject to gift, estate, inheritance, and other federal and state excise taxes.
- You can swap non-interest-bearing Series EE bonds for a minimum of $500 worth of Series HH bonds, which pay cash interest at a 4 percent rate. You must pay taxes on the cash interest for the tax year in which you receive the checks. But when you swap, you do not have to pay taxes on all the interest your EEs accumulated until you redeem the HHs. Series HH bonds mature in ten years.

- Yields on U.S. savings bonds are not fixed. Instead, for bonds issued May 1997 or later, they earn interest based on 90 percent of the average yields of five-year Treasury securities for the preceding six months. These bonds increase in value every month, and interest is compounded semiannually. The new rate is announced each May 1 and November 1. Series EE bonds issued from May 1995 through April 1997 earn short-term market-based rates during their first five years and long-term based rates from 5 through 17 years. The rate this bond earns is adjusted to market-based rates every six months. Series EE bonds issued before May 1995 earn market-based yields based on 85 percent of the average five-year Treasury yields, if you've held them for at least five years, as long as this rate is higher than the guaranteed minimum yields available at that time.
- The government no longer guarantees a minimum yield. For many years, the Treasury guaranteed that you would earn a minimum of 6 percent if you held a savings bond for at least five years. In 1993, the minimum was lowered to 4 percent, and in 1995, the minimum was dropped altogether for all newly issued savings bonds.
- A new savings bond known as an I bond was introduced in September 1998. This bond was designed for investors seeking to protect the purchasing power of their investment and earn a guaranteed real rate of return. I bonds are an accrual-type security, meaning the interest is added to the bond monthly and paid when the bond is redeemed. I bonds are sold at face value—you pay $50 for a $50 bond—and grow in value with inflation-indexed earnings for up to 30 years.
- If your modified adjusted gross income is up to $57,600 for individuals or $86,400 for couples married filing jointly at the time you redeem your savings bonds (this amount is adjusted slightly upward for inflation every year), the interest you earn from the bonds is either fully or partially tax exempt if you use it for college tuition for either yourself, your spouse, or your children. This version of savings bonds is called an *Education Bond,* and it can apply to any bond purchased after Dec. 31, 1989. Make sure to keep the savings bonds in your own name if you plan on using the proceeds for educational expenses.

As you can see, savings bonds have a lot going for them. If you sign up to receive them as part of a payroll savings plan, you receive an added benefit: you build capital automatically, which will come in handy if you need quick cash for an emergency or when you need capital to live on in retirement.

To find out more about how savings bonds work, you can contact any Federal Reserve Bank (see the list at the end of this chapter), or write the Savings Bond Office at the U.S. Treasury, 999 E Street, NW, Washington DC 20239.

You can call that office at 202-447-1775 or find the latest savings bond rates at 800-872-6637. Another good source of information is the Treasury's Web site <www.savingsbonds.gov> (see Figure 10.2), which answers frequently asked questions and includes a Savings Bond Earnings Report telling you what your bonds are earning. The site also includes a Savings Bond Wizard, which displays the current value and interest earned for each of your bonds and the total of all your bonds, and allows you to change the redemption date so you can see what the bond's value will be on the new redemption date.

Another source of information about savings bonds is the Savings Bond Informer (PO Box 09249, Detroit, MI 48209; 313-843-1910; 800-927-1901; www.bondhelp.com). This private-sector service will help you figure how much your savings bonds are worth, when the best time to redeem them arrives, and whether you have bonds that have stopped earning interest.

Figure 10.2   savingsbonds.gov

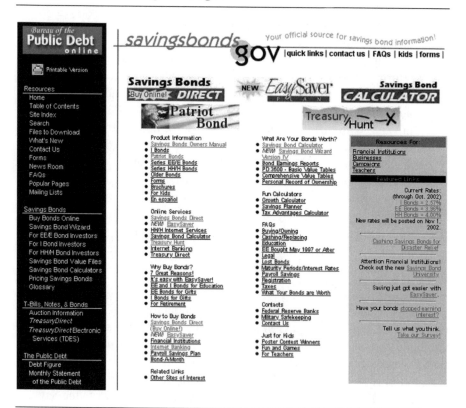

GOVERNMENT AGENCY SECURITIES

One notch more risky than Treasuries and savings bonds are the securities issued by a plethora of federal-government-backed agencies. Though they do not have the full faith and credit of the U.S. government behind them, you can be certain Congress would find a way to make sure these agencies don't default on their debt. Take the savings and loan crisis, for example. Congress appropriated a few hundred billion dollars to make sure depositors covered by the Federal Savings and Loan Insurance Corporation (FSLIC) would not lose their money. Though the specific laws backing each agency are different, the effect is the same: A default is almost unthinkable.

Because agency securities are not considered as completely risk free as Treasury securities, they pay slightly higher yields. If a Treasury bond yields 8 percent, a federal agency security of the same maturity might pay from 8.25 percent to 9 percent, for instance. Like interest from Treasuries, interest from agency securities is usually taxable at the federal level but exempt from state and local taxes. As with any bond, you must pay a capital gains tax if you sell a federal agency bond for a profit after holding it for at least one year. The two major exceptions to this rule are mortgage-backed securities of the Federal National Mortgage Association (Fannie Mae) and the Government National Mortgage Association (Ginnie Mae). The next section discusses mortgage-backed securities in more detail.

Unlike Treasuries, federal agency securities are not auctioned directly to the public; they are sold by a network of bond dealers and banks. Nonetheless, they are easy to buy through any brokerage firm. The dealer usually does not charge an explicit commission on agency securities (or on most other bonds), but he or she marks up the bonds and earns a profit on the spread between the price the dealer paid for them and the price at which he or she sells them. Depending on the agency, the bonds come in minimum denominations of $1,000 to $25,000.

The agencies that issue securities to the public are numerous and varied in their public purpose. The following are the biggest issuers of government-backed paper, with their acronyms or nicknames, where applicable:

- Asian Development Bank
- College Construction Loan Insurance Corporation (Connie Lee)
- Export-Import Bank of the United States
- Farmers Home Administration (FmHA)
- Federal Agricultural Mortgage Corporation (Farmer Mac)
- Federal Farm Credit System
- Federal Home Loan Bank System (FHLB)
- Federal Home Loan Mortgage Corporation (Freddie Mac)

- Federal Housing Administration (FHA)
- Federal National Mortgage Association (Fannie Mae)
- Government National Mortgage Association (Ginnie Mae)
- International Bank for Reconstruction and Development (World Bank)
- Resolution Funding Corporation (Refcorp)
- Small Business Administration (SBA)
- Student Loan Marketing Association (Sallie Mae)
- Tennessee Valley Authority (TVA)
- United States Postal Service

Some of these agencies are fully owned by the government; therefore, their securities are considered nearly as safe as Treasuries. Such agencies include the Export-Import Bank, the Farmers Home Administration, the FHA, Ginnie Mae, the TVA, and the Postal Service. Many of the agencies that are fully owned by the government issue securities through the Federal Financing Bank, established in 1974 as a central clearinghouse for federal agencies to issue debt.

Most of the other agencies listed were originally fully owned by the government but have since been transferred either to public ownership or to ownership by the organizations that benefit from the agency's services. For example, Fannie Mae, Freddie Mac, and Sallie Mae are all publicly traded corporations, with their stocks trading on the NYSE. The FHLB is owned by its member banks.

Whether a federal agency bond is right for you depends on its current yield and whether you feel comfortable with the slightly greater risk involved in owning one. For most conservative income-oriented investors, it can be a fine choice.

MORTGAGE-BACKED SECURITIES

You may not realize it, but when you take out a mortgage from your local bank or savings and loan, your monthly mortgage payments are probably funneled by the bank or S&L through a federally designed system to investors who buy mortgage-backed securities. These securities, which go by the names of the agencies that guarantee timely payment of the securities' interest and principal, such as Ginnie Mae, Fannie Mae, and Freddie Mac, offer higher yields than Treasury bonds at slightly higher levels of risk.

A mortgage-backed security works as follows: Soon after a bank or savings and loan issues a mortgage to a homeowner, the loan is sold along with thousands of other loans to a federal agency, which repackages them in the form of a mortgage-backed security. The federal agency then guarantees it will pay investors interest and principal as they come due, even if a homeowner is late with his or her mortgage payments or defaults on the mortgage. The homeowner continues to make payments to the local bank, which collects a fee from the agency for providing this go-between service. Once the bank receives this money, it can make another mortgage loan and start the process again.

From the investor's point of view, a mortgage-backed security provides regular monthly interest as it is paid by homeowners. In addition, each month, a certain amount of the mortgage principal is repaid, and that money is also passed through to the investor. The investor's brokerage statement will distinguish the two types of income received from the security each month.

The mortgage-backed securities market, which began in 1970 when Ginnie Mae introduced the concept, has mushroomed. Hundreds of billions of dollars' worth of outstanding mortgage-backed securities now exist, and billions of dollars' worth more are created every year. These securities are actively traded, and plenty of such bonds are always available from any major brokerage firm.

However, several problems exist for small investors buying individual mortgage-backed securities. First, the minimum denomination is $25,000, though some older issues trading at lower prices may require less than that. Second, the timing of interest and principal payments is not totally predictable. This is the biggest difference between a mortgage-backed security and a Treasury bond, which pays interest every six months and is not callable for years.

The interest and principal repayment schedule is uncertain because the homeowners making the payments can be unpredictable. If mortgage rates fall enough to make it worthwhile, they will refinance their higher interest mortgages. On the other hand, if mortgage rates rise, homeowners will hold onto their mortgages for dear life. And if a homeowner sells the residence, he or she may have to pay off the mortgage and take out another loan for his or her new home. Because the mortgage-backed security is a conduit through which homeowner payments pass, all of this activity greatly affects the cash flow received by investors.

In certain situations, the investors in a mortgage-backed security lose whichever way interest rates go. For instance, say an investor buys a Ginnie Mae filled with 10 percent mortgages, and mortgage rates drop over the next few years to 7 percent. Many of the homeowners in that Ginnie Mae pool will refinance their mortgages to lock in 7 percent, causing the investor to receive a flood of principal at a time when interest rates have fallen and it is impossible to replicate that 10 percent yield. In another scenario, if interest rates soar from 10 percent to 13 percent, exactly the reverse would happen. Few, if any, homeowners would refinance their mortgages at higher rates, so the investor would receive only a small amount of principal. With rates at 13 percent, though, the investor would love to receive principal so he or she could reinvest it at the higher rates.

As the mortgage-backed securities market has matured over the past two decades, these problems have become well recognized. The mortgage-backed securities industry has reacted in two ways: by raising yields and by creating new forms of mortgage-backed paper. To compensate investors for the uncertainty about the pace of repayment, mortgage-backed securities now pay between 1 and 2 percentage points more than Treasury securities of similar maturities. So, if a 10-year Treasury is paying 6 percent, you might be able to earn as much as 8 percent from a Ginnie Mae or Fannie Mae.

As though regular mortgage-backed securities were not complicated enough, a newer and even more complex version called a *collateralized mortgage obligation* (CMO) or a *real estate mortgage investment conduit* (REMIC), has been invented to ease the prepayment worry. In theory, a CMO or REMIC works by slicing a mortgage-backed securities pool into *tranches* (the French word for slice). All prepayments from underlying mortgages are applied to the first tranche until it is paid off. Then prepayments are applied to the next tranche until it is redeemed, and so on, until all the tranches are eventually retired. The idea behind this slice-and-dice routine is that investors can choose a tranche that most closely meets their maturity needs and will have a better chance that the security will last that long. Yet because tranches still do not guarantee prepayment schedules, investors receive a yield that is 1 to 3 percentage points higher than they would earn on similar maturity Treasuries.

Even though all this sounds extremely complicated, billions of dollars flow into mortgage-backed securities, CMOs, and REMICs these days, as people search out higher yields than are available from bank CDs and money-market funds. Realizing this, brokers market CMOs aggressively. Mortgage-backed securities may be right for you, as long as you understand what you are getting into.

In addition to mortgage-backed securities, there are several new classes of securities backed by other types of loans. These work exactly like mortgage-backed paper. The latest forms of asset-backed securities include pools of credit card loans, car loans, mobile home loans, and college loans. If you consider buying into one of these innovative loan pools, apply the same criteria you used with mortgage-backed securities.

MUNICIPAL BONDS

Though riskier than Treasury or agency securities, municipal bonds (munis) are extremely popular. These bonds, issued by states, cities, counties, towns, villages, and taxing authorities of many types, have one feature that separates them from all other securities: The interest they pay is totally free from federal taxes. In most cases, bondholders who are also residents of the states issuing the bonds do not have to pay state or local taxes on the interest either. Bonds not taxable by the resident state are known as *double-tax-free* bonds, and those also not taxable by a locality are called *triple-tax-free* issues. The exemption from federal taxation is based on the 1895 Supreme Court case of *Pollock v. Farmers' Loan and Trust Company,* which applied the constitutional doctrine of "intergovernmental tax immunity." The High Court ruled that this doctrine means that states are immune from federal interference with their ability to borrow money.

The fact that the interest from municipal bonds is federally tax free allows issuers to float bonds with yields lower than taxable government and corporate bond issuers must pay. Investors are satisfied to earn 6 percent tax free, compared to 8 percent on a Treasury, on which federal taxes are due. The higher an investor's federal, state, and local tax bracket, the more attractive munis become because they permit the investor to escape more taxes. At the same time, the lower yields that municipalities pay make it affordable for them to build roads, schools, sewer systems, hospitals, and other public facilities.

The market for municipal bonds is huge; well over a trillion dollars' worth of bonds are outstanding, and billions of dollars' worth of new bonds are issued every year. While there are millions of bonds and thousands of issuers, no centralized marketplace trades munis as it does stocks. Instead, municipal bonds are bought and sold by the many brokerage firms and banks that specialize in them. These dealers communicate with each other through a telephone and computer network. To buy municipal bonds, you must go through a broker or bank that can plug into this complex system of competing dealers. As with other bonds, brokers usually do not charge a separate commission to buy or sell your municipal issue. Instead, they make their money by marking up the bond from their cost by about 2 percent.

Municipal bonds are usually issued in minimum denominations of $5,000, though some are issued in lots as small as $1,000. Brokers usually require a minimum order of $5,000, but they prefer dealing in blocks of five bonds, or $25,000. Small orders invariably are hit with markups as high as 5 percent. Depending on the dollar volume of the bonds when they are issued, trading can be very active or almost nonexistent. Many municipalities have issued only a few bonds during their history, so the bonds are hard to buy or sell. If you plan to buy a bond and hold it until maturity, the fact that little trading activity occurs should be of little concern to you. When shopping for a municipal bond, ask how many years of protection against early redemption you will receive. Many municipal bond investors have been shocked in recent years when they received their principal back much sooner than they expected it.

The two main types of municipal bonds are general obligation bonds and revenue bonds. General obligation bonds (GOs) are issued by a state or local entity and are backed by the taxing power of that state, city, or town. In general, the proceeds from these issues are used to finance general capital expenditures, as well as ongoing municipal operations. Revenue bonds, on the other hand, finance specific revenue-producing projects, such as toll roads, bridges, tunnels, sewer systems, or airports. The interest and principal paid by the bonds comes from the economic activity generated by the bonds. For instance, a revenue bond might be floated to finance a new highway. The proceeds of the issue will be spent to build the road, and tolls collected on the road for the next several years will pay the interest and principal on the bonds. You can buy many other forms of revenue bonds, some riskier than others. For example, so-called private purpose bonds can be issued on behalf of hospitals, universities, or other nonprofit organizations. Industrial revenue bonds are sponsored by municipalities to finance construction of factories or industrial parks that will bring jobs into a district.

Aside from different kinds of general obligation and revenue bonds, some municipal issues can be taxable under certain circumstances. For example, some bonds are issued to be subject to federal income tax but exempt from state and local taxes to in-state residents who buy them. Other bonds, known as alternative minimum tax (AMT) bonds, can be taxed if the holder falls into the alternative minimum tax trap, which is designed to keep wealthy people from avoiding federal taxes altogether. If the holder will not be hit by the AMT, these bonds, which pay a slightly higher yield than regular munis, would provide totally tax-free income.

Debates rage among bond analysts over whether general obligation or revenue bonds are safer for investors. To some extent, the safety of the bond depends on the financial situation of the issuing entity and the revenue potential of the project the issue funds. Though defaults by states and cities are exceedingly rare, they can happen if political gridlock occurs in a state or city where expenses are soaring, revenues are falling and residents are moving out. Revenue projects normally are a safe bet as well, but they can be disrupted if an economic contraction (the area's economy takes a downturn) in the area of the project causes revenues to come in under projections. The best way to judge the safety of any particular issue is to look at the bond's safety rating by Standard & Poor's, Moody's, or Fitch.

If you would rather not worry at all about safety, a conservative alternative called *municipal bond insurance* is available on about half of all newly issued bonds today. You cannot buy insurance on your bonds individually, but you can purchase bonds that already have insurance attached to them. The municipal bond insurers, such as the Municipal Bond Investors Assurance Corporation (MBIA), the American Municipal Bond Assurance Corporation (AMBAC), and several others, guarantee that you will receive timely payments of interest and principal for the life of the bond if the issuer defaults. Insured bonds usually trade as though they have an AAA rating because no risk of default exists. However, the cost of the insurance is passed on to the investor; insured bonds usually yield a little less than similar non-insured bonds.

Determining your taxable equivalent yield. To calculate whether a municipal bond makes sense for you, compare its yield with taxable alternatives to see which bond leaves you the most money after taxes. The following exercise helps you determine the taxable equivalent yield of your muni.

First, deduct your federal tax bracket from 100. (This example uses a 31 percent tax bracket.) The result is known as the reciprocal of your tax bracket.

$$\begin{array}{rr} & 100 \\ \text{Tax bracket} & \underline{-31} \\ \text{Reciprocal of tax bracket} & 69 \end{array}$$

Divide the tax-free yield on the municipal bond you are considering by the reciprocal of your tax bracket. (In this case, assume the bond pays a 7 percent tax-free yield.)

$$\frac{7\% \text{ Municipal bond yield}}{69 \text{ Reciprocal of tax bracket}} = 10.14\% \text{ Taxable equivalent yield}$$

In this example you would have to buy a taxable bond paying 10.14 percent to end up with the same dollar amount after taxes that the 7 percent muni will pay. To earn that high a yield, you would normally have to take on far more risk than a municipal bond entails.

To make munis look even more attractive, go through the same exercise adding in your state and local tax brackets. For example, if your combined federal, state, and local tax brackets total 40 percent, the taxable equivalent yield of a 7 percent muni would be an astounding 11.6 percent! You can see why munis are so popular.

The following table will give you a few taxable equivalent yields for various tax-free muni yields. As you can see, the higher the tax bracket, the more you would have to earn in a taxable bond to end up with the same after-tax return.

Federal	Tax-Exempt Yield				
Tax Bracket	4%	5%	6%	7%	8%
15 %	4.71%	5.88%	7.05%	8.23%	9.41%
28	5.56	6.94	8.33	9.72	11.11
31	5.80	7.25	8.70	10.14	11.59
36	6.25	7.81	9.37	10.93	12.50
39.6	6.62	8.27	9.93	11.58	13.24

Which states tax which bonds. In almost every state, interest from bonds issued by that state is tax free to state residents. The only exceptions are Illinois, Iowa, Kansas, Oklahoma, and Wisconsin. For residents of those states, interest from some, but not all, in-state bonds is tax exempt.

The following states never impose state taxes on interest earned by residents who buy bonds issued by other states: Alaska, the District of Columbia, Indiana, Nevada, South Dakota, Texas, Utah, Washington, and Wyoming.

The following states do impose state taxes on interest earned by residents who buy bonds issued by other states:

Alabama	Kentucky	New York
Arizona	Louisiana	North Carolina
Arkansas	Maine	North Dakota
California	Maryland	Ohio
Colorado	Massachusetts	Oklahoma
Connecticut	Michigan	Oregon
Delaware	Minnesota	Pennsylvania
Florida	Mississippi	Rhode Island
Georgia	Missouri	South Carolina
Hawaii	Montana	Tennessee
Idaho	Nebraska	Vermont
Illinois	New Hampshire	Virginia
Iowa	New Jersey	West Virginia
Kansas	New Mexico	Wisconsin

Keep these taxation rules in mind when you are deciding whether it makes more sense to buy an in-state bond or an out-of-state bond. Your return will depend on whether the out-of-state bond is taxable and on your state tax rates.

Clearly, if you are in a high enough tax bracket, it could be quite worthwhile to investigate municipal bonds. They are not only safe; their after-tax yields can often beat any other taxable alternative.

CORPORATE BONDS

The next rung down the ladder of bond risk are bonds issued by corporations. While the U.S. government and its agencies, states, and municipalities are not going to disappear, corporations may not be around forever. Thousands of companies go bankrupt each year. Firms thrive or crash based on their success in the marketplace, and that is never ensured. Because corporations, no matter how solid financially, are thus perceived as vulnerable to changes in the business environment, the bonds they issue are considered riskier than government issues and therefore always pay a higher yield than government issues of the same maturity.

Still, only a tiny percentage of corporate bonds—typically less than 1 percent—ever default. Thousands of perfectly solid issues are outstanding, and many more come to market every year. Even in the worst-case scenario of a company going bankrupt, bondholders' claims are settled before stockholders receive any compensation.

As an individual investor, you have many opportunities to increase your income by holding corporate bonds. Most bonds pay interest semiannually and use the electronic book-entry system, so interest payments can be sent automatically to your brokerage account. Depending on the financial creditworthiness of the issuing company, a corporate bond can yield from 2 to 6 percentage points more than Treasuries of the same maturity.

As with all bonds, you can profit by buying them when interest rates are high and selling them after rates have fallen and bond prices have climbed. Corporate bond prices react to general fluctuations in interest rates, as well as the financial fortunes (or misfortunes) of the issuing companies. For example, a bond's price will rise if the company's finances improve because investors anticipate that the bond's safety rating from agencies like Standard & Poor's might be upgraded. On the other hand, a series of financial setbacks will cause the bond's price to sink, as investors fear a rating downgrade. If the situation deteriorates enough, the bond's price might plummet to very low levels because investors think the firm might declare bankruptcy and default on its bond payments.

Corporate bonds typically are issued in denominations of $1,000 and quoted in units of $100, like Treasury bonds. Most bond dealers don't like trading in lots of fewer than five bonds, or less than $5,000. For smaller lots, brokers' markups can be quite high. In some cases, brokers will charge a minimum per-bond commission of as much as $20.

Many of the thousands of outstanding corporate bonds trade quite actively and are therefore easy to buy and sell. Some smaller issues may not trade as frequently, which means there will be a wider spread between the buying price and the selling price.

As with municipal bonds, you must research your protection against premature calls carefully. Many corporate bonds offer ten years guaranteed against early redemption though call protection varies widely. Among the most frustrating experiences for investors is to have a high-yield corporate bond plucked from their grasp after interest rates have fallen sharply. Corporate treasurers will always do whatever is in the best interest of their stockholders— which is to refinance high-yield debt at the first possible moment.

Most corporate bonds are unsecured, meaning they are backed only by the companies' general ability to repay them out of cash flow and profits. Such unsecured bonds are generally called *debentures*. Other corporate bonds are secured by a particular asset, which becomes the property of bondholders if a company defaults. Examples of secured corporate bonds include mortgage bonds, backed by real estate, and equipment trust certificates, backed by equipment such as airplanes or railroad cars.

While most corporate bonds are fairly conservative, junk bonds allow riskier investment. An upcoming section describes junk bonds in more detail.

ZERO-COUPON BONDS

Zero-coupon bonds—called *zeros* for short—can, paradoxically, be the safest of all investments or the riskiest. It all depends on how you use them.

A zero-coupon bond gets its name from the fact that the bond is issued with a 0 percent coupon rate. Because people buy bonds to collect interest at the coupon rate, who would ever be interested in a bond that pays no interest? Plenty of people, and here's why: Instead of making regular interest payments, a zero is issued at a deep discount from its face value of 100, or $5,000. The return on a zero comes from the gradual increase in the bond's price from the discount to face value, which it reaches at maturity.

This slow but steady rise in value yields three benefits:

1. You know exactly how much money you will receive when the bond matures.
2. You know exactly when you will receive that money.
3. You do not have to worry about reinvesting the small amounts of interest regular full-coupon bonds pay.

Very few investments can guarantee you will receive a specific dollar amount years from now. Because zeros have a specific schedule of appreciation, you can use a zero as an integral part of a financial plan to fund specific expenses years in advance. For example, if you are the parent of a newborn, you know to the month when his or her first college tuition payment will be due. Therefore, you can buy a zero maturing in 18 years. Or, if you are a 40-year-old who plans to retire at age 65, you can buy a 25-year zero that will mature on the day your company gives you the gold watch.

When you contact a broker about buying a zero, he or she will usually quote the current price of a bond that will mature at a face value of $1,000 a number of years in the future (one advantage is that you can buy almost any amount, not a minimum of $5,000), and he or she will tell you what yield you are locking in at that price. The broker's quote will include the markup, so you do not have to figure in an additional commission. Markups can vary widely from broker to broker, so it is important that you shop around. Get at least three quotes, asking for:

- The amount of money you must invest now, including all fees and commissions
- The amount of money you will receive when the zero matures on the date you choose
- The yield to maturity you will be locking in for the years you hold the zero

Once you have the data for various zeros, choose the bond selling for the lowest price and boasting the highest yield to maturity for the date you want.

For example, if you want to have a lump sum of $10,000 available to you at various times in the future, the following is a table typical of one a broker might give you. It outlines your bond options and lays out the prices and yields you might achieve.

	Current Price	Cost in Dollars	Yield
5-year zero	$71.80	$7,180	6.05%
10-year zero	48.12	4,812	7.05
15-year zero	31.61	3,161	7.54
20-year zero	20.86	2,086	7.77
25-year zero	14.28	1,428	7.76

Notice that the longer in the future you want your money back, the fewer dollars you must pay now, because you are allowing more time for the zero to compound.

The other attraction of a zero is that your interest is reinvested automatically at the zero's yield. This can be a particularly significant advantage if you lock in a high interest rate. With a regular interest-paying bond, you receive interest checks every six months, which can be helpful if you need the money for living expenses. But if you would rather reinvest the interest to make your capital compound, prevailing interest rates constantly rise and fall, making it impossible to lock in a constant rate of reinvestment. Also, the dollar amount of your interest payment may be so small that you would not be able to afford the minimum needed to buy another bond.

Many issuers of zero-coupon bonds exist, but most investors buy zeros based on Treasury bonds. These zeros are commonly known as STRIPS, which stands for Separate Trading of Registered Interest and Principal of Securities. Like any other Treasury, they are backed by the full faith and credit of the U.S. government and are noncallable. Some brokerage firms have launched their own versions of STRIPS, with names like Salomon Brothers' CATS (certificates of accrual on Treasury securities) and Merrill Lynch's TIGRs (Treasury investment growth receipts). In a sense, U.S. savings bonds are also zeros; they work exactly the same way but are issued in much smaller denominations. Also, several large corporations issue zero-coupon bonds that allow you to lock in higher yields than do government issues. For the most part, though, it is best to invest in STRIPS because you do not want to wait 20 years with no payoff, only to discover that the issuing corporation went bankrupt recently.

If you want a diversified portfolio of zeros, you can buy shares in a zero-coupon bond mutual fund for a minimum of $1,000. The largest fund company offering zero-coupon funds is American Century Investments (PO Box 419200, Kansas City, MO 64141; 800-345-2021; www.americancentury .com). The company offers no-load funds called Benham Target Maturities Trusts that are set to mature every five years (such as 2005, 2010, 2015, 2020, and 2025). You pay annual expenses of .62 percent of your assets. You can avoid these expenses by buying STRIPS directly. But the fund does offer you a more diversified portfolio, and it is easy to buy and sell without having to pay the large spread some brokers charge.

Taxable zero-coupon bonds have one major pitfall. The Internal Revenue Service (IRS) has ruled that the scheduled yearly growth in the value of a zero-coupon bond (the IRS calls it the bond's accretion) must be considered interest income in the year it is earned, even though you do not receive any cash interest payments. The IRS publishes an accretion table, telling you how much "imputed" interest you must report each year. This rule can take much of the zip out of zeros because every year, you must pay taxes on interest without having received the interest to pay the taxes.

You have two ways to get around this dilemma: buying zeros only in tax-sheltered accounts or buying tax-free municipal zero-coupon bonds. If you buy a zero through an individual retirement account (IRA), a Keogh account, an annuity, a salary reduction plan, or some other vehicle that allows you to defer tax liability until you withdraw money from the account, the IRS accretion rules do not affect you. The zero compounds year after year, untouched by taxes. You pay taxes on the increased value only when you withdraw the money, usually at retirement.

Because you never owe taxes on the interest paid by municipal bonds, the same holds true for muni zeros. You can therefore buy muni zeros in your regular account and watch them compound tax free until they mature. The fact that muni zeros offer such superb benefits makes them extremely popular, which often means they sell out soon after they are issued. Therefore, if you think a muni zero is right for you, contact your broker before a new bond is issued so he or she can prepare to grab a few bonds while they last. When shopping for muni zeros, look carefully at the call provisions of the issues because many allow issuers to redeem them before their scheduled maturity, which could defeat your whole purpose in buying them. Figure 10.3 is an illustration of how a municipal zero yielding 7 percent would grow from $5,000 when you bought it to $20,000 in 20 years.

The risky side of zeros. So far, we have described zeros as the safest and surest way to fund a distant financial goal, despite one major pitfall. However, another far more volatile side to zeros exists if you use zeros to earn capital gains.

Because zeros lock in a fixed reinvestment rate of interest for a long time, their prices react to fluctuations in interest rates far more than does any other type of bond. For every one-point drop in interest rates over a year, for example, a normal 30-year coupon bond paying 8 percent would produce a total return (price change plus income) of 20 percent, while a 30-year zero with an 8 percent reinvestment rate would soar by 42 percent. Conversely, if interest rates rose by one percentage point over a year, the full-coupon bond would suffer a negative total return of 3 percent, while the zero would plunge by 19 percent. The fact that the zero compounds its yield automatically for many years magnifies the impact of interest rate changes.

Figure 10.4 shows how the total return of a 30-year zero-coupon Treasury bond with an 8 percent reinvestment rate is affected by interest rate changes of one percentage point upward and downward over a year, compared to the effect on a 30-year full-coupon bond paying 8 percent.

Notice that the effect of a one-percentage-point change is not symmetrical. A one-point drop yields a 43 percent gain on a zero, while a one-point rise yields an 18 percent loss.

Figure 10.3   The Growth of a 20-Year Municipal Zero-Coupon Bond Yielding 7%

$ Value

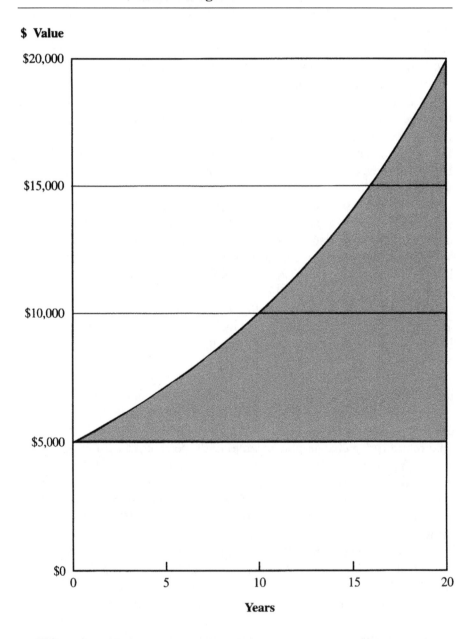

Source: Adapted with permission by Bond Market Association.

Figure 10.4   Zeros versus Full-Coupon Bonds

	Percentage Point Change in a Year								
	+4	+3	+2	+1	Unchanged	−1	−2	−3	−4
30-year zero	−64%	−53%	−38%	−18%	+8%	+43%	+89%	+139%	+220%
30-year full-coupon	−24	−18	−11	−2	+8	+20	+35	+54	+76

Source: Courtesy of Ryan Labs, Inc., a bond research firm in New York, New York.

The effect of interest rate changes on zeros is lessened if the zeros are of a shorter maturity. This is obvious in Figure 10.5, which illustrates the effect of interest rate changes of one percentage point upward and downward 5-, 10-, 20-, and 30-year zeros. (The table assumes 30-year Treasury rates are at 8 percent.)

Notice that if interest rates drop by four percentage points, the 30-year zero would soar 220 percent, while the 5-year zero would rise only 26 percent. On the other extreme, if rates shoot up by four percentage points, the 30-year bond would plummet 64 percent, while the 5-year zero would fall only 7 percent. This dramatically illustrates that the longer the maturity of the zero, the more volatile its price will be.

As a result of zeros' volatility, they are the favorite weapon for speculators who want to bet that interest rates will fall. This is a game for serious investors, however, because if interest rates raise instead of fall, they can lose big. For most investors, though, zeros are far from a speculative investment.

Figure 10.5   5-, 10-, 20-, and 30-Year Zeros Responding to Rate Changes

	Percentage Point Change in a Year								
	+4	+3	+2	+1	Unchanged	−1	−2	−3	−4
30-year zero	−64%	−53%	−38%	−18%	+8%	+43%	+89%	+139%	+220%
20-year zero	−47	−37	−25	−10	+8	+30	+56	+88	+117
10-year zero	−23	−16	−9	0	+8	+18	+29	+40	+53
5-year zero	−7	−4	0	+4	+8	+12	+17	+21	+26

Source: Courtesy of Ryan Labs, Inc., New York, New York.

CONVERTIBLE BONDS

Convertible bonds are hybrids—one part bond and the other part stock. In their role as bonds, they offer regular fixed income, though usually at a yield lower than straight bonds of the same issuer. In their role as stocks, convertibles offer significant appreciation potential and a way to benefit from the issuing companies' financial success. However, owners of convertibles will not benefit as much as common stockholders if the companies' fortunes soar. To some investors, convertibles offer the best of both worlds—high income and appreciation potential. To others, convertibles offer the worst of both worlds—lower income than bonds yield and less appreciation potential than common stock offers. Whichever way you view them, convertibles can make a solid contribution to your investment portfolio.

Convertibles come in two forms: preferred stock and debentures, which are unsecured bonds. Both pay a fixed rate of interest and are convertible into common stock of the issuer when the common stock reaches a certain price, known as the conversion price. That conversion price is always set at a level higher than the common stock's price at the time the convertible is first issued. It can be as low as 15 percent above the common price or as high as 50 percent above. When the underlying stock hits the conversion price, the convertible bond can be changed into a specified number of shares at what is called the *conversion ratio.* For example, ABC Corporation may issue a convertible that allows its holders to convert each bond into 50 shares of ABC common when ABC hits $100 a share.

Convertible bond prices are influenced by several factors. Because they are bonds, they are affected by the general ups and downs of interest rates. Also, the market evaluates convertibles as straight fixed-income securities. This gives them their investment value. The market also evaluates convertibles based on their underlying common stock. This gives them their conversion value. When the market takes a dim view of an underlying company, the convertible's investment value is more important than it would be otherwise. If the underlying company is a hot growth stock, however, the convertible will trade more on its conversion value because investors expect the common stock price to rise, and the convertible will eventually be changed into common shares.

You can judge what kind of growth potential the market expects of a convertible by looking at what is known as the *premium over conversion value.* As the underlying common stock rises in value, the convertible is viewed increasingly as a common stock. At a certain point, usually when the dividend on the underlying common stock is more valuable than the interest return from the convertible, it makes sense to convert into common shares. The price of the common shares will rise beyond the convertible price when this happens, signaling that it is time to convert.

The higher the conversion premium, the riskier the bond, however, because the premium can shrink quickly if the hot growth company stumbles. Any premium of more than 20 percent to 25 percent should be seen as a warning sign of increased risk. One way to protect yourself from paying too high a premium is to determine how long it will take to earn back that premium. The following example—in which the conversion premium is 20 percent, the underlying common stock yields 2 percent, and the convertible yields 7 percent—shows you how to do this.

First, subtract the common stock yield from the convertible yield.

Convertible yield	7%
Common stock yield	−2%
Yield difference	5%

Then divide the premium by the yield difference.

$$20\% \div 5\% = 4 \text{ Years}$$

The answer indicates how long it would take to recover your conversion premium if all else stayed the same. In this case, it would take four years.

Convertible prices tend to fall less than stock prices when the stock market declines because convertibles offer a higher level of income than most stocks, which tends to cushion the convertibles' descent. On the other hand, when the stock market surges, convertibles tend to rise less than stocks.

Convertible bonds are usually denominated in minimums of $1,000, though most brokers like to trade at least ten bonds, or $10,000 worth, at a time. Smaller trades will subject you to larger dealer markups. Depending on the size of the convertible issue, the stature of the issuer, and the credit rating of the bond from the ratings agencies, trading may be very active or inactive. As with other bonds, you must determine how much call protection the convertible offers. You don't want the bond redeemed quickly if interest rates fall and the issuer decides to refinance at a lower rate.

Convertibles offer no special tax breaks. All interest paid is fully taxable at the federal, state, and local levels. Although no taxes are due when you convert from a bond to common stock, you must pay all the normal taxes on the stock dividends. As with any other security, you must pay capital gains taxes if you sell a convertible for a profit after holding it for more than a year.

Before you buy any convertible, decide whether you want to own the issuer's common stock. If you think the underlying company has a bright future, the convertible can be an excellent choice to improve your current income and profit from the firm's success. However, if you are considering the convertible only for the income, and you would not want to be caught holding the underlying stock, move on to another option. Despite all the bells and whistles of convertibles, they are ultimately just another way to invest in a company's prospects.

If you want the benefits of convertibles without the complications discussed here, you can invest in a convertible bond mutual fund. It offers a high yield and appreciation potential, and the fund manager is an expert in picking through the somewhat bewildering world of convertibles.

For those seeking more information about convertibles, many brokerage firms publish research reports on widely traded issues. The best newsletter that tracks the field is the *Value Line Convertibles* (220 E. 42nd Street, New York, NY 10017; 800-535-8760; www.valueline.com).

JUNK BONDS

The riskiest types of bonds are known in the brokerage industry as high-yield bonds, but colloquially they are known as *junk bonds.* These bonds barely existed before the 1980s takeover, leveraged buyout, and junk bond boom made them famous—or infamous, depending on your experience with them.

Junk bonds are issued by corporations that have less than an investment-grade rating. That means Standard & Poor's and Fitch rate them below BBB, and Moody's rates them below Baa. Companies earn such low ratings for two reasons; they are either on their way up or on their way down, financially speaking. The up-and-comers are companies that do not have the long track record of sales and earnings that the ratings agencies require to merit an investment-grade rating. Just because they do not have a top rating, however, does not make them bad companies. It just means they need more seasoning before their rating rises from the BB into the BBB or level A category.

The companies on their way down, often called *fallen angels,* are a different story. These corporations attained an investment-grade rating in years past by diligently increasing sales and profits. But some event or series of events changed all that, causing the ratings agencies to downgrade the firms' bonds. Possible events include a takeover financed with millions of dollars in new debt, a failed market strategy that saddles a firm with operating losses instead of profits, or a general downturn in the economy that undermines a firm's profitability so severely that the ratings agencies doubt its ability to pay interest on its outstanding bonds.

While a low safety rating might be bad news for a company, it is good news for investors because it means that the firm's bonds will pay a substantially higher yield than will securities issued by blue chip corporations. How much more depends on which issuers you compare, but decent-quality junk bonds often yield between two and five percentage points more than investment-grade issues. That can translate into yields of 9 percent to 15 percent. Lower-quality junk issues can pay up to 20 percent.

Think you've found your dream investment? Well, hold onto your money because those higher yields obviously come with higher risks, chief among them:

- *The company can default.* The higher the yield, in fact, the more likely it is that the bond's interest rate will drop suddenly one day, from high double digits to zero, as the high cost of servicing the debt becomes too much for the company to handle. When a company seeks protection from creditors in bankruptcy, interest payments to bondholders often cease. Default rates on junk bonds vary and, to a large degree, depend on the overall health of the economy. A vibrant economy will allow companies to earn the profits they need to meet their interest costs, meaning only 1 percent or 2 percent of all junk bonds might default in a year. But in a recession, junk bond default rates can soar to 8 percent or 10 percent if reduced sales and profits make it impossible to pay bond interest.

- *The company's bonds can be downgraded further.* Though not as serious as outright default, a junk bond with a BB rating can be downgraded to a B or even into the Cs, which would pummel the bond's price.

- *Interest rates can rise.* While that hurts the value of all bonds, it can be particularly harmful to companies already in a weakened financial condition.

- *The stock market can fall.* Because a junk bond's price is tied closely to the fate of the underlying company, a general drop in stock prices can spill over to the company's stock price, which will affect its bond price negatively.

- *There can be an imbalance of supply and demand.* In the 1980s, when billions of dollars' worth of new junk bonds were brought to market every year, the supply eventually outran the demand, causing bond prices to decline sharply. In addition, because of junk-bond-related scandals and losses suffered by junk bond holders, Congress forced savings and loans to sell their junk bonds. Insurance companies were later ordered to liquidate their portfolios for the same reasons. Many other large institutions, such as pension funds, were also banned from buying junk bonds. All of this reduced demand for junk bonds even further. The main buyers of junk bonds now are individuals and mutual funds that raise money from individuals.

- *The liquidity of junk bond trading can dry up.* If bad news hits the market, such as an unexpected default, it can become very difficult to buy or sell bonds at a reasonable price. Dealers will execute trades only at enormous spreads that make it unattractive for investors to complete transactions.

- *Junk bonds can be called.* Companies do not voluntarily pay double-digit yields on their bonds; they are forced to do so. If their financial fortunes improve, or if interest rates fall, they will refinance those high-yielding bonds with lower yielding bonds at the first possible opportunity.

Despite the risks, junk bonds can provide very high returns if they are chosen well. In selecting a high-yield bond, look for a company with improving finances rather than worsening finances that you hope will turn around someday.

Most junk bonds come in minimum denominations of $1,000, but if they are depressed, they may sell for far less than that. Brokers normally like to sell bonds in lots of at least five, or $5,000. They will charge a wide spread or a steep commission on smaller orders.

The interest you receive from a junk bond is fully taxable at the federal, state, and local levels. If you sell the bond for a gain after holding it for a year, you must pay capital gains tax. If the company defaults on its bonds and ultimately liquidates, you can use the bond certificates to wallpaper your living room (unless you would rather not be reminded of your investment). You can also write off your losses against other capital gains and $3,000 of ordinary income per year.

If you feel skittish about buying individual junk bonds (and you should), a safer alternative is to buy a mutual fund that purchases a widely diversified portfolio of the toxic issues. That way, you have a professional manager picking through the junk for you.

Whether you invest in junk bonds depends on your ability to tolerate high risk in return for high yields and some potentially large capital gains. However, don't put too much of your money into junk bonds. The risk is just not worth the angst.

UNIT INVESTMENT TRUSTS

Unit investment trusts (UITs), sometimes called *defined asset funds,* buy a fixed portfolio of bonds and hold them to maturity. These contrast with bond funds, which constantly buy and sell bonds and never mature.

You can buy a UIT from any broker for a minimum of $1,000. You usually pay a sales charge of about 4 percent or 5 percent when you buy it, then minimal management expenses thereafter of .15 percent per year. The underwriter of the portfolio also profits by marking up the bonds it buys for the portfolio. Over the long term, though, these fees are less than the typical annual management fees of 1 percent or more on more actively managed bond funds. A few large brokerage firms, including Merrill Lynch, Nuveen, and Van Kampen, dominate the UIT business. The trusts are usually sold through syndicates of brokerage firms that unite to sell one trust after another.

UITs offer several advantages:

- You buy into a widely diversified, professionally selected portfolio that would be impossible to replicate on your own.
- You know exactly what assets the trust contains before you buy it. That is why they are called defined asset funds.
- You receive fixed monthly income checks, as opposed to payments every six months from individual bonds.
- If you need access to your capital, you can sell your units back to the sponsoring company, though you might have to sell at a discount.
- You receive your principal back when the portfolio of bonds matures (usually in about 20 years) unlike a bond fund, which never matures.
- You can choose a UIT that fits your income needs. Many trusts specialize in municipal bonds and therefore pay tax-free interest. Within that category, some trusts buy only bonds from a particular state, yielding double-tax-free income. For investors who want extra security, other municipal trusts buy only insured bonds. In addition to municipal bonds, UITs buy mortgage-backed securities, high-quality corporate bonds, foreign bonds, and even junk bonds.

Because they own fixed portfolios of bonds, UITs can get hurt if there is a problem with some of the bonds in their portfolios. For example, in the early 1980s, a consortium of municipalities that had banded together to build nuclear power plants in Washington state (called the Washington Public Power Supply System and commonly known as WHOOPS) defaulted on billions of dollars in bonds, many of which were held in UIT portfolios. While some of the bonds were insured, leaving trustholders unaffected, others were not. Thus, many UITs suffered losses and had to reduce monthly payouts. In extreme cases, UIT managers can sell bonds if they sense trouble coming, but such active management is the exception. When bonds are sold, however, the principal is returned to UIT holders because UITs are not allowed to add new bonds to a portfolio once it has been sold.

When shopping for a UIT, look carefully at the prospectus describing the portfolio. Notice the average maturity of the bonds, which may range from 10 years to as many as 30 years. Inspect the bonds' safety ratings, making sure that they fall in the A category if you want to depend on the trust for income for many years. Determine what kind of call protection comes with the bonds in the portfolio. Ideally, you would like at least ten years before the bonds can be redeemed.

With a little homework, you may find a UIT that meets your needs for dependable monthly income. You can request a free guide to UITs called "An Overture to Our Investment Strategy," by calling 877-DEFINED, 877-333-4633, ext. 3199. This guide is published by Merrill Lynch, Pierce, Fenner & Smith Inc.

RESOURCES

To learn more about bonds, read financial newspapers like *The Wall Street Journal* and *Barron's,* as well as personal finance magazines like *Money,* which feature articles about bonds regularly. For more in-depth information on bonds, consult the following books, newsletters, and trade associations.

Books

All about Bonds and Bond Mutual Funds: The Easy Way to Get Started, by Esme Faerber (McGraw-Hill, PO Box 548, Blacklick, OH 43003; 800-634-3961; www.mcgraw-hill.com). Simple, comprehensive book about bonds and bond funds. Includes new material on bond mutual funds, tax-free municipal bonds, international bonds, and bond funds.

All about Bonds from the Inside Out, by Esme Faerber (McGraw-Hill, PO Box 543, Blacklick, OH 43004; 800-634-3961; www.mcgraw-hill.com). Explains the basics of bonds, including the different types of bonds, varying levels of risk, how to spot undervalued and overvalued bonds, how to read yield curves, and calculations for interest rates and returns.

The Almanac of Online Trading: The Indispensable Reference Guide for Trading Stocks, Bonds, and Futures Online, by Terry Wooten (McGraw-Hill, PO Box 548, Blacklick, OH 43004; 800-634-3691; www.mcgraw-hill.com). Provides a nuts-and-bolts look at online trading and describes the tools and resources available online.

An Introduction to Bond Markets (The Reuters Financial Training Series) (John Wiley & Sons, 1 Wiley Drive, Somerset, NJ 08875-1272; 212-850-6000; 800-225-5945; www.wiley.com). Examines key debt market players, bond characteristics and valuations, credit agencies, ratings, and regulations.

Beating the Dow with Bonds, by Michael O'Higgins (HarperBusiness, PO Box 588, Dunmore, PA 18512; 212-207-7000; 800-331-3761; www.harpercollins.com). Provides a strategy when to buy stocks and when to buy bonds to maximize returns.

The Bond Bible, by Marilyn Cohen and Nick Watson (New York Institute of Finance, 1330 Avenue of the Americas, 10th Floor, New York, NY 10019; 212-641-6616; www.nyif.com). Explains everything from income streams and the Treasury yield curve to the advantages of federal agency bonds and the dangers of high-yield issues. Also addresses strategies, such as leveraging, credit rating agencies, insurance, bond funds, and unit trusts.

The Bond Book, by Annette Thau (McGraw-Hill, PO Box 548, Blacklick, OH 43004; 800-634-3691; www.mcgraw-hill.com). Explains how to assess the risks and opportunities of individual bonds, and shows investors where to get good information on the bond market. Covers bond market basics, Treasury securities, municipal bonds, corporate bonds, mortgage-backed securities, and bond mutual funds.

Bond Market Rules: 50 Investing Axioms to Master Bonds for Income or Trading, by Michael D. Sheimo (McGraw-Hill, PO Box 548, Blacklick, OH 43004; 800-634-3961; www.mcgraw-hill.com). Covers the basic nature and structure of bonds, how bond investing functions, the importance of interest rates and risk, and risk analysis.

Bond Markets, by Patrick J. Brown and Patrick J. Ryan (AMACOM, 1601 Broadway, New York, NY 10019; 212-586-8100; 800-262-9699; www.amanet.org). This book addresses how different bond instruments are normally quoted, how much accrued interest is payable by buyer in addition to traded price, the cost of a bond if quoted on a yield basis, normal settlement periods, how yields are quoted and calculated, and other related bond issues. Not for a beginner.

Bond Markets: Analysis and Strategies, by Frank Fabozzi (Prentice Hall, One Lake Street, Upper Saddle River, NJ 07458; 201-236-7156; 800-382-3419; www .prenticehall.com). Offers more sophisticated bond market strategies.

Bonds and Bond Derivatives, by Miles Livingston (Blackwell Publications, 350 Main Street, Malden, MA 02148; 781-388-8200). A good review of bonds and derivatives for a beginner.

The Fixed-Income Almanac: The Bond Investor's Compendium of Key Market, Product and Performance Data, by Livingston G. Douglas (McGraw-Hill, PO Box 543, Blacklick, OH 43004; 800-634-3961; www.mcgraw-hill.com). Provides years of performance data for the bond markets, including yield levels, measures of bond volatility, information on ratings upgrades and downgrades, and levels of new bond issuance.

Fundamentals of Municipal Bonds (The Bond Market Association, Publications Dept., PO Box 325, Congers, NY 10920; 212-440-9430; www.bondmarkets.com). An excellent overview of everything you need to know about municipal bonds.

Getting Started in Bonds, by Sharon Saltzgiver Wright (John Wiley & Sons, 1 Wiley Drive, Somerset, NJ 08875-1272; 212-850-6000; 800-225-5945; www.wiley .com). Guide for the novice bond investor. Covers basic concepts as well as explains the broader factors that affect bond prices. Well organized with solid fundamental bond information.

The Guide to Investing in Bonds, by David Logan Scott (Globe Pequot Press, 246 Goose Lane, Suite 200, PO Box 480, Guilford, CT 06437; 203-458-4500; 888-

249-7586; www.globe-pequot.com). An overview of bond investments and what factors to consider when planning investments.

The Handbook of Fixed-Income Securities, by Frank Fabozzi (McGraw-Hill, PO Box 543, Blacklick, OH 43004; 800-634-3961; www.mcgraw-hill.com). A complete guide to the bond market, with great detail on every aspect of the subject.

The Thomas J. Herzfeld Encyclopedia of Closed-End Funds (Thomas J. Herzfeld Advisors, PO Box 161465, Miami, FL 33116; 305-271-1900). Self-published encyclopedia of closed-end funds. Includes data on all funds and methods for choosing the best funds.

High Yield Bonds: Market Structure, Valuation, and Portfolio Strategies, by Theodore M. Barnhill, William Maxwell, and Mark R. Shenkman (McGraw Hill, PO Box 548, Blacklick, OH 43004; 800-634-3961; www.mcgraw-hill.com). Provides state-of-the-art research, strategies, and tools alongside the expert analysis of respected authorities to help you truly understand todays high-yield market.

How Municipal Bonds Work, by Robert Zipf (Prentice Hall Press, One Lake Street, Upper Saddle River, NJ 07458; 201-236-7156; 800-382-3419; www.prenticehall .com). Concise, readable, and offers a good understanding of municipal bonds.

How the Bond Market Works, by Robert Zipf (Prentice Hall Press, One Lake Street, Upper Saddle River, NJ 07458; 201-236-7156; 800-382-3419; www.prenticehall.com). An explanation of the ins and outs of the bond market.

Investing in Closed-End Funds: Finding Value and Building Wealth, by Albert Freedman and George Cole Scott (Prentice Hall Press, One Lake Street, Upper Saddle River, NJ 07458; 201-236-7156; 800-382-3419; www.prenticehall.com). Provides strategies for picking the best closed-end funds.

The Mortgage-Backed Securities Workbook: Hands-on Analysis, Valuation, and Strategies for Investment Decision Making, by Andrew S. Davidson and Michael D. Herskovitz (McGraw-Hill, PO Box 543, Blacklick, OH 43004; 800-634-3961; www.mcgraw-hill.com). Explains the complex world of mortgage-backed securities, including how to calculate prepayment risk and find the highest yields with the least risk.

Mortgage Securities: The High-Yield Alternative to CDs, the Low-Risk Alternative to Stocks, by Daniel R. Amerman (McGraw-Hill, PO Box 543, Blacklick, OH 43004; 800-634-3961; www.mcgraw-hill.com). Explains how to invest in mortgage securities, which are the highest yielding of all government-insured securities. Explains mortgage-backed securities mutual funds, how to buy and sell individual mortgage-backed bonds, how prepayment risk is factored into bond prices, and the difference between Ginnie Mae, Fannie Mae, and other issuers of mortgage-backed securities.

Savings Bonds: When to Hold, When to Fold, and Everything In-Between, by Daniel J. Pederson (The Savings Bond Informer, PO Box 9249, Detroit, MI 48209; 800-927-1901; www.bondinformer.com). Offers a full understanding of savings bonds, tips on the best time to redeem your bonds, details on swapping EE bonds for HH bonds, and tax aspects of bonds.

Yield Curve Analysis: The Fundamentals of Risk and Return, by Livingston Douglas (New York Institute of Finance, 1330 Avenue of the Americas, 10th Floor, New York, NY 10019; 212-641-6616; www.nyif.com). An explanation of how investing in different bond maturities can bring high returns and high risks.

Newsletters

Blue List, Bond Guide, Creditweek, Municipal Ratings Handbook, and *Unit Investment Trusts* (Standard & Poor's, 55 Water Street, New York, NY 10041; 212-438-2000; www.standardandpoors.com)

Bondweek (Institutional Investor, 488 Madison Avenue, 12th Floor, New York, NY 10022; 212-224-3800; www.bondweek.com).

Closed-End Country Fund Report (Suite 501, 725 15th Street, NW, Washington, DC 20005; 202-783-7051).

Closed-End Fund Digest (1224 Coast Village Circle, Suite 11, Santa Barbara, CA 93108; 800-282-2335).

Defaulted Bonds Newsletter (Bond Investors Association, PO Box 4427, Miami Lakes, FL 33014; 305-557-1832; www.bia.int.com).

Grant's Interest Rate Observer (30 Wall Street, 6th Floor, New York, NY 10005-2201; 212-809-7994; www.grantspub.com).

Investor's Guide to Closed-End Funds (Thomas J. Herzfeld Advisors, PO Box 161465, Miami, FL 33116; 305-271-1900; www.herzfeld.com).

Lynch Municipal Bond Advisory (PO Box 20476, New York, NY 10025; 212-663-5552).

Moody's Bond Survey (99 Church Street, New York, NY 10007; 212-553-0300; www.moodys.com/fis).

Public Investor (Government Finance Officers Association, 180 N. Michigan Avenue, Suite 800, Chicago, IL 60601-7476; 312-977-9700; www.gfoa.org).

Value Line Convertibles (220 E. 42nd Street, New York, NY 10017; 800-634-3583).

Newspaper

The Bond Buyer (One State Street Plaza, 27th Floor, New York, NY 10004; 800-982-0633; www.bondbuyer.com). A trade newspaper that covers the municipal bond business. Also available online.

Pamphlet

"Investing in Municipal Bonds" (North American Securities Administrators Association, 10 G Street, N.E., Suite 710, Washington, DC 20002; 202-737-0900; www.nasaa.org). Explains the basics of the municipal bond market.

Trade Associations

Association of Financial Guaranty Insurors (139 Lancaster Street, Albany, NY 12210; 518-449-4698; www.afgi.org). The trade group representing the insurance companies that insure municipal bonds against default. The following articles are available on their Web site: "Municipal Bonds—The Basics," "Insured Municipal Bonds," "Structured Asset Backed Securities," and "International Securities."

Bond Investors Association (PO Box 4427, 6175 NW 153rd Street, Suite 221, Miami Lakes, FL 33014; 305-557-1832; 800-472-2680; www.biainc.com). A non-profit group that educates the public about bonds and keeps statistics on defaulted bonds. Offers a pamphlet about the association titled "Staying Informed on Your Bond Investments in the 90's." Also offers subscriptions to three newsletters: *Bond Investors Association Newsletter, Defaulted Bonds Newsletter,* and *High-Yield Securities Journal.*

The Bond Market Association (40 Broad Street, 12th Floor, New York, NY 10004-2373; 212-440-9400; bondmarkets.com and investinginbonds.com). The industry group representing brokerage firms, dealers, and banks that trade government, municipal, and mortgage-backed securities. Offers the following guides on its Web site, or they can be obtained as pamphlets or small books for a nominal charge: "Investor's Guide to Bond Basics," "Bond Swapping," "CMOs," "Corporate Bonds," "High Yield Bonds," "Insured Municipal Bonds," "Mortgage Securities," "Municipal Bonds," "The Bond Markets," "Unit Investment Trusts," and "Zero Coupon Municipal Bonds." Also published a book called *A Guide to Certificates of Participation (COPs).*

Web Sites

The Blue List. Standard & Poor's offers daily updates on all municipal and corporate bonds coming to market. The site also provides commentary on the bond market and individual bonds. <www.bluelist.com>

The Bond Market Association. Offers a number of publications with extensive information on all types of bonds both online and as brochures, which can be ordered online. <www.investinginbonds.com>

BondResources. Education about bonds, lots of expert opinion about bonds and the bond market, and a database of more than 20,000 types of bonds. The site also has links to brokers. <www.bondresources.com>

Bonds Online. Lots of bond news and views. Connections to the best bond information available. Covers all types of bonds. You can get real-time prices for over 15,000 current bond offerings. <www.bondsonline.com>

Bondtrac.com. A Web-based fixed-income information system that provides quick and easy access to an expansive database of corporate, agency, and municipal bond offerings from the bond inventories of hundreds of firms. <www.bondtrac.com>

Bureau of Public Debt-Treasury Bills, Bonds, and Notes. The complete source for information about Treasury securities. You will be able to find out about upcoming Treasury auctions, and how the Treasury Direct program works. The site also answers frequently asked questions about Treasury bills, notes, bonds, and inflation-indexed securities. <www.publicdebt.treas.gov/sec/sec.htm>

Bureau of Public Debt—Savings Bond Division. The complete source for information about savings bonds. The site explains all the rules affecting savings bonds, including how to buy and redeem them and how to calculate their value. It also features the Savings Bond Wizard, which calculates the current redemption value of your savings bond holdings. <www.savingsbonds.gov>

CNN/Money.com. Research individual bond funds on this site and use their Portfolio Forecaster to see how they work with your portfolio. <www.money.cnn.com>

Convertbond.com. This site offers terms, analysis, news, and pricing relating to around 800 convertible securities that can be found in the U.S. convertible market. <www.convertbond.com>

eBondTrade. Provides access to a complete inventory of municipal bonds with clearly displayed bid and offer pricing. Register as an eBondTrader, log on to the Web site, and trade in bonds. <www.ebondtrade.com>

Emuni.com. Electronic Municipal Statistics (E-Muni) provides documents, news, developments, and financial information about the municipal bond market. <www.emuni.com>

Fitch Credit Rating Company. A Web site to look up the credit ratings of most corporate debt. Fitch is a major rating agency of corporate debt, and this site will let you find the ratings for American and international companies for bonds and preferred stock. It lists Fitch, Moody's, and Standard & Poor's ratings. You will also find ratings changes within the past 90 days and a list of companies on ratings watch, meaning that their ratings may be upgraded or downgraded soon. <www.fitchibca.com>

Investing in Bonds. You can learn about all kinds of bonds and calculate your personal taxable-equivalent muni yields. <www.investinginbonds.com>

InvestorGuide. This site has a bond section that explains the different types of bonds and has links to other bond quote services. <www.investorguide.com>

Moodys.com. Moody's maintains over 68,000 ratings on 16,000 municipal bond issuers, including the general obligations of governments, revenue bonds, and other municipal instruments. <www.moodys.com>

MorningStar.com. This is probably the most comprehensive bond information site available. You can get bond news, bond analysis, description of all the types of bonds available, and the performance of all bonds now trading. <www.morningstar.com>

Municipal Securities Rulemaking Board. Makes rules that govern the municipal bond business. They provide information to investors about investing in muni bonds. <www.msrb.org>

Standard & Poor's Rating Services. The largest rating service for corporate, municipal, and government bonds provides extensive listings in its Web site. S&P not only provides the ratings, but also why an issuer's rating has risen or fallen. You also can look at the Credit Wire for recent ratings changes. <www.standardpoor.com/ratings /index.htm.com>

The Next Move

No question, investing has its challenges, but the rewards can be well worth the effort. The choice is obvious. Do you want to spend a little extra time and effort putting together a lifetime investment program, or would you rather face a difficult and uncertain financial future? By committing yourself to a well-conceived investment program, you are helping assure a prosperous future and a comfortable retirement.

By now, after reading through the pages of this book, you should have a fair understanding of the stock, bond, and mutual fund universe. We've also listed plenty of other sources that can help you hone your investing skills. The next step is to begin building your winning portfolio one investment at a time. Whether you do that through a full-service broker, a discount broker, a mutual fund company, or an online brokerage service is up to you. The key is to take action, and to get the process started.

No matter how much time and effort you put into your investing program, you will have some investment decisions that simply won't work out the way you would like. You will buy some stocks or mutual funds that will decline rather than rise. In fact, there will even be times when a weak stock market will send your entire portfolio plummeting. But over time, with patience, persistence, and diversification, the portfolio you build will help you achieve a life of prosperity and financial security.

Glossary

asset allocation An investment strategy intended to reduce the volatility and risk of loss of an individual's holdings by assigning the holdings to several different types of asset classes, such as stocks, bonds, mutual funds, precious metals and real estate. Asset allocation is considered the main determinant of portfolio performance. The term can also apply to spreading assets across different regional and national markets.

asset classes The various types of investments, such as stocks, bonds, currencies, and commodities, that are available to investors.

basis points The smallest measure of the yield paid by a bond or note. One basis point is equal to 0.01 percent (one-one hundredth of a percent) of yield. If a bond's yield moves from 9.5 percent to 10.5 percent, that would be a move of 100 basis points.

beta A measure of volatility and risk that reflects the degree to which the price of a security or portfolio tends to rise or fall with the market. The higher the beta, the higher the volatility. The Standard & Poor's 500 has a beta of 1.

bear market A period of declining stock prices.

bill A short-term debt security, such as a U.S. Treasury bill with a maturity ranging from 13 weeks to a year.

blue chip The stock of the largest, most well-established companies. Also referred to as *large-capitalization stocks,* blue chip stocks are generally considered strong, growing companies with market values of in the range of $10 billion or more. Most blue chips pay dividends, and are considered to be the most stable, least risky stocks on the market.

bond A long-term debt instrument in which the issuing concern (usually a corporation or government body) is obligated to repay the debt on a given date, and must pay interest on the debt throughout the term of the bond. For example, a corporation may issue 10-year bonds to finance an expansion project, paying its bond investors a preset rate of interest each year, and repaying the original principal when the bonds mature after 10 years. Interest is usually paid semi-annually.

bond quality The safety of principal and dependability of interest payments of a bond. Quality depends on the financial soundness of the issuer. The lower the quality, the higher the interest rate an issuer must pay to attract investors.

book value The assessed value of a company's assets. Book value per share, which is frequently used in assessing the potential value of a company's stock, is defined as the per-share assessed value of a company's assets.

bottom-up analysis A stock market investment approach in which the emphasis is on analyzing individual stocks rather than broad economic trends. Opposite of the top-down analysis. Analysts try to identify stocks that are undervalued or have strong growth potential. It is far more popular than the top-down approach. (*Also see* top-down analysis.)

Brady bonds Named for former U.S. Treasury Secretary Nicholas Brady, Brady bonds were created to alleviate Latin America's debt crisis in the 1980s. Under the Brady plan, creditor banks exchanged existing bonds for new bonds with lower face value but with principal backed by U.S. Treasury bonds.

bull market A period of high and rising stock prices.

call An option that allows the option holder to buy an investment at a predetermined price until a preset date.

call option The right to buy a specific number of shares of an investment (such as stock) at a preset price by a certain date. With stock options, for instance, in exchange for a premium, a call gives the holder the right to buy 100 shares of a stock at a "strike" price at any time during a set period that may vary from 1 to 90 days. Call options are appropriate for investors who feel that a certain stock is going to increase in value. If the stock increases in value, the investor would exercise the option and collect a profit on the price increase. If the stock value drops, the investor would let the option expire, forfeiting the price of the premium. (*Also see* option.)

call provision A stipulation allowing some bond issuers to pay off their bond debt before maturity. Bond issuers tend to exercise call provisions when interest rates fall significantly, allowing them to issue new bonds at lower interest rates.

capital appreciation An increase in the market value of an asset.

capital market instruments Longer-term debt instruments, such as government and corporate bonds.

cash flow A company's annual profits plus depreciation.

coincident indicators Economic data that tend to coincide with the economic cycle. Examples include industrial production, employment, and personal income. In other words, during an economic upswing, industrial production, employment and personal income are all on the rise, while during a recession, they tend to be on the decline. (*Also see* leading indicators *and* lagging indicators.)

commercial paper Short-term debt instrument issued by corporations to facilitate their cash flow. Commercial paper is usually unsecured, with maturities of 2 to 270 days. The large denomination notes (at least $25,000) are normally issued by financial companies and large corporations.

commodities Bulk goods such as metals, foods, grain, livestock, currency, and lumber that are traded on a commodities exchange or a spot market.

common stock Unit of ownership of a public corporation. The vast majority of stocks traded on the exchanges are common stocks (as opposed to preferred stock). Typically, common stock owners are entitled to vote on company directors and important policy matters, and may also receive dividends from the company. (*Also see* preferred stock.)

compound annual return Measure of the rate at which an investment or portfolio has grown in value over a period of years, averaged out on a yearly basis. Varies from average annual return in that it measures what the fixed annual rate of return of an investment would have been based on its total long-term return. A stock that grew 75 percent in three years would have an average annual return of 25 percent (75% divided by 3 = 25%), and a compound annual return (calculated through a complex formula) of about 20 percent. In other words, if an investment were to increase in value 20 percent each year for three years, through compounding that would equal a total of a 75 percent return.

compounding Interest paid on interest from previous periods in addition to the principal. Though small at first, the additional returns can become substantial over time.

compound rate of return The annual return rate of an investment over a period of years, determined by calculating what fixed rate of return that investment would have to have earned in order to achieve its total return over that specific time period.

conversion price A preset dollar amount a stock must reach before convertible bonds or preferred stock may be exchanged for shares of common stock.

convertible bonds Bonds that pay a fixed rate of interest and are convertible to common stock if the stock reaches a certain price known as the *conversion price.* They offer regular fixed income—though usually less than bonds issued by the same company—and appreciation potential if the company is growing, but not as much as the company's common stock.

convertible preferred stock Preferred stock that may be converted to common stock at a preset price. Convertibles appeal to investors seeking higher income than common stocks provide, and greater appreciation potential than bonds offer. (*Also see* common stock *and* preferred stock.)

corporate bond A long-term debt instrument issued by corporations to raise capital. The issuing corporation is obligated to repay the bond debt on a specified date, and to pay a specified rate of interest on the debt throughout the term of the bond. While most bonds are backed by property or other assets, some bonds, known as *debentures,* are backed strictly by the word ("full faith and credit") of the corporation.

coupon rate The stated annual interest paid on a bond or other debt security. For instance, the coupon on a $1,000 bond that pays 10 percent interest would be $100. On coupon bonds, the owner must detach the coupon from the bond to present for interest payments.

current income The income an investor receives while holding a specific investment. Examples of current income include stock dividends and bond interest payments.

current returns Earnings from an income-producing asset, such as a bond that pays interest or a stock that pays dividends.

current yield The interest rate paid by a bond or other fixed-rate investment, calculated by dividing the annual interest payment by the current market price. Because the annual return is fixed, the yield automatically falls if the price rises, and vice versa.

cyclical industries Industries, such as automotive and other heavy manufacturers, that are subject to broad swings in economic activity. Cyclical stocks often anticipate changes in the economy, reaching their highs (or lows) just before major shifts in the economy.

cyclical stocks Stocks of cyclical industries, such as automotive and other heavy manufacturers, that are subject to broad swings in economic activity. Cyclical stocks often anticipate changes in the economy, reaching their highs (or lows) just before major shifts in the economy.

debt instrument A fixed-income investment, such as a bond, note, or bill, issued by governments and corporations. The issuer is obligated to repay the purchase amount on the date the instrument comes due (maturity date), and must pay a predetermined interest rate either during the course of the agreement or when the investment reaches maturity.

debt-to-asset ratio A measure used by value-oriented investor to help assess the strength of a company, and the value of its stock. The ratio compares a company's outstanding debt with its total holdings. A high debt-to-asset ratio indicates a company with high debt, and a shakier financial structure than a company with a low debt-to-asset ratio.

debt-to-earnings ratio A measure used by value-oriented investors to help assess the strength of a company, and the value of its stock. The ratio compares a company's outstanding debt with its annual earnings (profits). A low debt-to-earnings ratio is preferable, and indicates a low debt, and more stable financial footing.

derivatives Options, futures, and other investments that derive their value from other underlying assets, such as currencies, stocks, bonds, or commodities. In recent years, the variety and complexity of derivatives has grown dramatically.

discount Refers to a bond that is trading on the secondary market at a price below its issuing price. For instance, a bond issued at $1,000 par value may drop below $1,000 on the bond market if interest rates increase. A bond or other security that is selling at under par value is said to be trading at a discount. (*Also see* premium.)

diversification The strategy of investing in several different types of assets, (and, in some cases, investing in several different regions of the world) in order to balance the portfolio and protect against large losses and high volatility.

dividend income Monetary payment a stock shareholder receives from the company. The dividend, which is allocated from the company's earnings, is paid on a pro-rated basis in a fixed amount for each share of stock held. Dividends are usually paid quarterly. Dividends are not guaranteed, but many companies with consistent earnings pay them on a regular basis.

dividend yield The annual dividend payment divided by its market price per share. Example: If a stock is trading at $10 a share, and pays a $1 dividend, the dividend yield is 10 percent. While the yield may also be considered the current return on a stock, it does not take into consideration gains and losses in the trading price of the stock.

duration Referring to a bond or other fixed-rate investment: the number of years it would take to receive the present value of future payments, including both interest and principal, from the bond.

earnings Profit or income from a business. Usually refers to after-tax income.

emerging growth stock Stock of a small, rapidly expanding company. Emerging growth stocks offer great long-term appreciation potential, but tend to be the most risky and most volatile of all stocks.

equity investment A security (usually common or preferred stock) that represents a share of ownership.

exchange *See* securities exchange

face value The issuing price or *par value* of a bond, note, or security as stated on the certificate. For instance, many bonds are issued at $1,000 face value—and redeemed at maturity at that same $1,000 value. (The bondholder profits from the interest paid on the bond throughout the bond-holding period.)

fixed-income investment A debt instrument, such as a bond, note, or bill, issued by governments and corporations. The investment buyer is essentially making a loan to the issuer. The issuer is obligated to repay the purchase amount on the date the instrument comes due (maturity date), and must pay a predetermined interest rate either during the course of the agreement or when the investment reaches maturity.

fixed rate of return The annual profit from an investment that remains the same from year to year. For instance, a certificate of deposit may have a fixed rate of return of 5 percent per year over a five-year period.

floating rates Exchange rates (or interest rates) that are set by the market rather than by some type of governmental mandates.

futures contracts Essentially a promise to buy or sell a currency (or other type of investment) at a specified price on a particular date. The buyer is required to accept and the seller is required to deliver an investment such as currency or a security on that date at the specified price.

fundamental analysis A stock market investment approach based on the premise that a stock's value depends on the company's present and future earnings. The objective is to identify individual stocks or groups of stocks that have exceptional earnings potential or are currently undervalued relative to earnings potential, and therefore are likely to appreciate in the future. (*Also see* technical analysis.)

fundamentals Basic financial and economic factors affecting the success of a company and the price of its stock. Fundamentals of a company would include factors such as earnings and revenue growth, price-earnings ratio, dividend yield, and debt-to-equity ratio.

growth stock Stock of a small- to mid-capitalization company that is expanding rapidly. Growth stocks offer the greatest long-term appreciation potential, but are also the most volatile and vulnerable to changing business conditions.

high-yield bond Also referred to as a *junk bond,* it is a bond issued by a corporation or government whose ability to pay interest and repay the principal is in question to varying degrees. Normally, smaller, newer companies and third world countries must offer higher yields to attract investors. (*Also see* junk bond.)

income stocks Technically, any stock that pays a dividend, but income stocks are normally thought of as stocks that pay a higher-than-average dividend. Exactly what would be considered a high dividend depends on current interest rates, but generally, a dividend yield of 4 percent or more would be considered high. Income stocks tend to be the more established mid- to high-capitalization stocks.

inefficient portfolio An investment portfolio that is structured in such a way that it offers less than the maximum return potential for the risk assumed.

investment grade bond Considered among the highest quality bonds based on safety of principal and dependability of interest payments. Investment grade bonds are generally divided into four rating categories, led by bonds issued by the most stable governments and the largest, most financially secure corporations.

investment horizon The amount of time an investor expects to hold a specific investment. The longer the investment horizon, the less likely an investor will be to lose money on a volatile investment.

investment returns The profit (or loss) earned from a specific investment or a portfolio of investments over a specific period.

junk bond Also referred to as a *high-yield bond,* it is a bond issued by a corporation or government whose ability to pay interest and repay the principal is in question to varying degrees. (*Also see* high-yield bond.)

lagging indicators Economic data that trail the economy, rising or falling after the economy has shifted. Examples of lagging indicators include expenditures for new plants and equipment, commercial and industrial loans outstanding, and unemployment rates for medium and long-term unemployed.

large-cap (large-capitalization) stock Stocks of the largest, most well-established companies. Also referred to as *blue chips,* large-cap stocks are generally considered to be those with market values of $10 billion or more (such as Unilever, IBM, General Electric, and Sony). Most large-cap stocks pay dividends, and are considered to be the most stable, least risky stocks on the market.

leading indicators Economic data that usually predate turning points in the economy. Examples include average weekly hours, manufacturers new orders, unemployment claims, stock prices, inventories, money supply, and consumer confidence. (*Also see* coincident indicators *and* lagging indicators.)

market capitalization Can refer to a corporation or an entire national stock market. The value of a corporation—or an entire stock market—as determined by the market price of its issued and outstanding common stock.

market indicators Economic data that either predates, follows, or occurs simultaneously with turning points in the economy. Technical analysts track market indicators to time investment buy and sell decisions. (*Also see* coincident indicators *and* lagging indicators *and* leading indicators.)

market risk Also known as *systematic risk,* it refers to the risk attached to the overall market, rather than to an individual stock or bond. When an entire national bond or stock market rises or falls, most of the individual securities tend to rise and fall with the market.

market timing A classic buy low–sell high investment approach in which investors try to anticipate the ups and downs of the market, and make their buy and sell decisions accordingly. Market timers buy when they expect the market to go up, and sell—or lighten their position—when they expect the market to go down.

maturity (or maturity date) The prespecified date on which a financial obligation (such as a bond or promissory note) must repay the principal to the bondholder.

mid-cap (mid-capitalization) stock The stock of companies with market valuations of about $1 billion to $10 billion. They are larger than the small, emerging stocks, but smaller than the large-capitalization or blue chip stocks.

modern portfolio theory An investment asset allocation theory developed by 20th-century investment analysts and researchers that stresses diversification in order to reduce risk and increase long-term performance. Key assumptions of the theory are that investors prefer higher returns to lower, less risk to more, and that they have long-term time horizons. Under the theory, by adding a relatively risky, high-return asset to a portfolio, you can not only increase the expected return, you also decrease the risk.

money-market fund A mutual fund that invests in high-quality, short-term debt instruments such as Treasury bills or certificates of deposit. Money-market fund investors earn a steady stream of interest income that varies with short-term interest rates. Generally investors may cash out at anytime.

money-market instrument A short-term, low-risk security such as commercial paper, U.S. Treasury bills, certificates of deposit, and bankers' acceptances.

Moody's Investor Service A company that rates the quality of bonds issued by corporations and governments. The rating system includes a number of fine gradation between the safest investment grade bonds and the riskiest high-yield or junk bonds.

mortgage-backed security A debt instrument backed by a pool of mortgages issued by a mortgage lender or government agency that investors may buy to receive periodic interest payments and principal payments as the mortgages are repaid.

note A short-term debt instrument issued by a corporation or government, usually with a maturity ranging from 13 weeks to one year. Considered a cash equivalent investment, notes are also referred to as *promissory notes*.

option A contract that permits the option holder to buy or sell an asset (such as a stock or a currency) at a fixed price on or before a specific date. An option to purchase an asset is a call, and an option to sell an asset is a put.

options on futures An agreement that gives the buyer or seller the right, but not the obligation, to accept or deliver a futures contract at a strike price specified in the option contract.

par value The face value or issuing price of a bond. A bond issued at $1,000 would have a par value of $1,000. (*Also see* face value.)

preferred stock Like common stock, it is a unit of ownership in a corporation, but preferred stock pays a fixed dividend, set when the stock is issued. Although payment of the dividend is not an obligation, holders of preferred stock have the right to receive dividends before common shareholders. Should the company be liquidated, preferred shareholders would have claims satisfied before common shareholders. (*Also see* common stock *and* convertible preferred stock.)

premium A bond or other security that is trading on the secondary market at a price in excess of its issuing price. For instance, a bond issued with a $1,000 face value may increase in value to more than $1,000 on the bond market if market interest rates drop. A bond or other security that sells for more than par value is said to be trading at a premium. (*Also see* discount.)

price-book value ratio A measurement used by value-oriented investors to assess the value of a stock. Specifically, the company's share price divided by the book value per share (per-share assessed value of the company's assets).

price-cash flow ratio A measurement used by value-oriented investors to assess the value of a stock. Specifically, the company's stock price divided by its cash flow (profits plus depreciation) per share.

price-earnings (PE) ratio A commonly used measure of a company's stock price relative to its earnings per share. Specifically, it is a company's stock price divided by its earnings per share over the past 12 months. For instance, a company with a stock price of $10 and earnings-per-share of $1 has a 10 PE ($10 divided by $1). The higher a stock's PE, the more expensive the stock is relative to its earnings.

principal The purchase amount of a bond or other debt instrument.

promissory note *See* note.

quantitative analysis An investment strategy in which stocks are judged based on factors that can be precisely measured, such as earnings, revenue, assets, or liabilities. By contrast, qualitative analysis is based on subjective measures, such as the character and experience of management.

risk The level of volatility or variability of returns of an investment.

risk premium A higher yield offered by bonds and similar investments that carry a high risk rating. For example, government bonds are considered the safest bond investments, and pay among the lowest yields. Corporate bonds, on the other hand, must offer higher yields to attract investors because those bonds carry a higher risk than government bonds.

secondary market A trading market for bonds and other debt instruments after they have been issued. A bond may be issued at a par value of $1,000, but, depending on fluctuations in interest rates, it may sell for more or less than the $1,000 issuing price on the secondary market.

securities exchange A facility for the organized trading of securities such as stocks, bonds, and commodities. There are many national and regional exchanges around the world.

short-term, cash equivalent investment A highly liquid interest-bearing investment, such as money market funds or Treasury bills, that have a maturity of less than 12 months and are considered to be virtually as good as cash.

sinking fund A custodial account used by a bond issuer (such as a corporation or government body) to place a predetermined amount each year toward payment of the principal on its bond issue. The sinking fund helps an issuer receive a higher rating for its bonds by essentially guaranteeing that the money needed to redeem the bonds will be available at maturity.

small-cap (small-capitalization) stock The smallest, and generally considered to be the riskiest, class of stocks. Despite their risk and volatility, however, the small-cap stocks also tend to hold the greatest potential for appreciation, according to historical comparisons with mid- and large-capitalization stocks. Small caps have market values of under $1 billion. Sometimes referred to as *emerging stocks*. (*Also see* mid-cap stock *and* large-cap stock.)

standard deviation A measure of an investment's volatility. It summarizes in one number how far a portfolio's returns for individual years deviate from the average or expected return value. The higher the standard deviation, the more variable the returns and the riskier the investment.

stock An equity asset that represents a proportionate share of ownership in a company. The total number of shares is set by the company's charter. Stock shareholders may vote on directors and important corporate resolutions, and share in the profits and growth of the company through dividends and stock price appreciation. Stocks are traded on exchanges around the world.

technical analysis A stock market investment approach that examines recurring patterns in the market to predict price movements. Technical analysts assume that all information about the fundamentals of a stock, industry, or national market is fully reflected in the price of the stock. So, unlike fundamental analysts, technicians are not concerned with the financial strength of individual companies—only with the anticipated movement of the overall market. (*Also see* fundamental analysis.)

top-down analysis A stock market investment approach in which the emphasis is on economic trends rather than individual stocks. The opposite of bottom-up analysis. Analysts attempt to identify industries or geographic regions with the greatest potential for gain, and then invest in stocks of those categories. (*Also see* bottom-up analysis.)

total return The total profit earned from an investment. Includes the sum of the income plus capital appreciation over a given period, stated as a percentage of its value at the beginning of the period.

Treasury bills A government debt security sold in minimum amounts of $10,000, with a maturity date of 13 weeks to one year. Referred to as *T-bills,* they are purchased at a discount to face value, pay no interest, but mature at full face value.

Treasury bonds A long-term, interest-bearing government security with a maturity date of 10 to 30 years. U.S. Treasury bonds pay interest semiannually.

value-oriented strategy A stock market investment approach in which the emphasis is on identifying undervalued stocks—those that may have been knocked down in price by the market further than they should have been. Value-oriented investors try to buy those stocks when they appear to be poised for a rebound.

volatility A sharp fluctuation in the price of an investment (such as a stock, bond, or commodity) over a relatively short period. The more volatile an investment, the more risky it is considered to be.

yield The interest rate percentage a bond or other income investment pays to investors. A bond's current yield is calculated by dividing the annual interest payment by the current market price. Because the annual return is fixed, the yield automatically fluctuates if the market price for the bond rises or falls.

yield to maturity The rate of return investors would receive if they held a bond or other long-term, fixed-income investment to its maturity date. It takes into account not only the income stream generated by a bond, but also the capital gain (or loss) expected if an investor buys the bond at a discount (or premium) and holds to maturity.

zero coupon bond A bond that pays no interest but is priced at a discount to face value at maturity. The interest rate is stated as yield to maturity, compounded rather than simple interest. In other words, the bond pays no interest until it reaches maturity, at which point the issuer pays off the bond in full, including the principal and compounded interest.

Index